P9-CFD-542

Little Bighorn Battlefield NM

OCT 05 2016

Crow Agency, MT

Officers of the Seventh Cavalry (except where otherwise noted), **Ft. Lincoln, Dakota Territory, 1874.** (1) Lt. Bronson, 6th Inf; (2) Lt. Geo. D. Wallace, killed at Wounded Knee, 1890; (3) Gen. G. A. Custer; (4) Lt. B. Hodgson; (5) Mrs. T. M. McDougall; (6) Mrs. Custer; (7) Capt. T. M. McDougall; (8) Lt. Badger, 6th Inf; (9) Charles Thompson, (son of Capt. Thompson); (10) Mrs. James Calhoun; (11) Col. J. S. Poland, 6th Inf; (12) Lt. C. A. Varnum; (13) Capt. Tom Custer; (14) Capt. Wm. Thompson; (15) Mrs. M. Moylan; (16) Lt. James Calhoun; (17) Mrs. Donald McIntosh; (18) Capt. Myles Moylan; (19) Lt. Donald McIntosh; (20) Mrs. Yates; (21) Capt. G. W. Yates; (22) Miss Annie Bates; (23) Col. W. P. Carlan, 17th Inf.

TROOPERS WITH
CUSTER

Historic Incidents of the Battle of
The Little Big Horn

By

E. A. BRININSTOOL

University of Nebraska Press
Lincoln and London

Copyright 1952 by E. A. Brininstool
All rights reserved
Manufactured in the United States of America
⊗
The paper used in this publication meets the minimum requirements of
American National Standard for Information Sciences—Permanence of
Paper for Printed Library Materials, ANSI Z39.48-1984.

First Bison Book printing: 1989

Library of Congress Cataloging-in-Publication Data
Brininstool, E. A. (Earl Alonzo), 1870–1957.
Troopers with Custer: historic incidents of the Battle of the Little Big
Horn / By E.A. Brininstool.
p.   cm.
Reprint. Originally published: Harrisburg, Pa.: Stackpole Co., c 1952.
ISBN 0-8032-1213-5.   ISBN 0-8032-6101-2 (pbk.)
1. Little Big Horn, Battle of the, 1876.   2. Custer, George Armstrong,
1839–1876.   I. Title.
E83.876.B85   1989   88-31143
973.8'2—dc 19   CIP

Reprinted by arrangement with Stackpole Books, Harrisburg, Pennsylvania

DEDICATION

To that under-paid, overworked, yet ever-dutiful body of men who paved the way for the advance of civilization through a land whose every inch was contested by the Red Man of the Plains—the men who marched, fought, bled and suffered—the Indian Wars Veterans.

PREFACE

There is no fiction in the contents of this volume; no lurid tales of adventure with a historical setting against a background of make-believe, such as is found on the magazine stands of today. Personally, I believe such stories do far more damage than good; they are entirely misleading to thousands of readers, and are very apt to give the rising generation a decidedly wrong impression and conception of the old-time West, and of the breed of men who composed the population of our isolated army posts and frontier settlements in the days of the wild Indian and the buffalo.

The stories contained herein are all of actual happenings and actual participants; there are no fictitious names, no colored circumstances. They are a part of the real history of the West, and for that reason I am not ashamed to place this volume in the hands of any interested boy or girl, youth or elderly person, who may desire to know the truth about one of the leading Indian battles, and other important frontier happenings pertaining thereto, and the men who played leading parts therein. Every character mentioned in each chapter was a living, breathing person, and every incident related in this book can be vouched for and verified.

The author has taken the liberty, here and there, of putting certain words and sentences in parentheses or italics, in the interest of historical accuracy or a fuller understanding of the facts on the part of the reader. Unless otherwise noted, such interpolations are the author's.

There has been altogether too much "bunk" written around the history of the West. Many writers have drawn on their imagination to such an extent (and the "movies" have aided them) and have so distorted and twisted certain historical happenings, that any attempt to straighten them out and relate the TRUTH, is almost certain to meet with much opposition. Nevertheless, the writer intends to "hew to the line, let the chips fall where they may."

The Indian has been held before the young people of this country as a bloodthirsty, murderous, sneaking devil, always lying in wait for scalps, not to be trusted, and only good when dead. But the Indian was only what Uncle Sam himself made him in that respect. While the Indian is belittled, scarcely anything is said about the political parasites at Washington and elsewhere, who robbed, cheated, tricked, swindled, defrauded, deceived and imposed upon the red man at every turn.

Had Uncle Sam raised a few more thousand William Penns, the Indian would have had no excuse for taking to the warpath in retaliation for the wrongs inflicted upon him. The Indian never was bad until first made bad by his white brother, through his villainous whisky and still more villainous trickery and chicanery. Contact with the white race was the real undoing of the red man. The only wonder is that the Indian was not ten times worse than he really was, considering his unjust treatment by unscrupulous whites. He had every reason for going to the bad.

I believe that every old regular army man, in spite of what he may have received at the hands of the Indian, will agree with me in the foregoing assertion. There were too many dishonest, unprincipled Indian agents who did more to keep the regular army man out in the field, jeopardizing his life, than the great American public of this day realizes.

If these various chapters shall enlighten the reader in any manner on the last ill-fated expedition of the Seventh Cavalry, the author shall feel repaid for his hard work in gathering the actual facts.

E. A. BRININSTOOL

CONTENTS

LIST OF ILLUSTRATIONS

CHAPTER 1

THE CUSTER FIGHT IN BRIEF

TO THE AVERAGE AMERICAN little is known regarding the actual facts surrounding the battle of the Little Big Horn. Perhaps he has read brief extracts, or heard others discuss the affair, and it therefore seems fitting that the story of this greatest of Indian battles should be briefly told, the main reason being to correct some of the exaggerated stories which have been broadcast over the years, and to refute others which have been foisted on the public by persons who were not in possession of the actual facts.

The battle of the Little Big Horn was the culmination of the invasion of the Black Hills of Dakota (ceded Sioux territory) by white gold hunters. Custer, in 1874, led a government expedition into that then unexplored and unknown region, under orders to "spy out the land," and determine if the stories in circulation regarding its beauty and wealth were true. It was hinted that gold was there—in abundance—and where gold is, there the white man will go, regardless of treaties or the rights of anyone of whatever race or color.

After Custer had discovered and reported that there was gold in the Hills, a general stampede into the forbidden territory followed. In spite of the fact that the treaty of 1868 with the Sioux distinctly specified that "no white man should ever set foot in the territory without the consent of the Indians," no attention whatever was paid to this edict. Gold had been discovered—and what else mattered?

The Sioux resented this invasion of their ceded territory—

1

and rightly! But the government could not keep the gold-maddened miners out, although a feeble attempt was made in that direction. The protests of the Sioux went unheeded, and it soon became apparent that armed resistance was imminent.

Sitting Bull, the great medicine man of the Sioux nation—not a fighting chief in the strict sense of the word—was the leading fomenter among the Indians. He was a great schemer, a conjurer, with an immense following, particularly among the young men of the tribe. He was not an agency Indian but had a most bitter hatred for the "pale-face." He preferred to roam, refusing to accept the agency rations doled out to him by the "great Father" at Washington, choosing instead to live by the chase as long as the buffalo were plentiful. His camp, in 1876, was supposed to be located somewhere in the Big Horn country of Wyoming, or in the adjacent Montana wilderness—just where was not known, as that entire section, in 1876, was an unsettled and all but unexplored region.

To Sitting Bull's standard flocked thousands of the dissatisfied and rebellious among the Sioux. With them were allied many of the Northern Cheyennes. If the various Indian reservation agents were aware of these desertions from the agencies and the accessions to the ranks of the hostiles, they kept the information to themselves. This was one of the reasons why the Seventh Cavalry met with such disaster. They did not realize, nor for one moment dream, that the hostiles had been thus heavily reenforced.

These malcontents and dissatisfied among the Sioux were notified by the government, during the latter part of 1875, that if they did not cease their roving habits and come in and settle down on their reservations, where Uncle Sam could keep a watchful eye on their movements, armed forces of troops would be sent against them.

They did not obey Uncle Sam's mandate, and as soon as spring opened and the country was in condition to travel over, an expedition was formed to go out against these hostiles.

Sitting Bull, noted medicine man of the Sioux. He took no part in the Custer fight, although the camp was known as "Sitting Bull's Camp."

It was decided to send out three expeditions of troops from various points. The eastern column, under personal command of General Alfred H. Terry, was to start from Fort Abraham Lincoln, across the Missouri River from Bismarck, North Dakota; the western column, under command of Colonel John Gibbon, was to start from Fort Ellis, Montana, while the third column, under General George Crook, was to start from Fort Fetterman, Wyoming.

It was hoped, and confidently expected, that if the hostiles were in the region where reports had them located, they would thus be entrapped between the three commands, and be either crushed or compelled to return to their reservations.

It must be understood that at that time there was no telegraphic communication between Bozeman, Montana, on the west and Bismarck, North Dakota, on the east, while the nearest line to the south was at old Fort Laramie, Wyoming. Not a town, village, hamlet or settlement existed in all that vast stretch of country between the points named, unbelievable as it may seem at the present day, with that entire section now settled up and peopled by thousands, with cities, towns and villages galore in evidence. Seventy-six years ago the only means of communication was by mounted courier to the nearest telegraph line.

The eastern column, under personal command of General Terry, left Fort Lincoln, May 17, 1876. It consisted of approximately 600 to 650 men of the famous Seventh Cavalry, led by Lieutenant-Colonel George A. Custer, one of the greatest military figures of that time, and a cavalry leader whose superior the world has rarely seen—a man of unquestioned bravery, skill, energy and fighting ability, with a Civil War record second to that of no officer in the entire United States army. And Custer was but 36 years of age at his death!

It had been expected that Custer should go in command of the eastern column. Unfortunately, however, he had, a short time previously, incurred the enmity of General Grant, then President of the United States, and Grant had given orders that not only should Custer not go in command of the eastern division, but that he should not accompany the expedition in any capacity whatsoever, but should remain behind at Fort Lincoln.

This, to Custer, was a most humiliating condition in which he found himself. Smarting under the (to him) injustice of this edict of the President, Custer went to General Terry, whose headquarters were at St. Paul, and there begged (on his knees, so report has it) of General Terry that he intercede with the President to spare him the humiliation of seeing his regiment march away on a hostile Indian expedition and he not be allowed to accompany it.

General Terry, a most lovable and kindly man, and himself an army officer of distinction, at length agreed to take the matter up with Grant. The result was that the President finally reluctantly stated that if Terry really needed Custer, he would lift the ban and allow him to go at the head of the Seventh Cavalry, but not as commander of the expedition. Thus the expedition got under way.

Passing over the first few weeks of the march of the Seventh Cavalry (which were uneventful, so far as this article is concerned) Major Marcus A. Reno with six troops of the Seventh Cavalry, was sent out, June 10th, on a side scout in an endeavor to locate the hostiles.

Major Reno was an officer with a brilliant Civil War record, having received brevet after brevet, "for meritorious and gallant services in action." His skill, bravery and ability in handling troops in the field had been proven time and again.

Reno swung west as far as the Rosebud river, there discovering a fresh Indian trail leading up that stream. Unfortunately he did not follow this trail far enough to definitely ascertain in which direction its destination appeared to be, but after scouting over it but a short distance, he cut across the country to the encampment of the balance of the Seventh Cavalry at the mouth of the Rosebud.

General George A. Custer.

Here he reported to General Terry, the expeditionary commander, what he had discovered.

That night a conference was held in the cabin of the supply steamer "Far West," the boat chartered by the government for use during the campaign to carry supplies for the troops to the head of navigation, and which was now lying at the mouth of the Rosebud awaiting orders. This meeting was attended only by General Terry, Colonel Custer and Colonel Gibbon, the latter having arrived with the Seventh Infantry, a few companies of the Second Cavalry, and a Gatling gun division from Fort Ellis. Here General Terry laid his plan of operations before his subordinates.

Briefly this plan was as follows:

Gibbon, with about 400 men of the Seventh Infantry and Second Cavalry, with the Gatling guns, was to proceed west to the Big Horn river, which stream he was to follow up, with the expectation of arriving in the valley of the Little Big Horn on June 26th, or possibly the 27th.

Custer, with the entire Seventh Cavalry, was to march south up the Rosebud until he reached the point where Major Reno had discovered the fresh trail a few days before. Custer was then to ascertain definitely in which direction this trail led. If it led across the divide and over into the valley of the Little Big Horn (as Terry confidently expected) Custer was *not to follow the trail further,* but to proceed south up the Rosebud, another day's march, perhaps as far as the headquarters of the Tongue river, in order to give Gibbon's slower moving infantry time to arrive in the valley of the Little Big Horn where Terry expected to find the hostiles. Then—and not until then—Custer was to swing west toward the Little Big Horn, and upon striking that stream was to march north down stream, while Gibbon was marching south up it. Thus, if the hostiles were located on the Little Big Horn, it was expected that they would be entrapped between the two commands.

General Terry was to accompany the troops of Colonel

"Mitch" Buoyer, noted Crow scout, who warned Custer that he would be outnumbered by the Indians.

Gibbon, thus leaving Custer in supreme command of the Seventh Cavalry. Nothing had been heard of General Crook's column, which was expected from the south; but, unknown to any of the other commanders, Crook had fought the Sioux in a fierce battle on the Rosebud, June 17th, and had met with such determined opposition that he had been compelled to retire to his base on Goose Creek (near the site of the present city of Sheridan, Wyoming) and send a call back to Fort Fetterman for re-inforcements, in spite of the fact that his command numbered over one thousand men. (See note [1] at end of chapter)

The Sioux were greatly elated over the result of this battle, which had been disastrous to Crook, and were in trim for another—indeed it is stated that their leading chiefs, for some time afterward, thought they were fighting Crook's men again at the Little Big Horn.

Custer was warned by General Terry at the evening conference aboard the "Far West," that Colonel Gibbon's troops could not possibly reach the vicinity of the Little Big Horn valley *before* June 26th at the most, and Custer was instructed to so time his marches that both commands would reach the rendezvous *not earlier than that date.*

Unfortunately, Custer did not carry out his commander's plan for cooperative action. Indeed, Custer had stated to Colonel William Ludlow of the Engineer Corps of the U. S. army, on the streets of St. Paul, but a few minutes after having been notified that he was restored to the command of the regiment, that he was to accompany General Terry's column, adding a statement that his purpose would be at the first chance in the campaign *"to cut loose from (and make his operations independent of) General Terry during the summer,"* that he had *"got away with Stanley and would be able to swing clear of Terry."** This, after General Terry had used

---

* "The Campaign Against the Sioux in 1876." Col. Robert P. Hughes, in the *Journal of the Military Service Institution* for January, 1896. See also note 2 at end of chapter.

Looking West from Reno Hill into the valley of the Little Big Horn and the site of the great Indian encampment. Reno's first fight occurred near the bend in the river at the extreme upper right. A Brininstool photo.

his influence to have Custer restored to the regiment in order that he might accompany the expedition!

Upon reaching the trail which Major Reno had discovered, Custer gave no further attention to his commander's instructions, but at once, and with almost feverish haste, followed the trail over into the Little Big Horn valley, making forced marches and exhausting both men and horses. It will be noted that Custer (reaching the valley of the Little Big Horn shortly after noon of the 25th) was at least twenty-four hours in advance of the time he was instructed to be there, thus completely wrecking and upsetting all the carefully-laid plans of the expeditionary commander. The approach of Custer's troops having been discovered by the keen-eyed scouts of the hostiles, he had to do one of two things—fight, or see the Indians slip from his grasp. Needless to say, he chose to fight.

Unfortunately again, the written instructions to Custer from General Terry were not of a positive character, hence, for three-quarters of a century, dispute and bitter controversy has waged fiercely (and doubtles always will) as to whether Custer wilfully disregarded these instructions. In a confidential telegram to Washington, however, General Terry stated that he had warned Custer that Gibbon's troops could not possibly get to the Little Big Horn valley before the 26th at the earliest.

General Terry knew the impetuous and dashing make-up of Custer. He had tried to induce him to accept a battery of Gatling guns and some of the Second Cavalry from Gibbon's command as an auxiliary to his own forces; but Custer had declined this tender, arguing that he could, with the Seventh Cavalry alone, whip any body of Indians he was likely to encounter, and that the Gatling guns would only hinder and impede his progress.

The Indian village was strung along the west bank of the Little Big Horn river for a distance of over four miles, being pitched on a level plain. The east side of the stream washed the edge of broken, precipitous bluffs, all but impossible of ascent or descent by mounted troops, and there were fords only at certain places—all, of course, unknown to Custer. The village was from a half-mile to a mile in width across the valley, containing approximately eighteen hundred lodges, with many hundreds of single wicki-ups in addition, to accommodate the young braves who had "jumped" their reservations to join the hostiles. The entire population of the village was estimated at 15,000 men, women and children, with from 3,500 to 5,000 of the flower of the fighting strength of the Sioux and Cheyenne nations, armed with the best of repeating rifles, with unlimited stores of ammunition, in addition to their ever-present bows and arrows. It was the largest assemblage of Indians ever found in one camp on the American continent. Their pony herd contained from 20,000 to 30,000 animals.

Although this village was known as "Sitting Bull's camp," the fighting chiefs were Gall, Crazy Horse, Crow King, Hump, Two Moons and others. Sitting Bull was not, as previously stated, a fighting chief, but was a medicine man of great power and influence over his tribe. He took no part personally in the battle.

It is well at this point to make mention of the fighting capacity and armament of the Seventh Cavalry at that time. On this expedition Custer's regiment was only about sixty per cent full strength, the companies containing only from thirty to forty men each. From thirty to forty per cent of these were raw recruits—young men, principally from the cities, who were inferior horsemen, poor shots, unused to campaigning, much less Indian fighting, easily "rattled" and quickly stampeded in a crisis. They were armed with the single-shot Springfield carbine, caliber .45-70, and Colt revolver, caliber .45. The carbines were slow of fire, easily and quickly fouled, and defective of shell extraction—a prime factor in Custer's defeat. *No man, not even an officer, carried either saber or sword,* despite the efforts of Hollywood moving picture companies to depict the battle of the Little Big Horn

Gen. Custer shown resting with a fine trophy taken on one of his hunting trips.

otherwise. Each trooper carried on his person fifty rounds of carbine ammunition and twenty-four extra rounds of revolver ammunition. An additional fifty rounds of carbine ammunition was carried by each trooper in his saddle bags.

No wagons or transportation of any kind, save pack-mules, accompanied the Seventh Cavalry. All the extra ammunition (24,000 rounds) was carried on the pack-mules.

When Custer's Indian scouts reported to him the approximate location of the Indian camp (while yet nearly twenty miles away) he made preparations for immediate attack. Marching until within about fifteen miles of the village, he here made his first great error. He detached Captain F. W. Benteen, with three troops of the Seventh, with instructions to "move to the left, pitch into anything you come across, and report to me." With Captain Benteen, but marching well in his rear, came Captain Thomas McDougall with the pack-train, carrying all the supplies and reserve ammunition, and escorted by about 130 men.

It is well to remember this location of the pack-train, because all the ammunition which either Custer's or Reno's troops had, was the fifty rounds per man on the person and fifty more in their saddle-bags, besides the revolver ammunition mentioned. It will be seen, therefore, that none of the troops with either Reno or Custer were supplied with sufficient ammunition for any prolonged engagement. Further bear in mind, that both Benteen and McDougall were many miles away from Custer when so badly needed, with innumerable gullies, ravines, hills and canyons separating the respective commands, and further, *were there by Custer's own orders!*

After detaching Benteen and McDougall, with the pack-train, from the main command, Custer and Reno moved forward, side by side, to a point some twelve miles closer to the Indian village. Here Custer made the second division of the regiment. To Major Reno he gave three companies, with orders to "move forward at as rapid a gait as you think prudent, charge the village, *and we will support you.*" Reno's command consisted of exactly 112 men, his troops, like the others, containing a great percent of green recruits.

This left Custer with five companies, or troops, as they were then designated. These were Troops C, E, I, F and L.

Major Reno's command trotted away from Custer's column down to an Indian ford in the Little Big Horn river, at that time of year about belly-deep to the horses, caused by the melting of the snows in the Big Horn mountains. Reno crossed the stream, after allowing the command to water their horses, to the west side, and attacked the upper end of the great Indian camp, absolutely ignorant—as was every officer and man of the Seventh Cavalry (but not the Indian scouts)—of the overwhelming forces in the village.

The numerous and tortuous bends of the river practically hid the village from Reno's view until he had galloped out on the plain where he could see and note its extent and size. Here Reno saw at once that he was vastly outnumbered, and he immediately dispatched a courier to Custer (still following along in his rear, but on the other side of the river) with a note to the effect that "the enemy are in force in my front."

Reno's instructions were to "charge the village," and he has, absurdly and without warrant, been branded "a coward" by the general public because he did not carry out these instructions. Reno noted at once that to charge into that maelstrom of death with his puny force of but 112 men would mean the immediate sacrifice of his entire command. They would have been engulfed and swallowed up before he could have ridden five hundred yards among those Sioux tepees, swarming with thousands of blood-thirsty warriors. Custer, remember, had not attacked as yet. He had told Reno to make the initial attack and *he would be supported by the (Custer's) entire outfit.*

After notifying Custer of the overwhelming numbers of the enemy, Reno fought gamely and courageously as long as he had the faintest hope of driving the enemy before him, all the time looking for Custer, and wondering why he had failed to come to his support, as promised. But Custer had not followed nor supported Reno, and every second that Indian horde in front of him increased until there were fully a thousand yelling, exultant savages about him.

Why did not Custer stand by and support Reno as he had promised to do? Nobody knows to this day; but it is supposed by all who have carefully studied the details of this battle, that Custer had formed no battle plans up to that time. Benteen later contended that he had been given no order at all, save to go to the left and look for Indians; that there was no intimation from Custer as to what Custer expected him to do or the part he was to take in the battle.

"I always contended that it was a rather senseless order,"

testified Captain Benteen at the Reno Court of Inquiry, in 1879. " I could see no use of being sent away, over a practically impassable country, to look up more Indians when we all realized that there were already probably more ahead of us than we could take care of. Much less, nothing was said to me about effecting any junction with Major Reno."

John Burkman, Custer's "striker," who committed suicide at the age of 86 and who now lies buried in the National Cemetery, Custer battlefield. Brininstool photo 1924.

After Reno crossed the river, as ordered by Custer, and started the battle, Custer followed along in his rear for a mile or so, and then swung off to the right, over bluffs and ravines, sending no word whatever to Reno of this move, but with the evident intention of going down stream on his own side of the river, and attacking the village at its lower end. This, however, is only a supposition. Nobody knows what was in Custer's mind or what he intended to do, as there were no survivors of his command.

But Custer was not posted on the lay of the land, and he had to march over four miles of rough country before he could find a place where the steepness of the bluffs on his side of the river would allow him to approach a ford where his mounted men could cross and attack the camp—if such was his intention. But Custer never reached the ford.

For a quarter of an hour or so, Reno's men continued to pluckily hold out, their leader every moment expecting to hear the cheers of Custer's men charging to their support. The Indians had already stampeded the Arickaree scouts who held the left of the skirmish line, and the Sioux were now rapidly filtering through and working around to Reno's rear. Moreover, they were also firing upon his command from the bluffs across the river, and the two miles of country between him and the crossing which he had negotiated in advancing to the attack, were now swarming with the yelling hordes.

The situation was now desperate! What to do? Whatever was done must be done instantly. It would appear that Reno's chief had left him to "paddle his own canoe"; his raw recruits were firing away their ammunition hastily and without accomplishing much, and in another twenty minutes would be facing the enemy with empty guns. Then? Nothing but complete annihilation would be their portion!

And Major Reno has been branded "a coward" for using good judgment in such a crisis! Because he did not charge the swooping thousands in his front—not knowing the whereabouts of Custer, but supposing him on the way to his support!

Reno gave the command to mount and retreat to the bluffs on the opposite side of the river. It was the only chance of saving any of his command—of giving them the one opportunity of escaping with their lives. It was a most desperate chance, but Major Reno gamely took it, and to that move is to be credited the lives of all of the command who reached the bluffs.

In this din of battle, with the rattle of rifle-fire from the Indians, the resonant roar of cavalry carbines, the yells of the savages, making orders scarcely intelligible, and with billows of dust blinding everything fifty feet away, the order to "mount and get to the bluffs" was not generally overheard and

John Burkman, Custer's orderly, with Vic and Dandy, Custer's mounts. Custer rode Vic into battle where the animal was killed. Dandy was taken back to the pack train and later sent to the general's father at Monroe, Mich.

understood, and seventeen of the command were left behind in the timber, through nobody's fault but their own failure to hear the retreat order. Many of these eluded capture and joined Reno's command on the bluffs later, although some thrilling escapes were recorded.

In this retreat, or charge—and it was a most desperate fight for life every inch of the way—Major Reno lost twenty-nine men before the remnants of his shattered command reached the bluffs across the river, nearly two miles distant from the spot where the initial battle of the Little Big Horn was fought.

Charley Reynolds, Custer's chief of scouts and a plainsman of great fame and renown was among those cut off and killed, as was "Bloody Knife," the Arickaree scout and a special favorite of Custer's, who was killed at Reno's side just before the retreat was begun. Lieutenant Donald McIntosh, Lieutenant Benny Hodgson and Surgeon DeWolf also were shot dead, Hodgson dropping under the Indian fire after being towed across the river hanging to the stirrup of one of the troopers.

Just about the time that Reno's men were cutting their way through at the ford, Custer was being attacked down stream, and hundreds of Sioux, who had been arrayed against Reno, suddenly ceased harrassing him further, and swarmed down stream to concentrate against Custer. This was the only thing which prevented the complete annihilation of Reno's command. Had the savages followed his men up the bluffs with the same boldness with which they obstructed his retreat to the river, not a man of his command would have escaped!

Shortly after Reno's exhausted troopers had gained the bluffs, and were already digging in for their lives to form a barricade, Benteen's troops arrived in sight and joined him. Benteen had sighted no Indians at all on his little side scout, and had come to the conclusion that the best thing for him to do was to join the main column once more. The pack-train was yet almost an hour's travel in his rear, and Reno's com-

These Sioux Indians, with the exception of those in parentheses, all fought Custer at the Little Big Horn. Left to right, standing—(Jim Red Cloud), Red Hawk, Eagle Bear, Makes Enemy, Standing Bear, Sitting Hawk, White Bull, (Charles Little Hawk). Sitting—Blind Water, Iron Horse, Eagle Chase, Black Elk, Little Horse, unidentified and Conroy. Brininstool Photo.

mand had exhausted their ammunition to such an extent that they were practically unarmed.

Here again Reno has been branded "a coward' for not immediately hastening to Custer's relief! What could Reno have "supported" Custer with?· Not with ammunition, that is certain—and that was Custer's dire necessity right at that particular moment—ammunition, and plenty of it! Yet, there the pack-train was, miles away—*and by Custer's own orders*—at the time the entire command sorely needed to replenish its supply of cartridges! Besides, Reno had a great many wounded men, and these had to be supported by unwounded comrades, and this required six men to each suffering trooper!

As quickly as the pack-train arrived and ammunition could be distributed, Reno advanced in the direction of the sound of Custer's guns. Reaching a point where they could overlook the field, the Reno command observed that most of the firing had ceased, but that numbers of the Indians were riding about and apparently shooting at objects on the ground, but what they were could not be distinguished. Custer's command was not in sight, and it was the supposition that he had been repulsed and been obliged to retreat down stream in an effort to join Terry and Gibbon.

After Reno had advanced about one mile—having to carry all his wounded by hand, requiring six men to each injured trooper, the Indians (who had now annihilated Custer) again swarmed back to attack Reno for the second time. As their present position was not considered a good one for defense, Reno ordered the command back to its original position, far better suited for a siege, and upon higher ground.

Here Reno and Benteen fought throughout the afternoon of the 25th, until about 9 o'clock that night, as well as all day of the 26th, making one of the most heroic defenses against overwhelming odds in the annals of Indian warfare, and successfully keeping the savage hordes from getting inside their lines.

Late in the afternoon of the 26th, hovering dustclouds down the valley indicated the approach of another body of troops (Terry's and Gibbon's commands), whereupon the whole Indian village moved away in massed formation, broke up into small parties and scattered—and the battle of the Little Big Horn was over.

When Terry and Gibbon reached Reno's position, early on the morning of the 27th, the first question asked them was, "Where is Custer? Have you seen anything of him?" Not until then did Reno and Benteen have any idea of Custer's whereabouts, nor entertain the faintest suspicion but that he had been able to take care of himself. That he had met defeat and utter annihilation stunned and appalled them. It was unbelievable, incomprehensible!

Where *was* Custer, and what did he do?

The last man to see Custer alive, of the Seventh Cavalry, was John Martin, his orderly trumpeter, who had been sent by Custer, while enroute to the lower end of the Indian village, with a message to Benteen, that he had struck an immense Indian village, and to "come on, and be quick, and bring the packs."

This message did not reach Benteen until he was five or six miles distant from Custer, in the delivery of which Trumpeter Martin himself was fired upon by the Indians and his horse wounded. Besides, the packs were *not* in command of Benteen, but of Captain McDougall—and McDougall was a considerable distance in Benteen's rear when Martin arrived.

Benteen *did* hurry forward upon receipt of this message, leaving McDougall to hustle along the packs; but when Benteen stopped to water his horses at a morass, and just as his command was leaving, several of the pack-mules came rushing up, half-crazed with thirst, and waded into the slough. Many were "bogged down," and it took McDougall some time to extricate them. Benteen, meantime, went ahead, and reached the river—just in time to see the last drama of Reno's disastrous charge.

"I saw what appeared to be about a thousand Indians pursuing and killing a dozen or fifteen of Reno's troopers," he testified.

Benteen at once joined Reno on the hill, arriving just in the nick of time. Hurried preparations for defense were at once begun, but fortunately Custer's attack four miles down stream diverted the attention of the savages from Reno and Benteen for some time. Meantime, they were obliged to await the arrival of the packs and extra ammunition before any forward move could be made. And even at that, *had* there been plenty of ammunition, neither Reno or Benteen could by any manner of means have reached Custer, any more than Custer could have reached them. There were thousands of savages between the two commands, far better armed in every way than were the Seventh Cavalry.

This unfortunate separation of the regiment was unquestionably one of the prime factors in Custer's defeat. It was the same tactics he had employed at the "battle" of the Washita, in November, 1868, when he had surrounded and destroyed the village of Black Kettle. But it is very doubtful if Custer could have gained a victory over the Indians if he *had* kept the regiment together. It would have been a case of 600 against five to eight times that number, far better armed and equipped and far more skilfully led.

The actual discovery of the fate of Custer and his five companies was made in person by Lieutenant James H. Bradley, Seventh Infantry, chief of scouts for Colonel Gibbon, who, early on the morning of June 27th, was scouting ahead of the slow-moving infantry, on the east bank of the Little Big Horn. Suddenly his Crow Indian scouts called his attention to objects in the distance on a high knoll, which gleamed white and ghastly in the morning sun. Hastening forward, an awful sight met their gaze. Scattered about, here in groups and there singly or in twos and threes, lay the bodies of more than two hundred white men, all stripped naked, while lying about among them were the carcasses of dozens of horses all branded "7USC."

Capt. Myles W. Keogh, (Brevet Lt. Col.) Commanding Troop I, killed
in the Custer battle.

And this is all that ever was, or will be, known of the fate
of Custer, or his defeat and annihilation, because no man
survived to tell the tale. Had there been a survivor his fame
would have been world-wide from that day. How, or in what
manner, those five companies of gallant troopers and their
courageous, daring leaders were wiped out, no man can, with
certainty, say. All that is known is what the Indians tell who

fought against him—and their stories have been given hesitatingly and only under pressure, and are not dependable at the most. Dozens of alleged "survivors" of Custer's command have stepped into the limelight with the passing years; but all are prevaricators pure and simple. Not one man escaped the slaughter.

With Custer on that fatal field also died his two brothers, Captain Tom Custer, Seventh Cavalry, and Boston Custer, the general's younger brother. The latter was a civilian whom the general had appointed forage master of the expedition in order that he might accompany the command because of poor health, and it was thought the out-door life might benefit him. Custer's 19-year-old nephew, Armstrong Reed, who had accompanied the command just for the excitement and adventure of the trip, and Lieutenant James Calhoun, Custer's brother-in-law, also were among the slain.

Mark Kellogg, the reporter from the Bismarck Tribune, also lay dead on the field, the notes he had made on the expedition all ready to send east at the first chance, being found in his pockets. Colonel Lounsberry, editor of the Tribune, had expected to accompany the expedition, but was prevented at the last moment, and dispatched Kellogg in his place.

The only living thing found on the Custer field was one horse, the animal ridden by Captain Myles Keogh. This horse, named "Comanche," was discovered wandering aimlessly about, wounded in seven places. It was at first deemed advisable to shoot the animal and put him out of his misery, but after being examined by Dr. Porter, the only surviving surgeon (who was with Reno's command), his wounds were found not necessarily fatal. The horse was conveyed to the steamer "Far West," lying at the mouth of the Little Big Horn, carried down to Bismarck with the wounded, survived his injuries and lived to be 28 years of age, the pet and pride of the Seventh Cavalry to the day of his death. His mounted body yet stands in the museum of the Kansas State University at Lawrence.

Emmanuel Custer, father of the general, is shown mounted on "Dandy," Custer's favorite mount, which John Burkman was ordered to take to the pack-train just before the battle.

What were the causes of Custer's defeat? To the writer, at least, after years of study and research, it would appear that the chief reasons were these:

First: Positive disobedience of the orders of General Terry in bringing on an engagement with the Indians at least twenty-four hours in advance of the specified date of the arrival of all the troops of the expedition into the valley of the Little Big Horn.

Second: Neglecting to believe positive first-hand information from his scouts as to the overwhelming numbers of the enemy (although warned by them that the enemy were far more numerous than his own command); underestimating their strength, fighting ability and superiority in arms and ammunition, and being unmindful of the fact that the Indian leaders were familiar with every foot of the ground over which they fought—of all of which Custer was ignorant.

Third: The antiquated Springfield carbine used by the Seventh Cavalry—a single-shot, slow-firing weapon, with a shell extractor which was not dependable at all.

Fourth—and perhaps the chief factor—the fatal separation of the regiment into three battalions, none of which were within supporting distance of each other when so badly needed, and sending the pack-train carrying all the reserve of ammunition out with the first detachment while yet fifteen miles from what was later the scene of action—too far, by many miles, to have reached Custer in time to have aided him in the least.

Such are the main facts about the battle of the Little Big Horn. And yet, another fifty years will find speculation just as rife, controversy just as heated, dispute and acrimony just as bitter as to the causes of Custer's defeat. It can scarcely be otherwise, with no survivor of Custer's command to step forth and give that side of the story.

I can close this chapter with nothing more apropos than the words of Lieutenant-Colonel W. A. Graham, late Judge Advocate U. S. Army, himself a close student of the battle of the Little Big Horn:

"The tactics of the Indians on that day resulted in their doing to Custer exactly what Custer had planned tactically to do to them. And they were able to do it because they had the leaders, the arms and the overwhelming forces, none of which facts were known or appreciated by the Seventh Cavalry. Their numbers had been underestimated; their leadership and fighting capacity undervalued; their superiority in arms not even suspected. The Seventh Cavalry paid the penalty for national stupidity."

NOTE 1.

WHY CROOK DID NOT MEET TERRY, GIBBON AND CUSTER

Interesting Comments on the Rosebud Fight of June 17, 1876

The author has in his possession a most interesting and valuable letter from Mr. Robert E. Strahorn, of San Francisco, who, in 1876 was war correspondent for the New York Times, Chicago Tribune and Rocky Mountain News, of Denver. Mr. Strahorn was assigned to Gen. Crook's division, and took part personally in every battle and skirmish in which Crook's forces were engaged throughout the campaign. Mr. Strahorn is prominently mentioned and thanked by the then Secretary of War, for his courageous help in the Crazy Horse fight of March, 1876, and particularly mentioned in Capt. John G. Bourke's well-known work, "On the Border With Crook," for distinguished bravery and gallantry in action against the hostile Indians on every occasion in which Crook's troops engaged. There is no more competent authority on the part played by Crook's forces in the Sioux Campaign of 1876, than Mr. Strahorn. In explanation of Crook's fight on the Rosebud, June 17th, and his subsequent return to his base on Goose Creek, near the present city of Sheridan, Wyoming, Mr. Strahorn wrote:

"*Dear Mr. Brininstool:* Your question as to why Crook, with his 1,100 men retreated to Goose Creek after the Rosebud fight, and called for reinforcements, is easily answered. After some hours of pretty close fighting with a body of Indians estimated all the way from 2,000 to 3,000 or 4,000, and incidentally then retreat down a narrow gorge (known today as the "Dead Canyon of the Rosebud") toward their main command on the Little Big Horn, we happened to be riding with General Crook and his staff at the head of the column in pursuit. Suddenly halting, and rais-

General George Crook, who suffered a disastrous defeat in the battle of
the Rosebud, June 17, 1876, one week before the Custer battle.

ing his hand as a signal for that, he turned square back up through the ravine—of course facing the column all the way back—and with a disappointed look. I made bold to ask him why this move? He said that with all those wounded on our hands, and with an ambuscade clearly in sight, he would not take his men down into that hole.

"So we returned to the battlefield, camped there for the night, and buried our dead, which we had been carrying, and made campfires over their graves to mislead the Indians, if possible (who would naturally have dug them up to gratify their usual appetite for plunder.)

"That night Crook took the necessary steps to discover just the situation down that canyon and below, assigning the duty to Frank Grouard (his chief of scouts) and, I think, one other scout. Upon their return they reported all sorts of preparations on the sides of the canyon, and in the 'cul-de-sac' at the bottom, for a massacre, if we had gone down a little bit further.

"Crook thus took the only course open, and rode back to his wagon-train and sent for reinforcements. He had felt the Indians out very effectively, much to his credit following the safe course. He was on the offensive throughout the fight, took his time to return to his base—and wasn't whipped.

"I was with Crook in every foray or movement throughout the Sioux war, and am sure that his undoubted courage, absolute devotion to duty, and unequaled experience in Indian warfare, would have led him to persist in his march to effect a junction with Terry on the Yellowstone, except for the needless sacrifice of troops involved in certain further encounters with the savages, whose overwhelming numbers were absolutely unknown until then. Remember, that with every fourth man taking care of the horses in a fight (because you can't fight Indians mounted); also providing adequate protection of the wounded and pack-train, and exhaustion of half his ammunition, Crook was actually in nearly as poor shape to advance as was Custer when he rode to his doom a week later.

"Doubtless the Indians he engaged there would have returned with much larger forces had Crook continued northward; and while I think he was too adroit a campaigner to have duplicated the Custer fiasco, there is no telling how great a loss of men might have been suffered, but for his return to his base."

(Signed) ROBERT E. STRAHORN

NOTE 2.

THE CHICAGO TRIBUNE'S OPINION

On July 7th, 1876, the Chicago Tribune printed a column-length editorial on the Little Big Horn battle, in which it attributed the disaster to Custer himself, saying among other things:

"Custer . . . was a brave, brilliant soldier, handsome and dashing, but he was reckless, hasty and impulsive, preferring to make a dare-devil rush and take risks rather than to move slower and with more certainty, and it was his own mad-cap haste, rashness and love of fame that cost him his own life, and cost the service the loss of many brave officers and gallant men. No account seems to have been taken of the numbers or leadership of the Sioux, . . . no account was even taken of the fact that General Gibbon was coming to the Little Big Horn with reinforcements, only a day's march behind, *although General Custer was aware of it.* He preferred to make a reckless dash and take the consequences, in the hope of making a personal victory and adding to the glory of another charge, rather than wait for the sufficiently-powerful force to make the fight successful and share the glory with others. *He took the risk, and he lost.*"

And on June 5, 1932, the same Chicago Tribune said: "Printed at a time when it could not be popular, the Tribune utterance was a masterpiece of editorial judgment and courage."

CHAPTER 2

A TROOPER'S ACCOUNT OF THE BATTLE.

Author's Note—In the following thrilling account of the battle of the Little Big Horn, given to the author in 1920, William C. Slaper, Los Angeles, California, formerly of Troop M, Seventh Cavalry, under comand of Capt. Thos. H. French, (which troop fought with Major Reno's battalion) recounts his own personal experiences in this greatest of Indian battles upon the American continent. Mr. Slaper's story can be depended upon as absolutely reliable and accurate insofar as his own personal observation is concerned. No two men would likely have witnessed things exactly similar under the exciting conditions which existed on the occasion of the Little Big Horn fight. Mr. Slaper's escape from an awful death was miraculous, and his story is the clear, concise truth of a trooper in the ranks. Mr. Slaper died at the Soldiers' Home, Los Angeles, Nov. 13, 1931.

I WAS BORN AND RAISED IN CINCINNATI, Ohio, November 23, 1855, working there at various employments until I attained my twentieth year. Early in September, 1875, I found myself out of a job, and while walking along the street, wondering what I had better try next in the work line, I observed the sign, "Men Wanted," in front of the United States Army Recruiting Station. Although I had passed that sign numberless times before, it never held any attraction for me until that morning.

I stopped and read it. Then I wondered if they would take me as a soldier. Half-heartedly I went upstairs to the office, almost hoping I would be rejected. I told the recruiting officer what I was after. He asked me many questions, and finally I was requested to disrobe for a physical examination. This examination was a very rigid one, because out of ten applicants that morning, but two were accepted, I being one of them.

There and then I took an oath to serve Uncle Sam to the best of my ability, for the regal sum of $13 a month "and found." The $13 were always forthcoming, but the "found" part I often found wanting. At that time, any young man wearing the uniform of a United States soldier was looked upon as an idler—too lazy to work. Being in my own home town, and well known, I felt somewhat ashamed of being seen in my uniform.

I had a sweetheart, of course, and naturally wanted to see her, although I remained indoors most of the time. However, as the time of my departure drew near, I ventured forth one afternoon to pay her a visit. I thought by making use of back alleys and unfrequented streets, I might reach her home undetected; but someone who knew me reported it at my home, and this brought my older brother down the following morning to investigate the matter, and, as he said, "to get me out of the army." As I was under age, it was lucky for me that I managed to get my brother's ear before he reached the recruiting office. I took him to the room I had been occupying, and told him if he "gave me away" they could send me to prison for two years for making a false statement regarding my age. He finally concluded to let me go ahead, but first commanded me to go home and see my mother, as she knew where I was and wanted to see me.

I found she had met with an accident whereby she had broken her arm in two places. When she saw me in army uniform, she fainted. That was too much for me! Kissing her, I rushed from the house, leaving my mother in the care of my sister. Mother had a dread of war—and with good reason. My father, my mother's brother, her brother-in-law and a cousin all lost their lives during the first year of the Civil War. It had made life hard for her, as there were five of us

Wm. C. Slaper, Troop M, Reno Battalion, shown at the spot where he dipped up water for his wounded comrades while under fire of Indians across the stream. Recipient of Congressional Medal of Honor. Brininstool photo 1926.

children. Doubtless she feared that I never would come back home to her again—but I did, after five years' service. Mother lived only three months after my return, however.

A few days later, twenty of us recruits were sent to Jefferson Barracks, St. Louis. Here we remained about six weeks, where we were instructed in the dismounted drill, and given some preliminary training at stables. We were taught how to groom a horse in regulation style, by a crusty old sergeant named "Bully" Welch, a character whom all old cavalrymen of that day will remember.

Then came an order for several recruits to be sent to join the Fifth Cavalry. Many of the twenty young fellows who had come to St. Louis with me, were taken. Soon after this, three or four of us were selected to become troopers in the Seventh Cavalry. General Sam Sturgis was then at St. Louis on recruiting service, and commanded Jefferson Barracks. He was also in command of the Seventh Cavalry, and his son, Jack, who had graduated from West Point, was there with him. Jack was appointed a second lieutenant in the Seventh, and was to accompany the recruits. I well remember when we were all in line to receive our instructions, Gen. Sturgis told us he was going to send his son with us to the Seventh Cavalry, and for us to take good care of him—which we gladly promised to do. Poor Jack! His service was a short one after that. He was killed with Custer's command in the Little Big Horn fight, and his body was one of those never found—at least, not recognized, when we buried the dead.

Both Lieut. Sturgis and I were assigned to M Company. We left St. Louis in good marching order, our destination being Fort Abraham Lincoln, near Bismarck, Dakota, on the Missouri River, then headquarters of the Seventh Cavalry.

A little incident that took place en route will perhaps amuse the reader. While stopping for coffee and something to eat at Fargo, Dakota, we had about two hours to wait. An Irish sergeant in charge of our car—seemingly an old veteran—instructed a bunch of recruits to go to a certain

Captain Thomas W. Custer, commanding Troop C, a brother of Gen.
Custer.

saloon not far from the station, take their canteens and guns,
and pawn or trade the weapons for liquor, and to bring the
liquor back in their canteens. On their return with the
whiskey, he then took a squad of recruits, armed them as
guards and marched them over to the saloon. Here he

threatened the proprietor for buying government arms, and immediately confiscated the pawned weapons! He thus secured plenty of whiskey at no expense. I thought myself that it was a pretty clever trick. Needless to say that from Fargo to Bismarck that night, the sergeant's car contained a bunch of noisy and hilarious troopers. However, we reached Bismarck in good shape, where we were ferried over the Missouri River to Fort Lincoln.

Here were six companies of the Seventh Cavalry stationed. We fresh recruits were lined up and assigned to our respective companies, I being, as stated previously, assigned to M Troop, which had just got in from a scout. A day or so later we were started for Fort Rice. Here we passed an uneventful winter, and here I got a taste of real cold weather, the thermometer often reaching 40 degrees below zero. I remember that among other duties, we cut ice and filled the big ice house—later to be enjoyed by the infantry who were sent to guard the fort, while we of the cavalry were out campaigning on the hot, dry, dusty plains, drinking alkali water.

When spring arrived, we were ordered back to Fort Lincoln, where we went into camp, having received instructions to make ready to join the expedition to be sent out against Sitting Bull and his hostile warriors of the Sioux nation, who were then leaving their reservation in large numbers, and committing all sorts of depredations. There were many sub-tribes of the Sioux who "jumped" their reservations with their families and plenty of extra ponies, all heading to meet at a general rendezvous, later found to be established along the Little Big Horn River, in the territory of Montana.

Some months previously, Capt. Tom Custer, brother of the general, had been sent to Standing Rock Agency, on the Missouri River, about 40 miles below Fort Rice. The object of his trip was to arrest an Indian named Rain-in-the-Face, who was wanted for the murder of Dr. Honzinger, an army veterinarian, and a Mr. Ballaran, an army post sutler, who had strayed from their command. After some hazardous

Rain-in-the-Face, prominent Sioux in the Custer fight.

maneuvers, Capt. Custer, through the assistance of Charley Reynolds, General Custer's chief of scouts, secured the Indian, and took him to Fort Lincoln, where he was placed in the guardhouse. One night, several prisoners broke out, among them being Rain-in-the-Face, who immediately joined the hostiles and swore eternal vengeance against Capt. Tom Custer.

It was on the 17th day of May, 1876, that my regiment left Fort Abraham Lincoln. Gen. Alfred H. Terry was the commanding officer of the entire expedition, but the Seventh Cavalry itself was under the immediate command of General Custer. It was said to be the best equipped regiment as to horses, men and accouterments, that Uncle Sam had ever turned out. Custer was known to be very strong for getting only the best in horses and men, and for securing all the conveniences which that early day afforded. There was little enough in the way of comfort at that time on the then un-settled plains of the northwest.

Being only a "kid" at the time, I paid but little attention to passing events, such as keeping a diary, as some of the older men did, so at this distant day I am unable to give dates, names of camping places, etc., as readily as I would wish. I was only in the "shavetail" class, having had no real ex-perience in roughing it, much less of Indian fighting. But I was destined to get my full share ere another six weeks had passed.

The first day's march was a very lengthy one, and we camped on Little Heart River. There was some excitement on on this first day's march, as some of the horses were very un-ruly and hard to manage after their long winter's rest; and having been well fed, they were ready to "go." In camp that night, there was more excitement. The prairie all about us was on fire, and we were kept busy fighting the flames to prevent their spreading through the camp. However, it did but little damage, and we shortly thereafter had a chance to rest

Chief Gall, a Hunkpapa, who led the final charge against Custer. Photo by D. F. Barry.

All went well until June 1, when we were in the Bad Lands of the Little Missouri. Retiring as usual that night, we were surprised the following morning to discover that we had been snowed in. We were using "pup" tents, two men to the tent, which left but little room for anything else. It turned very cold, and was mighty uncomfortable for both men and horses, but we passed through it with no great harm being done.

Nothing worth special mention occurred thereafter until we reached Powder River. Attached to the expedition were four companies of the Second Cavalry, some artillery and some infantry. At the Powder River, our wagons were all sent back. Our sabers were also here boxed and returned; no one, not even an officer, retaining his. The regimental band also was sent back. Thereafter pack mules carried the rations, extra ammunition and supplies of whatever nature were taken along. Some scouting was done from here, and taken altogether, it looked very much as if trouble would loom on the horizon ere long. Rumors of all sorts were floating about the camp, but nothing official was reported.

On June 22d, we left our Powder River Camp. General Terry had tendered Custer the use of four companies of the Second Cavalry, but they were declined, Custer remarking that he could whip any Indian village on the Plains with his own regiment, and that extra troops would simply be a burden. He also declined the tender of the Gatling guns.

Nothing of special interest occurred on the 22d, the march being but a short one, probably of twelve or fifteen miles. The next day we marched about thirty miles (as I recollect) and the following day about the same; but at some hour in the night we were called out and made ready to make a night march. This has always been a puzzle to me, since it was given out that we were to meet General Terry in the neighborhood of the Big Horn River, with the balance of his command on the morning of June 27th. I do not claim to know what orders General Custer had from General Terry about this, save from the written instructions given Custer by Terry, which are now public and which doubtless every student of the Custer fight has read. It seemed to be the general understanding among the men that Custer and Terry were understood to have agreed to meet somewhere in the valley of the Little Big Horn on June 27th.

This forced night march had much to do with the worn condition of our horses during the battle of the Little Big Horn. The grazing had been poor for several days, and as we were traveling in light marching order—that is, without wagons—there was little, if any, grain for our horses.

As I recall, it was about daylight when we halted and made coffee. I remember this very distinctly, because I did not get any of the coffee, having dropped down under a tree and fallen asleep, holding to the bridle-rein of my horse, and I did not awaken until called to fall into line. We did not unsaddle at this halt, so the animals secured but little rest.

This was on the fateful morning of June 25th, when so much was destined to happen. We all knew that we were on a hot Indian trail, and likely to run into the savages at any moment. Excitement began to grow, and every move was watched with curiosity and intense eagerness. Throughout the morning we were traveling quite rapidly. Toward noon there was a halt, and General Custer called his officers together and gave them their instructions. It so happened that my company M, under Capt. Thomas French, Company A, under Captain Moylan, and Company G, under Captain Wallace, were elected to go under the command of Major Marcus A. Reno. Of course we did not know at that time what General Custer's plans were, or how many companies he took with him, but later learned that Companies C, E, I, F and L were under his immediate command, and Captain Benteen was given Companies H, K and D, while Company B was to guard the pack-train, under the command of Captain McDougall.

As I recall it, it was Benteen and his command which

Captain Thomas W. French, Troop M, Reno Battalion.

started on to the left. General Custer and his command went straight ahead along the little tributary of the Little Big Horn River, but on the right bank of the stream, while Reno and his command marched parallel to Custer on the left bank.

Soon after this, Adjutant Cooke came direct to Reno from Custer with some instructions. Then we took a rather sharp angle to the left, and things began to liven up. We were then trotting our horses and going down a long hillside which took us to the Little Big Horn River, which we crossed. I believe it was Company M which had the advance and was the first to ford the river, Company A following, with G Company in the rear.

Soon commenced the rattle of rifle fire, and bullets began to whistle about us. I remember that I ducked my head and tried to dodge bullets which I could hear whizzing through the air. This was my first experience under fire. I know that for a time I was frightened, and far more so when I got my first glimpse of the Indians riding about in all directions, firing at us and yelling and whooping like incarnate fiends, all seemingly as naked as the day they were born, and painted from head to foot in the most hideous manner imaginable.

We were soon across the stream, through a strip of timber and out into the open, where our captain ordered us to dismount and prepare to fight on foot. Number Fours were ordered to hold the horses, while Numbers One, Two and Three started for the firing line.

Our horses were scenting danger before we dismounted, and several at this point became unmanageable and started straight for the open among the Indians, carrying their helpless riders with them. One of the boys, a young fellow named Smith, of Boston, we never saw again, either dead or alive.

In forming the firing line we deployed to the left. By this time the Indians were coming in closer and in increasing numbers, circling about and raising such a dust that a great many of them had a chance to get in our rear under cover of it—where we found them on our retreat!

It was on this line that I saw the first one of my own company comrades fall. This was Sergeant O'Hara. Then I observed another, and yet another. Strange to say, I had recovered from my first fright, and had no further thought of fear, although conscious that I was in great peril and standing a mighty good chance of never getting out of it alive.

The Indians were now increasing in such hordes and pouring such a hot fire into our small command, that it was getting

Spotted Tail, a Brule Sioux Indian.

to be a decidedly unhealthy neighborhood for Reno's command. In a short time word came to retreat back to the horses in the timber. We got back there about as quickly as we knew how. In this excitement, some of the horseholders released their animals before the riders arrived, and consequently they were "placed afoot" which made it exceedingly critical for them. It was said that before Reno gave the order to mount and retreat, he rode up to Capt. French and shouted, "Well, Tom, what do you think of this?" Capt. French replied, "I think we had better get out of here." Reno thereupon gave the order, although I did not hear it. Neither did I hear any bugle calls or other orders or commands of any sort. I could hear nothing but the continual roar of Indian rifles and the sharp, resonant bang-bang of cavalry carbines, mingled with the whoops of the savages and the shouts of my comrades.

When I got to my horse there were not many of us left in the timber that I could see. Soon after, Private Henry Koltzbucher who was "striker" for Capt. French, was shot through the stomach, just as he was in the act of mounting his horse. He fell to the ground, and I saw Private Francis Neely dismount to help him. I thereupon got off my own horse and helped Neely drag the wounded trooper into a clump of heavy underbrush, where we thought he might not be found by the Indians. Wm. E. Morris, another comrade, came up at this juncture and helped us care for Koltzbucher. We saw that he was probably mortally wounded, so we left him a canteen of water and hurriedly mounted again, dashing toward the river in the wake of our flying trooper comrades. After the battle we found the body of Koltzbucher where we had dragged him. He was not mutilated, and consequently had not been discovered by the Indians or their squaws in their fiendish work of killing and mutilating our comrades who had been helplessly wounded in the river bottom.

I cannot say that the retreat from the river bottom—and further on—had a very military appearance, but I can say that I saw nothing disorderly about it, although so many had gone on ahead of me and were so far in advance that what they did, or in what order they retreated, I cannot say with positive certainty. I did not strike the river at the regular ford, so was compelled to jump my horse into the stream at a point where the bank was about six or eight feet high. My animal nearly lost his footing when he struck the water. As I glanced about me, the first thing that engaged my attention was Trumpeter Henry Fisher of M Troop, riding in the river some distance up, with Lieut. Benny Hodgson hanging to one stirrup. Hodgson had been wounded and was on foot in the stream, when Fisher came dashing into the water. Noting Hodgson's helpless condition, he thrust one of his stirrups toward him, which Hodgson grasped and was thus towed across to the opposite bank, under a galling fire from the Indians, who were now riding into the stream, shooting into the ranks of the stampeding troopers, and actually pulling many of them from their horses right there in the river. As Fisher gained the opposite bank, dragging Hodgson at the end of his stirrup, and the latter was trying to struggle up the incline, another shot rang out and Hodgson dropped. I did not see him move again, and suppose he was killed right there.

My own position was decidedly precarious. As I urged my horse through the water I could see Indians in swarms about the ford above me, and many lashing their ponies to reach that spot, paying no attention to me. One reason for this was that I was alone, and they were doubtless looking for bigger game. Bullets were cutting the air all about me, however, as there were Indians on both banks, as well as in the water, fighting hand-to-hand with the troopers. Death seemed to ride on every hand, and yet a kind Providence must have been watching over me, for I crossed the stream unscathed. It was at the ford crossing where many of the men met their death, but in the retreat to the river and the climb up the steep bluffs on the opposite side, some twenty-nine troopers were killed.

I believe one reason why so many of the men escaped was because of the intense dust which was raised by the horses and ponies of the combatants. It hung in dense clouds, and it was almost impossible to see fifty feet ahead in any direction. With fully twenty-five hundred or three thousand Indians racing their ponies about through that dust-laden plain, one can understand better the explanation of the situation.

After getting across the river, I had the steep bluffs to climb. These were so very abrupt that many of the already-wearied horses were unable to carry their riders to the top, and many of the men had to dismount and lead their exhausted animals, all the time being under a murderous fire from the Indians hidden in the brush along the river. On the way up I passed the body of Dr. De Wolf, one of our surgeons, who had been shot and killed while trying to gain the top.

I arrived at the crest of the hill without even a scratch. Here I came upon Captain French with about twenty of the men, and I joined them. Capt. French was as "cool as a cucumber" throughout the entire battle, and although I searched his face carefully for any sign of fear, it was not there. He had such perfect self-control that I had to admire his courage and bravery, and was indeed glad to be under his leadership. I was, however, considerably worried about the rest of the command, and where Custer was and why he had failed to support us as he had promised to do. It looked to me as if we could be wiped out before any assistance arrived, as the Indians were now swarming up the bluffs after us, seeking places of advantage where they could completely surround us.

It was not long before Capt. Benteen was seen coming our way. I did not know where he had been or what he had been doing with his three companies, but I do know that they did not show the wear and tear of the Reno "remains." Had Reno not made that move out of the river bottom when he did— just in the nick of time—we could all have fared the fate of Custer and his men, without any assistance from any one.

Lieut. James Calhoun, commanding Troop L, who was married to Margaret
Custer, a sister of the General.

Even yet, I cannot understand why Benteen was not at hand
where he could have assisted Reno in the fight in the river
bottom. Of course he had his orders, but what they were I do
not know. But after he joined us on the hill, we shortly thereafter all mounted and started in the direction that Custer was
supposed to have gone. But we did not get very far. The Sioux
had such a countless horde of warriors there, and they met
our advance with such a staggering fire, that we were com-

pelled to turn about and retreat to our first position on the hill. Even here, we were not in a protected position. There were higher ridges than the one we were on, which were immediately occupied by Indian sharpshooters, who poured heavy volleys down upon us.

However, we were in the best position we were able to get in the limited time at hand. Here we laid out a hospital, with the horses staked around the outside. We then formed in line of battle outside the horses, and the fighting commenced with renewed vigor on both sides. We were ordered to lie flat on our stomachs and stay down, and not to expose ourselves, for the least sight of any portion of the body was the signal for a volley from the Indians. It was not long before we were carrying more wounded men to this improvised hospital.

There were many redskins on the higher hills which our short-barreled carbines could not reach. Finally our first sergeant joined the line at this point. He carried a special make of rifle—his own private weapon, and with it was enabled to throw bullets into the midst of the Indians there, and he soon silenced their fire. While in this line, Capt. French was about in the center, giving orders as coolly as though it was a Sunday school picnic. He would sit up tailor-style, while bullets were coming from the front and both sides. I could but marvel that he was not hit. Without appearing to be in the least excited, he would extract shells from guns in which cartridges would stick, and pass them loaded, then fix another, all the time watching in every direction.

We were not very well entrenched, as I recall that I used my butcher knife to cut the earth loose and throw a mound of it in front of me upon which to rest my carbine. At one time a bullet struck the corner of this mound, throwing so much dirt into my eyes that I could scarcely see for an hour or more. That same afternoon while lying face down on the ground, a bullet tore off the heel of my left boot as effectually as though it had been sawed off! That was as close as the Indians ever got to me, but I saw many of my comrades who fared worse.

With all the sad happenings in that hell-hole, there were yet some amusing incidents. In my company was a young fellow known as "Happy Jack," because of his jovial disposition. During all that leaden hail that fell about us, I could hear "Happy's" hearty laugh ring out at a distance, although I could not imagine the cause of it, as I didn't see anything to laugh at; but it cheered me and made me feel a bit braver. Another time I was helping drag a wounded comrade into the hospital. We were compelled to drag him because we dared not expose ourselves. On the way back we started to walk out from the hospital site, instead of creeping out. My comrade had just reached the horse line when a bullet struck him behind the ear. Fortunately it was merely a glancing shot, passing through his ear. He tumbled to the ground and rolled over and over until I had a chance to examine him and assure him he was not seriously hurt.

I had only just returned to my position on the firing line when the man next to me was shot through the shoulder and disabled.

The firing was very heavy all through the afternoon of the 25th, and continued until dusk, which was about 9 o'clock in that region at that time of year. After that, we had a little respite, and took occasion to strengthen our defenses and make better breastworks. At peep of day on the 26th, the fighting again commenced with renewed vigor. Just about daylight a stray pack-animal with the pack yet on its back, wandered past our line, and in order to relieve the poor beast of its burden, two troopers and myself arose to our feet. Having done some packing, I was quite handy in untying the ropes, but we had only just started when some Indians caught sight of us and gave us a volley. A stray shot cut off the corner of a hardtack box in the pack. We managed to get the pack loose, but did nothing more, getting back to our places on the line as quickly as possible. These were the first shots fired on the morning of the 26th, which was another busy day all around for both troopers and Indians. We had been kept awake the night before by Major Reno and other officers who walked about among us to see that none were asleep. It was a hard task to refrain from dropping off, after the excitement of the previous day, but we had little chance to relax.

When the ball opened on the 26th, Dr. Porter, who was the only surviving surgeon of the entire command, came up and said that the wounded were crying for water and ought to have it. Volunteers were called for to venture to the river. This was extremely hazardous, as the Indians were occupying the brush along the opposite bank of the stream and commanded every approach to the water. I did not go out with the first detachment sent for this purpose, but did with the second. We had to creep cautiously down the hill through a coulee until we arrived at its mouth where it debouched into the river. It was about thirty feet from the mouth of the coulee, and we had to cover this thirty feet entirely exposed to Indian bullets at short range, fill the canteens or camp kettles from the stream, and go back again under fire. When the first squad went out, nobody had the forethought to post a bunch of good shots at a point where they could fire volleys into the brush to silence the fire of the Indians; but when my detachment went for water, several expert riflemen were instructed to fire volleys into the brush while we were getting the water and running back into the coulee. In spite of this, an Indian managed to put a hole through the camp kettle I carried, so that I lost a good amount of the water. However, after several attempts, we managed to fill all the vessels and get back to the hospital, where it is needless to say the water was a God-send.

I have read in Capt. Godfrey's account of these water volunteers that all the men were rewarded with medals of honor by Congress. I never received any such medal, nor do I think any other man did. If so, I never heard of it.

In our venture to the stream, we found Trooper Mike Madden lying in the coulee, shot through the ankle. Mike was a big husky fellow and had accompanied the first detachment.

Looking East across the Little Big Horn, toward the hills to which Reno's command retreated. Photo taken 1886 on the 10th anniversary of the battle.

He lost his leg in the hospital, where it was amputated. An amusing incident happened in connection with it. Before amputating the member, the surgeon gave Mike a stiff horn of brandy to brace him up. Mike went through the ordeal without a whimper, and was then given another drink. Smacking his lips in appreciation, he whispered to the surgeon:

"Docthor, cut off me other leg!"

Lat' on, Mike was employed in the harness depot of the department at St. Paul.

I had made the trip for water with a young comrade named Jim Weeks. On our way back, Jim was hailed by Capt. Moylan, requesting a drink. I was surprised to hear Jim blurt out, "You go to hell and get your own water; this is for the wounded." Nothing more was said, but I know that must have been a hard pill for Moylan to swallow.

After carrying the water to the hospital we returned to our places on the firing line. I had just laid down when the man on my left (Henry Rutten) was shot through the shoulder. And thus it went for the balance of the day, with Capt. French still sitting up tailor-style, superintending the firing and defying the Indian bullets without flinching once. I was no longer frightened, in spite of the fact that there seemed no chance of our getting out alive, surrounded as we were by thousands of Indians far better armed than ourselves, and outnumbered a hundred to one.

I must say that I had to admire Major Reno during the entire fighting on the hill. I also saw him twice in the river bottom, and he did not seem to be at all ruffled. To a man in such a responsible position it must have been a trying time, without the support in sight which Custer had promised him. Our ammunition had been nearly exhausted during the fighting in the bottom, and had we not retreated to the hill, we certainly would have been wiped out in a very few minutes.

I observed Reno several times during the fighting on the bluffs, and can well remember his walking about among the men through the night. He would tap a man with his boot and remark, "Don't go to sleep, boys." I cannot understand why he was not shot down while walking about, as none of the troopers were able to make a move without drawing the fire of the Indians. I know it encouraged his fellow-officers as well as the troopers. I have read articles pertaining to this part of the battle of the Little Big Horn in which it was stated that Reno was drunk. This I brand as a lie. At no time did I observe the least indication of drunkenness on the man, nor seen him use any liquor.

At dusk that evening of the 26th, the Indians had withdrawn to such an extent that we were enabled to lead our poor famished horses down to the water. I could not locate my own, so grabbed another—a fine black animal, which I later learned belonged to Capt. Weir.

After this, I heard no more firing, but we kept our places in line throughout the night. The next morning we had roll call of the company, and many were missing. Through the kindness of John Ryan, who was first sergeant of my company, I have a copy of that roll call as the dead and missing were marked off.

Later we observed an immense dust-cloud coming our way up the valley. Some remarked that it was the Indians coming back, but we soon received word that it was Gen. Terry's command. It must have been an awful shock to him, as he was to meet Custer that very 27th of June so they could attack the Indian village together. When he arrived at our position, he told us, with tears in his eyes, what he had seen of the Custer command. It did not seem possible. This was the first intimation we had as to Custer's fate. It was an awful blow to us, as every man lost friends who were in the companies commanded by Custer. Nobody even dreamed that he could possibly meet with such an overwhelming defeat.

Everything was then made ready to move the wounded. Many horses which were badly wounded and unable to go further had to be shot. We were then ordered over to the spot where Custer and his men fell. Here, with a few spades,

we were set to work to bury them. We had but a few implements of any sort. All that we could possibly do was to remove a little dirt in a low place, roll in a body and cover it
with dirt. Some, I can well remember, were not altogether
covered, but the stench was so strong from the disfigured,
decaying bodies, which had been exposed to an extremely hot
sun for two days, that it was impossible to make as decent a
job of interring them as we could otherwise have done. There
were also great numbers of dead horses lying about, which
added to the horror of the situation.

I did not have time to go over the field and make notes,
but from what I did see, I gathered that these men were surprised here and killed in a very short space of time. It struck
me that many of them had evidently shot their own horses
and used them as breastworks until killed. In one instance we
found two men lying between the legs of their dead horses.
From what I saw of the field, it appeared to me that there was
very little time for Custer and his men to make any sort of a
defense whatever. All the bodies seemed naked, which would
indicate that as soon as the warriors had finished their bloody
work, the squaws had ample time to rob the bodies of clothing and valuables and strip the horses of their saddles and
trappings and pack it away unmolested.

Doubtless while doing this, the mutilation of the bodies
occurred. Some of these disfigurations were too horrible to
mention. After being scalped, the skulls were crushed in with
stone hammers, and the bodies cut and slashed in all the
fleshy portions. Much of this was doubtless done to
wounded men. Many arrows also had been shot into some of
the bodies—the eyes, neck, stomach and other members. I
observed especially the body of Capt. Tom Custer, which was
the worst mutilated of all. Many arrows bristled in it. It is
said that he was killed by Rain-in-the-Face in revenge for
being arrested the previous year at Standing Rock agency.
His body was lying about twenty feet from that of the general,
and close beside that of Adjutant Cooke, one side of whose

Lieut. William W. Cooke, (Brevet Lt. Col.) adjutant 7th Cavalry, who wrote the famous message, "Benteen, come on, be quick, big village, etc."

face had been scalped, taking with it his magnificent sideburn whiskers. His body also was badly mutilated.

The body of Gen. Custer had not been touched by the Indians. He had been shot twice. Some say the Indians do not mutilate the chief officer, out of respect for his bravery. Others said it was because the Indians wanted to make sure that his white friends would recognize him and know that he had been killed.

Boston Custer was found near the bodies of his two brothers. That of Mark Kellogg, the reporter for the Bismarck Tribune and New York Herald, who had accompanied the expedition, was close by. These bodies were on the line nearest to the river, making it appear that they were halted by an overwhelming force, which closed in on them so rapidly and in such superior numbers that they were given but little chance to put up a fight.

I was working a spade on this end of the line of dead and so had a hand in burying this group. I am sure that we used more earth in covering Custer's body, and made a larger mound for it than for any of the others. I have heard it said that there was no certainty that the body of the general was really identified when a party went to the field the following year to remove the bodies of Custer and the officers. I do not think this can be possible, as he was not in the least mutilated. The large mound we erected over his body should have been sufficient to identify his burial spot.

It must have been a great satisfaction to the Indians to know that he was killed, as they had a dread and a fear of Custer, as he was known as the hardest-fighting white chief against them. He was a fearless and brave soldier, and many will agree with me that he was also a hard leader to follow. He always had several good horses whereby he could change mounts every three hours if necessary, carrying nothing but man and saddle, while our poor horses carried man, saddle, blankets, carbine, revolver, haversack, canteen, 10 days' rations of oats and 150 rounds of 45-caliber ammunition, which itself would weigh more than ten pounds—and we had no extra horses to change off. With the forced night march we made to get to the Little Big Horn, it is no secret why our horses played out before going into action. A number of these worn animals were brought in by the rear guard. A comrade friend of mine—a member of one of the companies with Custer, was fortunate in being detailed to go with the rear guard. His horse had played out and he could not go into action.

In doing this forced marching, it was generally understood that Custer disobeyed the orders of Gen. Terry, insofar that we were expected—as I have stated—to meet Terry's command on the 27th. I have before me now a copy of the written instructions from Terry to Custer. This order reads in part that Custer should conform to the orders unless he saw sufficient reason for departing from them; and again it reads: "But it is hoped that the Indians, if upon the Little Big Horn, may be so nearly enclosed *by the two columns* (Terry's and Custer's) that their escape will be impossible." So while this order does not flatly designate June 27th as the time for meeting, yet it shows that Gen. Terry expected to be there with his command when the time for the attack was ripe. It was understood that Custer was under arrest on an order from President Grant, and that his object in going into the fight without Terry, was that if he were going to win, he would get all the glory himself, and likely the charges against him would be dismissed. This may have spurred him on to take a desperate chance and make a fatal error. When he first viewed the village from the ridge and saw the immense number of tepees, he must have then observed that his puny force was totally inadequate to cope against the thousands of warriors in the valley below, far better armed than his own command.

Again, I, like many others, think he made a mistake in dividing his command in this fight. Had he kept them together and struck the village at one end, he might have mastered them, or at least, have put them to flight.

A year or so after the battle I was cooking for Capt. French, and we often had a heart-to-heart talk about the Little Big Horn fight. One day I asked him what he would have done had he been in Custer's place. His answer was, "There would have been no fight." Officers, as a rule, are loath to say anything against another officer, no matter what may be in their mind. So that in all statements made by officers who took part in the battle of the Little Big Horn, none has shown a willingness to speak his mind as to whether

Custer did right or wrong in dividing his regiment, or going into the fight before Terry arrived.

After we had buried all the dead on the Custer field, the site of the Reno battle in the river bottom was investigated. The dead there were all buried where they fell. All had been horribly butchered. Isaiah Dorman, a negro scout and interpreter, was found with many arrows shot into his body and head, and badly cut and slashed, while unmentionable atrocities had been committed. Corporal Henry Scollen of M Troop was found badly mutilated, with his right leg severed from his body. Jim Turley's body was found with his hunting knife driven to the hilt in one eye. Three others, Gordon, Myers and Summers of M Troop were in an awful state of mutilation. I did not see the body of our chief of scouts, Charley Reynolds, who was Custer's favorite guide, and who was killed in the river bottom, but I am sure his body was not respected by the red fiends. Many others were scattered about through the timber, but I did not see them all. In making this retreat from the river bottom, the number of Indians all about us, with the unnumbered hundreds constantly reinforcing them, proved that we only got out just in the nick of time. I consider it lucky that Reno had the good sense and foresight to act when he did and give us a chance for our lives. I recollect that in my dash for the river an Indian rode so close to me that I could have reached him with a saber, if I had had one. My comrade, Smith, whom I have mentioned, and whose horse ran away with him into the Indian lines, may have been captured alive. From our position on the bluffs we could see many fires in the Indian village the night of June 25th, with the Indians dancing about the fires, and it occurred to me then that they might have been burning and torturing some helpless captives at the stake.

After the burial of the dead had been completed, the next task was to move the wounded of Reno's command. Because of the meager facilities at hand, transporting them down to the supply steamer "Far West," which had been lying at the mouth of the Little Big Horn awaiting orders, was no easy task; but we did all that was possible to make them comfortable. Many were carried on travois made from tepee poles left in the deserted Indian village, and while this sort of conveyance was not very desirable over such a rough country, it was the only possible manner of transporting them.

After the wounded had been started down the river on their long journey of nearly 1,000 miles to Bismarck, the remainder of the regiment joined forces with Gen. Crook's command, and with all the force then at hand, we were strong enough to wipe out any detachment of savages we might meet. But we did not meet them—for reasons known best to Gen. Crook. Buffalo Bill Cody was at the head as chief of scouts with Gen. Crook. He did not remain with us very long, because of a misunderstanding with Gen. Crook, the nature of which would be but hearsay to me.

Since the Little Big Horn fight I have met with many imposters who have recounted their "experiences' on that fatal field, but who were not there at all. I have read, I dare say, a hundred accounts of the death of "last survivors of Custer's command." All such stories are absolutely false, and there were no survivors of Custer's command—every man was killed. One of Custer's Crow scouts, "Curley," long posed as the only living man who escaped. For "Curley" I will say that I do not believe he ever got to the Custer forces, but skirmished his way around the outside until a chance presented itself for him to make his escape undetected. I am certain he was not in the fight.

CHAPTER 3

CAPT. BENTEEN'S OWN STORY
OF THE CUSTER FIGHT.

FOREWORD

by the Author

For the first time since he testified before the Reno Court of Inquiry at Chicago, in 1879, Capt. F. W. Benteen, senior captain of Custer's regiment, the famous Seventh Cavalry, here relates the part he played in that most disastrous of Indian fights on American soil, over which more controversy has raged than over any other battle fought against the red man in the United States.

Much of the account is from his own testimony at the Reno Inquiry; some of it is from an article he wrote, but never published, and some of it from the personal letters of Capt. Benteen in my possession. Certain charges were made against Major Marcus A. Reno and Capt. Benteen by Frederick Whittaker, Custer's biographer. At the last moment Whittaker withdrew his charges against Capt. Benteen. He also utterly failed to substantiate his charges against Major Reno, the verdict of the Court being that "there was nothing in his conduct which requires animadversion from this Court, and that in view of all the facts in evidence, no further proceedings are necessary in this case."

The testimony at the Reno Inquiry developed the fact that both Capt. Benteen and Major Reno had done the best that could be done with what they had, after Custer's fatal separation of the regiment; and that, but for their extraordinary heroism and bravery in the fight on the bluffs, following Custer's complete annihilation four and a half miles down the Little Big Horn river, the troops under their charge would likewise have been wiped out.

Capt. Benteen's testimony and extracts from his letters prove absolutely that Custer had formed no battle plans at the time he made his battalion assignments; or, if he had such plans, he did not reveal or communicate them to either Major Reno or Capt. Benteen.

While the number of the attacking Indians has been variously estimated by participants in the engagement at from 1,500 to 4,500, Capt. Benteen stated that, in his opinion, they numbered *eight or nine thousand.*

"TRUMPETS SOUNDING, HORSES PRANC-ING, guidons waving proudly, the twelve troops of the Seventh U.S. Cavalry passed in review before Brigadier General Alfred Terry, commanding the Department of Dakota, at noon, on the 22d day of June, 1876.

"The scene of the review was in Montana Territory, on the bank of the Yellowstone River, in close proximity to the junction of Rosebud Creek with said river.

"After passing the reviewing officer, the regiment 'ployed into column, and the line of march was taken for Rosebud Creek, the distance marched that afternoon being twelve miles.

"On the night of that day, the officers of the Seventh Cavalry were summoned to appear at the bivouac of Lieut. Col. Custer, commanding the regiment, and upon the assembling of the officers, Lieut. Col. Custer gave some directions about what formation of the troops should be made, in case of an attack upon the camp by Indians.

"Evidently the meeting of the officers was not 'called' for the promulgation of the directions which were given out by Lieut. Col. Custer, as directions were wholly rudimentary, and as the regiment had been campaigning for the past nine years with nearly the same officers, during which term of years Col. Custer had never before seen fit to counsel or direct us as to the A, B, C of our profession. At this, however, no one felt injured, and Col. Custer drifted into saying 'that while HE was willing to accept recommendations from the junior second lieutenant of the regiment, such recommendations must come to him in proper form; and moreover, that he (Custer) was aware that his official actions had been

talked of and criticized by officers of the regiment to officers
of the Department Staff during the march from Fort A.
Lincoln, D.T., and that he now notified all such officers that
such criticisms must cease, or that the officers offending would
be proceeded against as the regulations of the army provided.'

Capt. F. W. Benteen, commanding Troop H, whose
controversial scout to the left, ordered by Custer, has
long been an interesting topic for students of the
Indian Wars.

"It was then patent to us all for what purpose the 'call' had
been sent forth, and as my relations with Lieut. Col. Custer
were not of the warmest personal nature, I was anxious to
learn the names of the officers whom he evidently mistrusted.
So I said, 'General, will you not be kind enough to inform
us of the names of those officers who have so offended?'

"Custer stammered slightly and said: 'Colonel Benteen,
while I am not here to be catechised by you, I take pleasure

in informing you, for your own gratification, that you are not among those officers whom I have alluded to.'

"The meeting then dispersed, each proceeding in the direction of his own bivouac.

"On the morning of the 23d of June I reported to Lieut. Col. Custer for orders as the new officer of the day. Lieut. Col. Custer told me the letters of the three troops of the battalion I was to take charge of as guard to the pack-train for the day, and ordered that I was to march the battalion in rear of the last mule of the train. Soon thereafter Lieut. Col. Custer marched at the head of the column of the other nine troops.

"It took exactly one and a half hours to get the pack-train across Rosebud Creek, so by that time Custer's column was all of six miles ahead of my train, and out of sight. For some time I marched the train and the battalion as I had been ordered by Lieut. Col. Custer, but as the train was much scattered—so much so that I could exercise no control of it from my position in rear of the whole of it, and as I would be held responsible for safety of the same, in case of an attack by Indians, I determined to put the troops in such positions along flank of train, that, in case of attack, the command was prepared to defend it.

"For such purpose I placed one troop on flank at head of train, second troop at center of train, while I remained with the third troop on flank and at rear of train. Our march that second day was about thirty-five miles, and up the Rosebud Creek.

"On arrival with the train and battalion at the place of bivouac for the night, I found the regimental adjutant, Lieut. W. W. Cooke, awaiting my arrival for the purpose of designating the place each troop of my train-guard was to occupy in the camp.

"I said to Cooke that 'General Custer had ordered me to march the whole battalion in rear of the last mule of the train, and that I had carried out his orders until I feared to longer do so, as I might have lost a great portion of the train in case it had been attacked,' telling Lieut. Cooke the manner in which I had marched the guard to protect the train, and requested that he would communicate the same to General Custer, so that the next officer in charge should not receive such orders as had been given to me regarding the marching of the train. Lieut. Cooke replied, 'No, I will not tell General Custer anything about it. If you want him to know it you must tell him of it yourself.'

"On the morning of the 24th of June, General Custer rode by my bivouac of the night before. I approached him and reported that on account of fearing for the safety of the train the day before, I had placed the battalion on guard differently from the manner he had ordered. Custer stammered slightly, and said, 'I am much obliged to you, Col. Benteen. I will direct the officer who relieves you to guard the train in the manner you have done.' As my duties ended on delivering the train at camp on the 23d, I did not have to report to the commanding officer with the new officer of the day.

"The march of June 24th was interrupted by frequent and sometimes quite lengthy halts of the column, but on what account I was not aware; but on arriving at Mud Creek, which was to be our place of bivouac, I was loudly called to by Col. Keogh to come where he was; that he had been saving me a snug nook with beautiful grass in it for me, that I might camp next to him. The reply to this was characteristic of the Plains, something like 'Bully for you, Keogh, I'm your man!'

"After our frugal repasts which went for dinner, Col. Keogh and his lieutenant, Porter, came over to my bivouac, where, sitting around, were four or five officers engaged in listening to Lieut. DeRudio's yarns. However, I placed my saddle in position for a pillow, spread my saddle blanket for a bed, and notified the gentlemen 'that I was going in for what sleep I could pick up, as I was impressed with the belief that we would not remain in that camp all night.' The officers, however, went on with their conversation, and before I had caught a wink of sleep, an orderly from regimental headquarters came, with the information to us to meet at once at headquarters.

"It was then pitch dark, so I called up my first sergeant and directed him to see that everything was in order for an immediate move, as I didn't think we would be allowed to remain in that camp all the night. The sergeant assured me that everything was in good shape; so I then started to find General Custer's headquarters. I had not gotten far on the way thereto when I stumbled across Lieut. Edgerly, who informed me that it was not necessary to go any further, as the only orders were that we were to move at 11 o'clock that night—at which hour we did move.

"However, there was an hour and a half consumed in getting the pack-train across Mud Creek. Col. Keogh had charge of the packs on that move, and the column remained impatiently on the other bank of the creek while Keogh was superintending the crossing of the pack-train. Some little time after, the column got started on the march. The only guide of direction I had for my troop was the pounding of the cups on the saddles of the men in rear of the troop preceding me in the column.

"About this time Col. Keogh rode up to me, complaining that he couldn't tell head or tail of the pack-train—didn't know where in sheol they were—and what was he going to do about it? I told him to take it easier, that nothing but an Indian could run one of those mules off. Some of the packs, of course, might slip off and be left behind, but we could recover the same at daylight—and the tin cup pounding on the saddles of the troop ahead of me went on, all of which suddenly ceased. The column was at a halt, pack-train and all spread out together.

"I should think an hour and a half after this, daylight began to peer through, and I noticed General Custer pass me on horseback. Custer went on, saying nothing to me. Just then

Captain E. S. Godfrey, Troop K, Benteen Battalion.

I noticed Major Reno and Lieut. Hodgson on the other side of a ravine, about to sit down to breakfast; so, not knowing where I would get a breakfast, I went over and assisted them in disposing of what they had.

"In course of half an hour or so, without orders or bugle sound, the column in advance commenced moving forward, which movement was, of course, followed by the troops, and pack-train in the rear. I should think we went about a mile and a half, when the column again halted. I am of the belief that an orderly was sent to notify the officers that General Custer wished to see us; at all events the officers gathered where he was.

"General Custer then told us that he had just come down from the mountains where our Crow Indian scouts had been during the night, and that they had told him *they could see tepee tops, lots of Indian ponies, dust, etc.*, but that he had looked through their telescopic glasses *and that he could not see a thing, and did not believe that they could, either, see anything of the kind.*

"Now, in 1875, I had a very similar experience with Indians in Dakota, and as the statements of the Indians then were absolutely confirmed by what was afterward proved, I was strong in the belief that the *Crow Indians only reported what was shown them by their superior keenness of vision, and that the hostile village was where they located it;* but as no opinions were asked for, none were given.

"The column then advanced, I should think, a mile or so, and the officers were summoned to General Custer. On arrival of all, General Custer desired to know whether the requirements of a regimental order which were issued on the Yellowstone River, were being carried out, which order was to the effect that every troop of the regiment should have a non-commissioned officer and six men on duty with the pack-train, in immediate charge of the mules of each troop, and that one hundred rounds of carbine ammunition and twenty-four rounds of pistol ammunition should be issued to each trooper;

that the first officer who first notified him that these requirements were being observed, should have the advance of the
regiment for his troop.

"I am really of the opinion that General Custer neither expected or desired that I should have the advance of the regiment; nor do I think he was of the opinion that I would
volunteer to be the first to assure him that all orders were
being carried out to the letter in my troop. However, my troop
being right on top of us, as it were, I saw no way of evading
the question as to whether we were a dutiful lot of officers
in H Troop but by notifying him—that to my certain knowledge the requirements of the order he had alluded to were
being carried out as a matter of course.

"With a slight stammer, General Custer said, 'Then, Col.
Benteen, you have the advance, sir.' The last officer to report was to catch the pack-train to guard, as the penalty for
not being more rapid in reporting; and this, I opine, few
cared for.

"After all had reported, I was notified by General Custer
to move my troop to the right of the regiment, which was
then in column of fours.

"The regiment had moved but a short distance when Custer
rode to the right of the column and remarked that I was
setting the pace too fast. He then remained in front, halting
the column after a mile or so had been passed over.

"General Custer and the regimental adjutant, Lieut. Cooke,
went a few yards in advance of the column, just out of ear-
shot, and were diligently engaged in talking and making notes
in a scratch-pad. After fifteen or so minutes of this work,
I was called by the adjutant, and was informed by General
Custer that I was to mount D, H and K Troops, which were
then in column dismounted, and proceed to a line of bluffs
about two miles off, at about an angle of 45 degrees; to send
a well-mounted officer and ten men in advance; to pitch into
any Indians I could see, and, in such case, to notify him at
once.

"I at once mounted my battalion and set out, sending
Lieut. Gibson and ten men in advance. To say the country
terrain was rough is but putting it mildly—expletives could
be worked in front of 'rough' that would be more truly
descriptful, and by no means exaggerative of the lay of the
land. But on we went, with high intent from embankment to
embankment. Perhaps a mile or so had been covered when
the chief trumpeter of the regiment overtook me with 'the
compliments of General Custer to Col. Benteen,' that if I
came across, or could see nothing, from the first line of bluffs,
to go on to the second line of bluffs, pitch into anything I
came across, and to notify General Custer of same at once.

"Again we went on, from 'the second line of bluffs.' Nothing but more and more bluffs; still further on. But by this
time we had been overtaken by another messenger from
General Custer, this time in the person of the sergeant-major
of the regiment bearing the 'compliments of General Custer';
that if Col. Benteen saw nothing from the second line of bluffs,
then to proceed to the valley, to pitch into anything I came
across, notifying General Custer of same at once.

"Forward again once more, but no valley nor sign of valley was to be seen. *The last glimpse we had gotten of General
Custer's column was the sight of the gray-horse troop at a
gallop.* Well, one couldn't tell much about the simple fact of
seeing that much of a column at an increased pace, as owing
to the roughness of the country the troop might have lost distance, and had only increased the pace to recover its distance.

"But through the whole oblique to left, the impression went
with me that all of that hard detour was for naught, as the
ground was too awfully rugged for sane Indians to choose to
go that way to hunt a camp—or, for that matter, to hunt anything else but game.

"I knew that I had to come to some decision speedily, when
I had given up the idea of further hunting for a valley and
being thoroughly impregnated with the belief that the trail
Custer was on would yield quite a sufficiency of Indians;

that for the present any little undiscovered band might be
safely left for future garnering—and—none of us, too, desired to be left out of the fight, which all were absolutely
sure could be found at the other end of the trail that Custer
was following; so the question with me was, shall I 'valley
hunt' any more, or shall I hasten with these three troops to
where I feel sure of getting all the fighting they can want, and
maybe help someone out of a hole there?

"My real, Simon-pure, straight orders were to *hunt that
valley;* but I didn't know where the valley was, and thought
that perhaps an opportunity might happen later to search for
it; but just then I believed I hadn't time to do it. So, shoulder-
ing the responsibility of not having found the valley, I pitched
off with the battalion at a right oblique to reach the trail
Custer's column had followed, endeavoring by speed to make
up for the precious time that had been lost in our futile hunt
for the valley. My battalion reached the trail Custer had followed, just in advance of the pack-train, and pretty close to a
boggy place where I thought water for the animals could be
gotten. So, perhaps fifteen minutes were consumed in watering them.

"Just as my battalion pulled out on the trail from the
watering-place, the advance mules of the pack-train flound-
ered into the bog, going up to the packs in mud. However. I
couldn't spare the time to assist in extricating them, as this is
wholly one of those perquisites of the owner of that duty—
i. e. guard to pack-train, and is by no means a labor of love.

"About two miles from this bog, we passed a burning tepee,
the tepee being quite handsomely decorated in colors in Indian
art style. Dismounting from my horse I peeped into the tepee.
and on a bed made of forks of (and small limbs of) trees, was
stretched the body of an Indian warrior. As I hadn't time to
investigate as to the causes of his having been made a 'good
Indian', I remounted my horse and kept the battalion pushing
on at a stiff walk.

"A mile or so further on, I met a Sergt. Kanipe coming

Sergeant Kanipe, Co. C, identified by Captain Benteen as carrying a verbal message from Custer to the Commander of the pack train to join him.

from the adjutant of the regiment with order-—written *for the commander of the pack-train.* I told the sergeant the pack-train was about seven miles back, and he could take the order to the commanding officer of the pack-train to hurry up the packs, as I had nothing to do with that—that Capt. Mc-Dougall was in charge of the pack-train.

"About a mile or so further on I met Trumpeter Martin,

who had brought a written order, which I have. It has no date. It says: *"Benteen, come on; big village; be quick, bring packs. P. S. Bring pac's. COOKE.'*

"It was about two miles from where Major Reno first crossed the Little Big Horn that Martin met me, and about two and a half miles from the burning tepee. I did not know whose trail I was following. I asked Martin, after reading the note, about this village. He said the Indians were all 'skeddadling,' therefore there was less necessity for me to go for the packs. I could hear no firing at that time.

"I was then riding four or five hundred yards in advance of the battalion with my orderly. Captain Weir was about two hundred yards in my rear. I waited until he came up, then handed him the note. I asked him no questions, and he did not volunteer advice.

"Well, by this time I had acquired a tolerably fair 'lay of the land.' If I went back for the packs, I feared much valuable time would be lost. If I halted where I was, waiting for the packs to come up, the conditions weren't being at all bettered, and this sight of the 'lay of the land' was sufficiently convincing to me that no Indians could hope to get between my battalion and the pack-train.

"So on I kept the battalion moving, now quickening the pace to a trot, willing to assume an added responsibility as regarding safety of the packs. A couple of miles or so brought me to where Major Reno's battalion crossed the Little Big Horn. That was my first sight of it. There I saw an engagement going on, and supposed it was the whole regiment. There were twelve or thirteen men in skirmish line that appeared to have been beaten back. The line was then parallel with the river, and the Indians were charging through those men. I thought the whole command was thrashed, and that was not a good place to cross. To my right I noticed three or four Indians, four or five hundred yards from me. I thought they were hostile, but on riding toward them I found they were Crows. They exclaimed, 'Heaps of Sioux' and said there was a big 'pooh-poohing' going on. Just then I saw the advance of Reno's battalion appear on the bluffs, on the side of the river I was then on. I formed my battalion in line, and moved up the bluffs. Then Reno, hatless, came riding down to meet me.

"I inquired where Custer was, showing him the order I had gotten. Reno read the order, replying that about an hour ago Custer had sent him across the river with orders to charge a body of Indians in the valley, *promising that he would support Reno with the whole outfit;* that since that time, he (Reno) had seen nothing of Custer, and knew nothing of his whereabouts, but had heard some firing down the river, and supposed he was in that direction.

"Now it had become imperative that I should speedily connect with the pack-train, and Reno dispatched Lieut. Hare, Seventh Cavalry, to go to the train and hasten it along. In an hour or less the pack-train came up. Some carbine ammunition was then unpacked from it, and was issued to some of Reno's men.

"I heard very little firing at all after the time I got on the Reno Hill. Not more than fifteen or twenty shots. While at the river I could both hear and see it, about two miles away. My effective force was about 125 men. I reached Reno about 3 p. m. The pack-train was not yet in sight.

"Reno was not present when Custer ordered me to move off to the left.

"Reno's men appeared to be in good order, but pretty well blown, and so were the horses. They were not in line of battle, but were scattered around, I suppose to the best advantage. They all thought there was a happier place than that, I guess.

"I had no knowledge or impression where Custer was, or on which side of the river. My impressions from Trumpeter Martin were that the Indians were 'skeddadling,' but my first sight of the fight showed that there was no skeddadling being done by the Indians.

"Reno did not explain to me why he had retreated from the river bottom to the hill; nor did he express any solicitude or uneasiness about Custer. Nor did I. I supposed General Custer was able to take care of himself.

"The only firing I heard which came from the direction Custer had gone was fifteen or twenty shots that seemed to come from about the central part of the village. I have heard officers disputing about hearing volleys. *I heard no volleys.*

"About this time I saw one of the troops of my battalion proceeding to the front, mounted. It was Capt. Weir, who sallied out in that direction in a fit of bravado, I think, without orders. That was about half an hour after we arrived. It was before the packs came up. Upon this, I followed with the other two troops, Major Reno having his trumpeter sound the halt continuously and assiduously; but I had to get in sight then of what I had left my valley-hunting mission for.

"Capt. Weir, with his troop, had gone down a gorge. Indians were riding around the bluffs on either side of this troop, signaling. I then threw forward a troop, dismounted, at right angles with the river, and one on the bluffs parallel with the river, so that if Custer's forces were near, our position would be defined.

"Just then, up the gorge, *pell-mell* came the troop which the commander had so fearlessly sallied forth with, and the preparations I had made allowed him and his troop to come to a less frantic style of going. Then came the necessity of getting into a good shape, as 'twas clearly apparent that we were in for a good long fight. A movement could have been made down the river in the direction Custer had gone, but we would all have been there yet! The whole command could have gone as far as I went, but no farther. We were driven back.

"From my position was my first sight of the village, and the only point from which it could be seen. *I saw about eighteen hundred tepees;* no sign of troops or fighting, at that point.

"Slowly we fell back to just about the very point where

Reno reached the bluffs from his retreat from the valley, and with the little time allowed us we formed a line which stemmed the tide of Indian fire while the fight lasted, which was till dark on the 25th, and until the retreat of the Indians, on the 26th of June.

"The line was formed in an irregular ellipse. There was a flat where our pack animals and horses were corraled, and the line formed around it in the shape of a U (horseshoe), one prong of the horseshoe extending further than the other. The Indians surrounded us there, and kept it pretty lively as long as they could see. I was in the prong of the horseshoe; the short prong was turned in at right angles. Capt. Moylan had that.

"I had left one company on the ridge with orders to hold it at all hazards, but that company got back as quick as the others. Then I sent Capt. Godfrey's company to another hill to check the Indians till we could form. I saw Reno there. He came back with me and talked with me. I don't know that he gave any orders to retire from the advanced position. *Orders were not necessary about that time.* The first I knew as to the formation of a line was when I told Lieut. Wallace to place his company at a spot I pointed out; but he said he had no company—only three men. I told him to go there with his three men, and I would see that he was supported; and from that the line was formed. I thought then there were about twenty-five hundred Indians surrounding us, *but I think now that there were eight or nine thousand.*

"At the angle of the line was Company A; then followed G, D, B, M and K. I was not assigned to any particular part. My company was on the extreme left. After our line was formed, it was about as lively a fire as you would like to stand up under. You had only to show a hat or a head, or anything, to get a volley. It was about 5:30 when we got our line finished, or maybe later. We were under fire from two and a half to three hours.

"The Indians had picinic parties as large as a regiment

standing around in the river bottom, looking on. There was
no place to put them. Fully two thousand were around us,
waiting for a place to shoot from!

"The Indians close to us did not expose themselves. The
only thing you could see would be the flash of a gun. They
came so close that they threw arrows and dirt over at us with
their hands, and touched one of the dead men with a coup-
stick. That was the next morning. That afternoon was like
the second day—we could see nothing to shoot at. We got
volleys, but could not return them.

"The night of the 25th Major Reno was upon the hill
where my company was, and ordered me to build breastworks.
I sent for spades, but there were none. I thought it unnecessary, but the next morning the fire was much heavier, and I
had a good deal of trouble keeping my men on the line.

"I had to run them out of the pack-train, and I brought up
sacks of bacon and boxes of hard bread and pack saddles, and
made a redoubt. I took twelve or fifteen skulking soldiers and
packers, and turned the redoubt over to my first lieutenant,
and told him I intended to drive the Indians from the ravine.
I did so, and we then got water. Major Reno at the time was
on the other end of the line. He thought the main attack
would come there.

"After getting to the water I sent word to Reno to get
all the receptacles together, and fill them. I then told Reno I
was being annoyed by a cross-fire from every quarter, and
was unprotected, save the breastworks, and asked him if I
might drive those Indians out. He said 'Yes,' and we did it. I
gave the order, and told the men to go, and went in with
them.

"I may say I was with Major Reno all the time the night of
the 25th. I saw him every fifteen to thirty minutes, till 3 a. m.
I laid down in his bed. He was as sober as he is now. He is
entirely sober now and was then. There was no time, during
the 25th or 26th when there was any indication of drunkenness on the part of Major Reno.

" I know nothing about any altercation with a packer except by hearsay. I know they robbed the packs, and robbed me, and I also know there was not enough whiskey in the whole command to make him drunk. I had occasion to go to the pack-train many times during the 25th and 26th, to drive out skulking soldiers. There was much complaint about stealing in the pack-train.

"I might have joined Reno in the timber, but would not have attempted it without first getting the pack-train, but my losses would have been much greater. What we did was the best that could be done. If I had to do it again I would go over the same trail. I could not improve it.

"The timber position first taken by Reno was an A-1 defensive position, and could have been held five or six hours, depending on the size of the attacking force. Against nine hundred it was defensible, but the nine hundred would have been reinforced by another nine hundred, and the next morning we would all have been killed.

"Eight or nine hundred Indians was only a small part of what they had. It could not have made a particle of difference so far as Custer was concerned. The seven companies would have been as completely corraled there as on the hill. General Custer would have had to look out for himself, the same as we did.

"There was not a foot of unoccupied ground in that country. There were Indians everywhere, from twelve feet to twelve hundred yards away.

"I think Custer went to the right of the second divide, and not to the river at all. On the morning of General Terry's arrival, I asked permission to take my company and go over the battlefield of General Custer. I did so, and followed down the gorge; *but I am now satisfied that he did not go down that way.* The nearest body to the middle ford was six or eight hundred yards from it.

"I went over the battlefield carefully, with a view to determine how the fight was fought. I arrived at the conclusion

I have right now—*that it was a rout, a panic, till the last man was killed; that there was no line formed.*

"There was no line on the battlefield. You can take u handful of corn and scatter it over a floor, and make just such lines. There were none. The only approach to a line was where five or six horses were found at equal distances, like skirmishers. Ahead of them were five or six men at about the same distances, showing that the horses were killed, and the riders all jumped off, and were heading to get where Custer was. *That was the only approach to a line on the field.* There were more than twenty killed there to the right; there were four or five at one place, all within a space of twenty to thirty yards. *That was the condition all over the field.*

"Only where General Custer was found was there any evidence of a stand. The five or six men I spoke of were where Capt. Calhoun's body was; they were of his company. There were twenty-two bodies found in a ravine, fifty to seventy-five yards from the river. They had, I think, been killed with stones and clubs. They were unarmed; I think they were wounded men who had gone into the ravine to hide. There was a trail leading to a crossing about a hundred yards above that ravine.

"I counted seventy dead horses and two Indian ponies. I think, in all probability that the men turned their horses loose without any orders to do so. Many orders might have been given, but few obeyed. *I think they were panic-stricken; it was a rout, as I said before. . .*

"The village, as I saw it from the high point, I estimated at three to four miles long; about eighteen hundred tepees; four to seven warriors to the tepee. I saw it when it moved away (on the 26th). It started about sunset, and was in sight till darkness came. It was in a straight line about three miles long, and I think a half mile wide, as densely packed as animals could be. They had an advance guard, and platoons formed, and were in as regular military order as a corps or division.

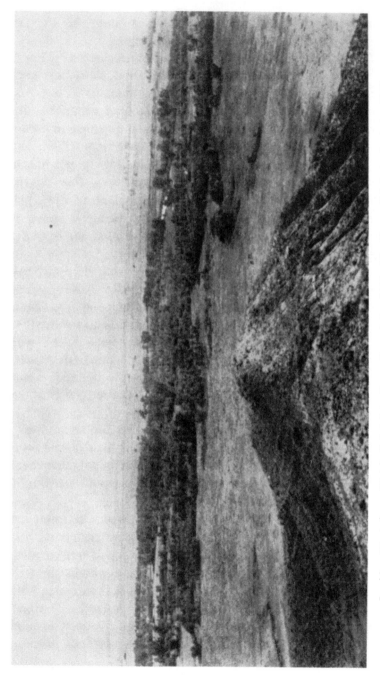

Looking West from Weir's Point into the valley of the Little Big Horn. Brininstool photo 1913.

"*I saw no evidence of cowardice on Major Reno's part.* I found it necessary at one time to caution him about exposing himself. I told him to be careful how he stood in front of the point, as volleys were coming constantly.

"When I received my order from Custer to separate myself from the command, *I had no instructions to unite at any time with Reno or anyone else. There was no plan at all.* My orders were 'valley-hunting' ad infinitum. The reason I returned was because I thought I would be needed at the ridge. I acted entirely on my own judgment. *I was separated from Reno fifteen miles when at the greatest distance.*

"I had a very fast walking horse, which I think can walk five miles an hour easily. We had to go by files through defiles and circuit around rugged hills which were too steep to ascend, and that is why I tell you we were at a trot from the time we left Custer until we watered the horses at the morass. From that time until we reached the place where Reno crossed the river, the gait was the same. It was not necessary to give a command to trot, because the men would all be trotting to keep up with me. We were going then as fast as we could go without going at a gallop.

"Reno could not have expected me to join him. There were no orders to do so.

"When I left, I did not know that Reno had a command. The division had not been made yet, and I don't think Reno knew anything about it at the time I left. When I passed, he asked me where I was going, and I told him I was going to the left, with instructions to pitch into anything I came across. The next time I saw Reno was on the hill.

"The farthest down stream that any company of Reno's got was about a half mile below that highest point. I planted a guidon there as a guide to our position for Custer. His battlefield is not visible there; *I know that positively,* though some officers think it was

"Not a soul in the command imagined Custer had been destroyed till Gen. Terry came up. That was our first intimation. Up to that time we were wholly ignorant of his fate. From all the circumstances *it is my judgment that the fight lasted from fifteen minutes to half an hour or an hour; not more than the latter.* I do not think it would have been possible to have communicated with him, even if we had known where he was.

"It was after we had marched eight or ten miles the morning of the 25th when General Custer said *he did not believe there were any Indians in that country.* It was about 10 o'clock that morning. I started off to the left shortly after 12 o'clock.

"It was the belief of the officers on the hill, during the night of the 25th, that General Custer had gone to General Terry, *and that we were abandoned to our fate.*

"Major Reno knew I went off to the left, but not what orders I had. If different parts of a command are expected to cooperate, I should think it very necessary to communicate orders to other officers. When I left, Reno had no command that I knew of. Reno had no reason to think I was near, or following, the same trail. I scarcely knew myself what to do. As I said, I was 'valley hunting.' He had no right to expect any assistance from me whatever.

"If there had been any plan of battle, enough of that plan would have been communicated to me so that I would have known what to do under certain circumstances. Not having done that, I do not believe there was any plan. In *General Custer's mind there was a belief that there were no Indians, nor any village.* I do not know, except that I was sent off to hunt up some Indians. I was to pitch into them and let him know; and if I found them, the distance would have been so great that *we would have been wiped out before he could get to us.*

"It would have taken me an hour and a quarter to bring up the packs after I got the Martin order. I could not have expedited it by going back after them, as a sergeant had already done that. I heard no firing until I arrived at the ford, when I both heard and saw it—about nine hundred Indians engaged in demolishing about thirteen men.

"The order I got from Custer *did not indicate that he expected me to cooperate in any attack on the village.* The first two were things he forgot to tell me as he started off, while the column was in plain sight. The order to send him word if I found anything showed that *he did not believe there was any village there.*

"*I am convinced that when the order brought by Martin reached me, General Custer and his whole command were dead.*

"It was not evident to me that he expected me to be on the trail. He could have expected no such thing. From the orders I started with, *he could not possibly have known where to find me within ten or fifteen miles.*

"My going back was providential—or accidental—or whatever you may be pleased to term it. I supposed Custer had found what he sent me out to find, and he wanted me as quickly as possible. *And I got there as soon as I could.*

"From my orders, I might have gone on twenty miles without finding a valley. Still, I was to go on to the first valley, and if I did not find any Indians, I was to go to the next valley. *Those were the exact words of my order—no interpretation at all.* I at least had to go to the second valley. I understood it as *a rather senseless order.* We were on the main trail of the Indians; there were plenty of them on that trail. We had passed through immense villages the preceding days, and it was scarcely worth while hunting up any more. *We knew there were eight or ten thousand Indians on the trail we were following.*

"General Crook had fought these same Indians seven days before we did, *and he saw enough of them to let them alone.* He had a larger force[1] than we had; yet he remained from the 17th of June until 15th of August awaiting reinforcements, *and did not think it prudent to go after those Indians.*

[1](Note by Author: Crook had over eleven hundred men against the six hundred and fifty in the Seventh Cavalry.)

Looking north from Reno's entrenchments toward Custer's position, showing the dangerous and difficult four miles between the two commands.

"*Why I was sent to the left I don't know. It was not my business to reason why. I went.*

"I considered that I violated my orders when I struck to the right. If I had carried them out, I would have been *at least twenty-five miles away. As it was, I was certainly too far to cooperate with Custer when he needed me.*

"I think after Custer sent Reno across to charge the Indians, his intentions were to get in the rear of the village and attack them from the left. His plan of attack was, therefore, *known only to himself and not to Major Reno, for he* must naturally have expected his assistance *to come from the rear and not from the front.*

"The position of the bodies on the Custer battlefield indicated that the officers did not die with their companies, for only three officers were found with their companies. *That shows they did not fight by companies.* All the officers, except Keogh, Calhoun and Crittenden, were on the line with Custer. That would not be the fact if the command was overwhelmed making a stand. If there had been a charge, the officers would have led it; there is no royal road to death in a charge.

"The officers' bodies, including General Custer's were in a position which indicated that they had not died in a charge. There was an arc of a circle of dead horses around them.

"Lines could have been formed, but lines were not formed—they probably had not time to form lines. General Custer might have fled the field and saved a part of his command; and I think discretion would have been the better part of valor if he had done that.

"The sergeant who came to me had verbal orders to the commanding officer of the pack-train, and I did not consider that an order to me. *The pack-train was not a part of my command or column.*

"My supposition in regard to Custer's whereabouts was that he had found more Indians than he could conveniently handle with his battalion of five troops, and that he had fallen back to connect with Generals Terry and Gibbon.

"My battalion got to the point in time to save Reno's forces; *but from not knowing the position or needs of Custer,* it was without the bounds of possibility to render him any assistance. That my battalion made such an attempt is clear enough. It is also clear to me that after the occurrence, the whole seven companies of the regiment could have rendered no assistance to Custer after Reno had been defeated, even had there been time and we had known the lay of the land.

"And the reason for this is: that there were a great deal too many Indians who were powerful good shots, on the other side. We were at their hearths and homes; they had gotten the bulge on Reno; their medicine was working well, and they were fighting for all the good God gives anyone to fight for.

"Had I known of the defeat of Custer's force at this time, my only surprise would have been, why they didn't get us too!

"The fact is, all the talk about Reno's being able to re-inforce Custer is simply absurd. *Custer himself was responsible for the Little Big Horn action, and it is an injustice to attribute the blame to anyone else.*

CHAPTER 4

WITH COL. CHAS. A. VARNUM
AT THE LITTLE BIG HORN.

ON CUSTER'S LAST EXPEDITION, Lieutenant Varnum had charge of the Crow and Arickaree Indian scouts, and as such was operating independently of the main command, spending most of his time in the saddle, scouting far in advance of the regiment, with his Indian allies.

This story of his experience in Custer's last battle begins on the morning of June 25th, when he, with his Indian scouts, attached themselves to Major Reno's command. After crossing the Little Big Horn river, and the engagement with the hostiles commenced, Lieutenant Varnum's Indian scouts broke and fled, leaving him without a command. He thereupon voluntarily joined the troop under Captain Weir.

Colonel Varnum's story presents an interesting array of facts regarding this most disastrous battle between United State troops and hostile Indians. In discussing his experience with the writer many years ago, he said: *"If we had remained in the river bottom twenty minutes longer, not a man of us would have escaped. We were nearly out of ammunition when we did leave. What was left of Major Reno's command did not average five cartridges to the man when we reached the bluffs."*

His account, which follows, is taken in large part from his testimony in the official Record of the Reno Court of Inquiry, held at Chicago during January 1879, but also from personal conversations with the writer in San Francisco, in the year 1927.—The Author.

"I was absent from the command nearly all the time, scouting with the Indians under my lead, and I heard none of the instructions given to any of the subordinates. When I reported to General Custer, Major Reno was passing the general and his staff about a mile from the ford where Reno afterward crossed the river with his command.

"I joined Major Reno's command there. I started on ahead with my Indians and fell in with the command as I went on. I saw the battalion going into the fight, and I happened to be in the front and dropped in and crossed the ford. I was then riding on the flank of the command. About one company of the battalion had crossed already, and I joined the head of the command as it was forming over there. I don't know whether the Indians could be seen from Major Reno's command at the time I started from General Custer. As for myself, I had seen a large force of Indians on the river bottom an hour or more before, but I had been out on the hills, and I am not certain whether they could have been seen from where Custer and Reno separated.

"Major Reno's three companies moved out in columns of fours; I think at a rapid trot. They moved down to the ford and crossed the river. After I had left Gen. Custer's column I did not see it again while I was on that side (east) of the river.

"When I left Gen. Custer he was at the head of a column of troops and they were moving at a walk, and Major Reno pulled out at a trot. I think, from what I have seen of the country since, that Custer must have turned off somewhere there, so that it was impossible for me to judge what the relative positions of the two commands were. I don't know what direction the two commands took respectively. I could not tell what the distance between the two commands was at that time. I had seen a portion of the Indian village before Custer and Reno separated.

"I can't recollect what time Major Reno's command separated from General Custer's column. The last time I recall

Lieut. Charles A. Varnum (photo taken in 1872), commanding Indian Scouts, attached to Reno Battalion.

looking at my watch was eight o'clock in the morning. That was on top of the mountain, on the divide between the Rose-bud and the Little Big Horn. I can just calculate from that point, and I have very little to base my opinion on as to the time, unless I connect with somebody else's statement, which would simply be his own opinion. I think that Major Reno's command must have separated from General Custer's column soon after two o'clock in the afternoon, or about two. I base that opinion a great deal on other people's opinion, combined with my own, as to the time. The separation must have oc-curred soon after we passed a tepee that stood on the tribu-tary of the Little Big Horn river. There was a lone tepee there. I did not go down to it. I was out of the column when we passed it, and came back into the column, I think, soon after passing that tepee. The crossing was made ten to fifteen minutes after the separation. The water was quite deep at the ford, and the river was perhaps twenty-five or thirty feet wide—possibly more, and in a column of troops going across, there was necessarily a delay, as we could not keep closed up in the water. There was some delay in the first company crossing; I can't tell how much of a stoppage. Everything seemed to be moving over pretty rapidly.

"I had not ridden near the troops from the morning of the 24th, having been out in the hills, and I was so com-pletely exhausted that I could hardly sit in the saddle. Noth-ing but the excitement of going into action kept me in the saddle at all. I had traveled about twenty miles further than the troops, and I can assure you there was a vast difference between going along on the trail and scouting all over the hills.

"There were eight or ten Indian scouts with me at the time I joined Reno, and as soon as the column had passed I was joined by Lieut. Hare, who had been detailed to assist me in scouting.

"We started out fifty to seventy-five yards ahead of the command. The river bottom opened out wider as we went down stream. There was quite a large body of Indians a little ways off, and they appeared to be running away from us, and then running back and forth across the prairie and toward us, in every direction, apparently trying to kick up all the dust they could. In fact, there was so much dust in the air that it was impossible to judge anywhere near as to the number of Indians there.

"At times they appeared to be running way, as I have stated, then halting and circling around. Suddenly I observed that they had stopped and turned backward, and I glanced back to ascertain the cause, and noticed the battalion deploying from column into line. The command then moved forward again and we also rode on, I suppose fifty yards in front of the command, and as we went down the river bottom we worked out toward the bluffs—toward the left of Major Reno's line. The Indians let us come closer and closer as we went down. We could see about half way down to where the final halt was made. There we observed a number of Indian tepees, and as we worked out toward the left, we could see yet more. The Indians were meantime circling and raising a dust which did not uncover the village very much.

"We went on down possibly two miles. The line then halted and dismounted. I was not present—that is, close enough to hear any of the orders, so I do not know what orders were given.

"When the line halted, I rode with Lieut. Hare in toward the line, and the Indian scouts were gone—I don't know where. My old company that I belonged to was on the line—Captain Moylan's troop—and I went back and reported to him, and told him I should stop with his company during the fight.

"The point where Major Reno's skirmish line was formed was about two miles from the nearest point of the Indian village, and I should think about two hundred yards further around the bend of the river to where the nearest tepees were, and the main bulk of the village was below that. There must have been a pretty solid lot of tepees right in front close together, in that bend. After crossing the river, Major Reno's command moved right down the valley of the stream, but owing to the bend in the river we moved closer to the timber, and then out on the prairie, following the general course of the stream.

"The Little Big Horn river is a very crooked stream. The course of the troops was very nearly a direct one. It was probably fifteen to twenty minutes after Major Reno's command crossed the river until they halted and deployed as skirmishers. Going from the crossing to the point where the command halted, there was no absolute contact between the command and the Indians.

"It was about half-past two in the afternoon of June 25th when the skirmish line was deployed, assuming that my statement about the time is correct. The ground between the right of Major Reno's command when it was deployed as skirmishers, and the river, along the edge of what was called the second bend in the bottom, contained some very heavy timber—large trees, with dense underbrush, and little paths, made by animals, through it; and then there was a rather open glade, or grassy place. Also, there were willows and rushes and small trees down near the river, and brush or smaller timber nearer the bank of the stream. It might have been a hundred yards from the right of the skirmish line down to the river. At the time the line halted and formed the skirmish line, there had been a few shots fired, and there was a sort of an engagement between some of the scouts and the Indians. The ground immediately in front of the skirmish line in the direction of the village was open prairie, with some ravines.

"The village was situated along the left bank of the Little Big Horn river. Owing to the bend in the stream and the timber around the left bank as you go down the bottom, it was almost impossible, unless one was well out on the plain, to see much of the village in coming from the direction that

F. F. Girard, interpreter with the 7th Cavalry. Left behind in Reno's retreat from the river bottom, he rejoined the command after a miraculous escape.

we came. We could see some of the tepees, but it was impossible to note the extent of it or how large the village itself was. I don't think I made much, if any, estimation on the strength of the Indians I had seen—there were certainly more Indians than I ever saw together before. It was a very large village—I could see that very plainly, because I had seen immense numbers of Indians from the tops of the bluffs I was on when I was out scouting, and I knew there was a very large village there.

"The position we occupied in the timber was as good as

any on the left bank of the stream as far as I can judge. At
that time I did not know much about the country up and
down the stream. The position we held in the timber (I do
not know exactly its size) was large enough so that with the
number of men we had in the timber—those three companies,
numbering 112 men, that were under Major Reno—I do not
think we were able to cover the position which must necessarily be held to keep the Indians out of the timber. We
could not let them come in there with us. We had to occupy
the position as the ground lay, in order to hold it at all. It does
not seem to me that we had men enough to hold the entire
circle of the river bottom.

"When the skirmish line was formed I saw a good many
excited men shooting right up in the air. There was very
heavy firing going on on both sides, and I was lying in
the timber with Fred Girard, the interpreter, and Charley
Reynolds, our chief guide. Reynolds was very anxious to get
a drink of whiskey out of his flask, and, to tell the truth, I
was paying more attention to that than I was to the Indians.

"At that time the heaviest firing of the Indians was toward
the right of the line. The Indians at that point were about
three or four hundred yards distant, and fewer and fewer as
one passed around the line; and away around to the left there
were only scattering Indians here and there. There were a
good many of them at long range. They would pass around
us and keep out of range, circling around.

"At the time I was with Girard and Reynolds there were
about four or five hundred Indians in front of the line. There
may have been a great many more. The heavy firing came
from these Indians on the front, and it was so rapid that
there were bullets in the air all the time. As a rule, the Indians
fired from their ponies; they were just scampering around us
and pumping those Winchester rifles into us as fast as they
could. The heaviest dust was about seven or eight hundred
yards off possibly a thousand yards distant.

"From the commencement of the fight in the woods until

Major Reno's command fell back and left the woods, the
engagement lasted about half an hour. I don't know how
many men were killed up to the time the command left the
timber. All I am sure about was my old first sergeant and
my orderly. The troops lay right on the edge of the woods,
and when a man was shot, he would drop right over into
the timber and I would not see him at all.

"There certainly was a feeling of uneasiness in the command regarding Custer while we were fighting in the river
bottom. I was thinking 'Has he got in the same fix we are
in? What has become of him? Has he been thrown off?'
Custer had promised to support Major Reno, but he was not
there. However, the idea that his command had been cut up
and wiped out—well, I simply didn't even think of such a
thing. I don't know as there was any such feeling as that.
It was 'What in the world has become of him? Has he been
corraled as we are?' There was no feeling at all that he had
been completely used up. My impression was that he had
gone to connect with General Terry's command, knowing
Terry was coming up.

"At the time that I saw a detachment of troops on the
bluffs I did not know it was General Custer's command, or
a part of it, inasmuch as I did not see what companies he
had with him then. But at the time Major Reno's line dismounted on the river bottom, just as. I joined them with
Lieut. Hare, at the time the skirmish line was being deployed,
in looking up to the bluffs on our immediate right—right
across the general direction of the river—I saw the gray
horse company of the battalion moving along the bluffs, and
as I know now that the gray horse company was with Custer,
I suppose that was his command. I just looked up there,
but as we had plenty to do down below, I didn't attach any
importance to it.

"The point where I saw them was back from the actual
edge of the bluff, and I could see, from the glance that I
made, that the head of the column was just behind the edge

Mouth of Reno Creek on
north side of Yellowstone
July 6th 1876

My Dear Daughters
When the Steamer Far West
left here on the 3rd I could not write you
as I was too tiered & suffering from Rheuma-
tism. I am now getting better but am for
him small. You will no doubt see by
the papers that Gen Custer's command had
a fight with the Indians on the Little Big
Horn where Gen Custer & 12 Officers and
nigh on to 300 men were killed. during
the fight; I with 3 others became separated
had to hide in the brush for 2 days & one
night & had a narrow escape from drowning.
I escaped through the grace of God; many a time
there did I think of you all & wonder whether I
would ever see you again, If I ever return
to Lincoln I shall never go out again with an
expedition. I lost many good & true friends
I write you now to ask you if my
safety, will be sure & let you another way from
here, there is no paper now & to be had
I doubt whether we get back to Lincoln before
November & may get in by the last of September
with much Love & many Kisses I am
Your Affectionate Father
F. F. Girard

Letter written shortly after the Custer battle by F. F. Girard, interpreter,
to his daughters.

of the bluffs. They were crossing, I suppose, so that my glance happened to take in that part of the column—I think the whole of the gray horse troop. It was probably about three-quarters of a mile from where we were. General Custer always rode a very fast walking horse which would make the whole command trot when he was riding at the head of the column; and I think that was the gait at which the command was moving when I saw them—that it would be going pretty rapidly to keep up with that horse of the general's in front. I do not say that General Custer was riding that particular horse at the time, but that was my impression from the gait his command was moving.

"When I had been on the line ten or fifteen minutes I heard somebody say that Company G was going to charge a portion of the village down through the woods—or something like that, or to that effect. I heard some of the men calling out 'Company G is going to charge.' I was on my horse at the time, and I rode down into the timber to go with the company that was going to charge the village. In the timber there was a little glade or opening, and I recalled that in riding into this opening I could see the stream in one direction, so we must have been near the stream, and I could see the line of the opening in front, and also that there was a detached portion of the village on the other side of the stream, and that is where they were going. I heard no order. It was just a rumor that I followed, and I saw Major Reno there. He was right with G Company, evidently deploying it, or assisting to deploy it, to go through the woods. The company was on the down stream side of this opening, and I said, 'I am going to charge', or something like that—meaning that I was going to accompany the troop that seemed about to charge the village. I rode to where Major Reno was, and he asked me if I had just come from the line in front, and I told him I had a few minutes before. In coming down there I was delayed by the narrow, intricate paths in the first edge of the timber, and had trouble getting through there with my horse.

"Major Reno said to me, 'I wish you would go back there and see how things are going on, and then come back and report to me.'

"So I turned back on my horse, and was riding across this opening when I met Lieut. Hodgson. I asked him if he had just come from the line, and he said he had. I told him that Major Reno wanted to know what was going on on the line, and asked if he would report to the major while I rode up, and that I would be back again a few minutes afterward.

"A few minutes later I was with Hodgson again. He thought his horse had been shot, and he was anxious to know about it, and that delayed us a minute. Then I went up on the line. I went up thru the paths to where the line was. At that time it appeared to have fallen back to the edge of the timber—that is, it was lying on the edge of the timber instead of being perpendicular to it. The command was in the timber, and I could not see all of the men. I saw Captain Moylan when I got to the edge of the line, and he called out—I don't know that he intended the remark for me—that the horses the men had dismounted from, were beyond the left flank of the line; that the Indians were circling into the timber toward his left flank, and would cut off our horses and our extra ammunition, which was all there in the saddle-pockets, and that something must be done. I told him I would bring the horses up and I went back.

"In order to go down the line I had to travel through the woods to this opening I have spoken of. I rode down to the left of the line and called out for all of A Company men to follow me with their horses. Then I guess all of the other companies followed me. I went up with my own company, and we came right in the rear of where Captain Moylan was. He was about at the rear of his own line. I dismounted and went up on the line, and as I did so I heard Captain Moylan call out that his men were out of ammunition, and he ordered that each alternate man should fall back from the line and get ammunition from their saddle-bags, and then return to the line and let the others go back on the same errand.

"Then I got up to the right of the line, and it was there that I met Girard and Charley Reynolds. I stopped and was talking with them two or three minutes, when I heard cries of 'Charge, charge, we are going to charge!' There was quite a bit of confusion and I jumped up and said, 'What's that?' and started down through the woods and grabbed my horse. Everybody was mounted. I didn't hear any orders. I just understood hearing the men calling out that they were going to charge, and I grabbed my horse and mounted him. This was in the bushes, and as the other men were mounting just outside the bushes it hindered me, and I couldn't get out until the men had passed.

"As soon as they passed so that I could get out into the path myself, I did so, and came out with the men. The head of the column was then about a couple of rods, or something like that, from the edge of the timber as I came out. I was riding a Kentucky race horse, and I gave him his head and pretty soon overtook the head of the column. I had a very fast horse. As I came up with the head of the column it was probably about half way from there to the ford at which we crossed soon after.

"I came up on the left-hand side of the column, and didn't see any officer at the head—that is, as I came up. I supposed there had been a charge started, and that the first men out of the timber had struck some Indians and wheeled and started for those, and the others might have followed them. I didn't know what was up, and I yelled at them to stop. But my horse was plunging about like mad and he was hard to manage. Not seeing the command at all on the left, I supposed they were up there; and then they went from there to the river and crossed the stream.

"I have stated all I know about the command leaving the timber, and know nothing beyond what I have told here. I did not hear any bugle or trumpet calls from the time Major Reno's command left General Custer until the evening of the 25th. If there had been any in the timber, I would undoubtedly have heard them, and it is possible I may have heard them and not remembered it; but I don't think I heard any calls. I have no idea how the order to charge or fall back was communicated to the troops. All I heard was some men yelling that they were 'going to charge,' or something like that.

"In reference to the danger to the command in the timber I would say that it was hardly a safe place. They were fighting a force of Indians who outnumbered them, and there was that danger.

"At the time the retreat from the timber was made, a good many bullets had begun to drop through the woods from our rear. It was brush there near the stream. Whether the bullets came from the bluffs above or from the river bottom, I don't know. But I know there was quite a lively shower came in from our rear, toward the river. I don't know that any efforts were made to ascertain where the firing from the rear came from. I don't know that any point was designated where the command should rally or retreat on. The point to which Major Reno retreated, taking the road we went, was about four hundred yards from the crossing. It was right up a steep hill, on a straight line. It was about three-quarters of a mile from the crossing to the place in the woods where the skirmish line was formed. It took the troops about six or seven minutes to reach the crossing in retreat.

"When we rode out of the woods, I came out on the left of the column, and there were a good many Indians scampering along with their rifles across the saddle, working the levers of their Winchesters on the column. When we got to the top of the hill, most of the Indians withdrew. Between us and the stream I saw fifteen or twenty in the timber, and I have understood since that there were several troopers' bodies found in there where I saw the Indians dodging and running through that light brush.

"On the retreat some of the troopers were using revolvers. The command had to go into the river pell-mell on the jump, because it was a straight bank down to the water, with a drop of several feet, and a straight bank to climb up after leaving the water on the other side. I know my horse nearly threw me off, he jumped up so straight. I don't know whether any of the men fell back into the river there.

"When I rode out of the river I turned toward the left and started up a ravine. Ahead of me I could see Dr. De Wolf and his orderly. Some of the men were yelling at me, but I could not hear what they said, except that they kept pointing ahead and beckoning me to come where they were. I finally concluded to ride over and see what their racket was about. Dr. DeWolf was still toiling up the steep incline and I turned to watch him. Suddenly some shots rang out and I saw both the doctor and his orderly pitch forward, dead. That would have been my own fate if those men had not yelled and warned me to come where they were.

"At the crossing, the water was four or five feet deep. I do not think the Indians followed us clear to the river, because the firing receded as we came to the river. On the retreat almost everybody I saw was considerably excited. They were in that condition when they went into the engagement, for that matter. They were very much demoralized when they got on the hill after the retreat, but they had left a good many behind them.

"At the time I left the skirmish line, when we were fighting down in the river bottom, there was some man in Company A who was left down in the woods. He was killed before the command left. I heard people speaking about this man, but I don't remember who he was. I don't remember where Sergeant Hyde and a man named Strode were shot. One was shot through the knee. He was on his horse when I saw him, but whether he managed to get on his horse with a ball through his knee, I don't know. That is all I know about the casualties in the river bottom. The movement from the timber on the retreat I knew was a movement to get out of there, and to get to higher ground some-

Looking East toward the bluffs where Major Reno was besieged. Up these steep bluffs Reno's command retreated under heavy fire. White dot top center is marker where Dr. DeWolf was killed on his way up. Little Big Horn river hidden by fringe of trees. Photo by the author.

where. When I got out on the prairie I was satisfied our men were getting away from the Indians as fast as they could.

"I think a good many casualties must have occurred in the timber about the time we left—that is, in the rear part of the column, and there were certainly a number killed and wounded on the retreat from the timber to the bluffs; also some there at the ford. We lost a good many men about that time. I don't know exactly where they were killed or how. Some of them must have been killed in the edge of the timber, because there were a number of dead bodies left in there. The Indians did not charge into the tail end of Major Reno's column on that retreat. They would ride some little distance off on the flank, varying from fifty to a hundred yards, with their rifles right across the pommels of their saddles—which would be about the proper height to strike a man mounted— just pumping those Winchesters into us, and not even taking time to throw the gun to their shoulders. A great many of them followed the command that way down the river bottom in retreat, but as we neared the river they began to draw off and go the other way. If they had had the sense to have followed us right up the bluffs, I doubt if a man of us would have escaped alive.

"Lieutenant Hodgson, Lieutenant Wallace, Captain French and Lieutenant McIntosh were all behind me in the retreat. Hodgson was killed at the ford and McIntosh was cut down before he reached it. I don't know what they were doing. The rear of the column was scattered as I came out of the timber, and there were still men behind me. I don't know that any wounded men were left in the woods. There were men left there when we were surrounded, but I supposed they were dead. Every man who was so shot or disabled that he could not follow the command was probably left there. They would be likely to have been killed at once. I don't know how many dead men were left in the woods, but there were some there, and some out on the plains.

"There was no charge made, from the position where the

skirmish line was, toward the Indian village. The only charge that I know anything about was when Major Reno started down through the woods with G Company, as I understood it to charge the Indian village, and I started to go with them.

"As to my riding for the head of the column after leaving the timber, I had no special object in mind in going to the head at all. I was foot-loose to go where I pleased, and the column was retreating, and I had no special object other than to go where the head of the column was, and if there was anything to be done, to do it.

"My horse was a high-stepper, and I had to saw his mouth with the bit to keep him from getting way ahead of the column. When I reached the head of the command I said something like 'This won't do, this won't do; we have got to get into shape,' or something like that—I don't remember the words. My idea was—thinking there was no officer at the head of the column—to take command and see that it was conducted by somebody. But just then I discovered that Major Reno was there himself, so that my supposition in thinking there was no other officer there but myself was entirely wrong.

"I don't know whether there were any Indians in the timber before the command left or not. I didn't see any myself. When we first got a chance to talk about it, after we got on the hill, I heard there were Indians behind us in the woods. Some of the men were making such a remark. When I went to get the horses I had no trouble getting them. There were no Indians in where the animals were. Some of the men who had been left as horse-holders were probably firing. The line on the left of the timber was under the same hill that the horses were. All I had to do was to ride down the skirmish line, to and beyond the left of the line. Captain Moylan said the Indians were getting in on his left, and that the horses were not covered by the skirmish line, and that the Indians would probably get in there. I didn't see any Indians in there; neither did I find or see any horses that had been struck by bullets.

"After Major Reno's command got on the hill, there was quite a number of the men firing. I went to the wounded men. I did not watch particularly as to the number of Indians, but I know from the sound of the shots that there were some Indians firing on us. They were just scattering shots. If the men happened to see any Indians riding along they would fire, if the savages were within range.

"On the other side of the stream where we crossed was a very steep and high hill to the yet higher bluffs beyond. I know the horses were pretty well tuckered out, panting and climbing that awful grade. I don't know exactly what did happen at that time at the head of the column, because my orderly who had been with me was very badly wounded. His horse also was shot and fell with him and I stopped to pick up a loose horse and mount him.

"The head of the command halted there, or there was some sort of a delay, and somebody said they were going to move on up to the top of the hill, as there was no use stopping there. When we reached the crest of the bluff I found there were several wounded men, and two or three of them were from my own company—the first sergeant and one or two others. I stopped and helped them down off their horses.

"A few minutes later a column of troops was in sight coming down stream toward us, and we stopped there ten or fifteen minutes until they arrived. It was Captain Benteen's battalion. At that time I don't recollect that Captain McDougal's company, with the packs, was in sight. I remember that Lieut. Hare started out soon afterward to hurry them up. We waited there five or ten minutes, when Major Reno told me to take a detachment and go down and bury Lieut. Hodgson's body. There was nothing there to dig a grave with, and I told him I would have to wait until the packs arrived. He said he had been down to the river and got some little trinkets from Hodgson's body, but that his watch was gone.

"We remained there until the packs came up, about three-quarters of an hour later. I then got two spades from the packs and started with about six men to go down to the river and bury Lieut. Hodgson. About two-thirds of the way down, I saw a lot of men coming out of the woods. There was a citizen and quite a number of soldiers who came out of the timber dismounted, and were climbing the bluffs, coming up out of the river bottom.

"As I started with the men to bury the bodies, somebody —I think it was Lieut. Wallace—called to me that they wanted me to come back, and then I started immediately up the hill. When I arrived there most of the command had started to move down stream along the bluffs, with the exception, I think, of Captain Moylan's company, and possibly some of the others. Moylan had most of the wounded—in fact, I think they were all from his troop, and the men he had left and who were able to travel, were hardly sufficient to carry them along. There were very few men there belonging to A Company after the fight, and they moved very slowly. I remained with them some time, and think Capt. McDougal's company sent a platoon to assist in carrying the wounded. I started along with A Company for awhile. I had no company myself at all. About a mile and a half from there I joined Capt. Weir's troop. That was on the far point of the long range of bluffs which ran along the right bank of the Little Big Horn. I went where his company was dismounted and firing at the Indians, who seemed to be coming from out of the prairies. It was quite long range, but the Indians also were firing at his command. All the Indians in the country seemed to be coming after us again as fast as they could travel.

"Soon after this, we turned and gradually dropped back. I did not see the troops leave that further point, but I went back to Captain Moylan and helped with the wounded a little while. I rode back slowly to the rear, and the troops gradually fell back to the point I think a little further up the stream than where we touched the bluffs. It was quite a slow

Captain Myles Moylan, Troop A, Reno Battalion.

movement, as one or two of the companies were dismounted. They got their horses and fell into line and dropped back into the position that was selected and on which we afterward fought.

"The firing was kept up. The entire Indian force seemed to have turned back against us, and we had to fight falling back dismounted to cover the retreat, to the position where we were later located. The firing continued as long as we could see—a very heavy firing against us, and the men fortified as well as they could, using tin cups, knives and whatever came to hand to dig into the flinty soil.

"I supposed the object of the move down stream after Benteen came up, was to go in the direction General Custer was supposed to have gone, and that we were to unite with him.

"The night of the 25th, when the line was first formed, I laid right down on the line with the men while the firing was going on, and until it ceased, and as soon as it slackened I fell asleep—or in a very few minutes afterward—and I didn't know a thing until the bullets commenced to fly around the next morning, and then I got up. I was lying on a little knoll when daylight came, and it was rather exposed, so I started over for French's line and laid down in the trench with him.

"The men had been fortifying in the night, and that was my first sight of how they had been throwing up their fortifications—or rather, digging out the little holes they were occupying. That was the first time I noticed exactly where Major Reno was. He was down on Captain Weir's line to the right. I think there were one or two companies intervening between his position and French's troop.

"I presume most of that day I lay with Captain French in that little hole. I think we were there two or three hours anyway. In fact, the Indians were firing very rapidly at us, and so we just laid still and made no reply to them whatever. We just let them shoot. Occasionally they would start to make a rush on us, and then we would jump up and open on them and they would run back. That sort of tactics alternated for a long time.

"About nine or ten o'clock I went to Captain Moylan's line. I endeavored to get some scouts to try and get outside of the lines with a dispatch. I finally got two or three Crow scouts to say they would go if the 'Rees would also go. I went over to see Major Reno to get a note. I think he wrote four copies of the note, and I sent it out with the scouts. That was probably on the afternoon of the 26th. The Indian scouts did not get through the lines at all, nor do I think they even made the attempt.

"I don't know exactly how to describe the movement of the Indians on the hill. They would lie behind a ridge from two hundred to five hundred yards off. There was one place where I don't think they were over one hundred yards away. We had to charge on them ourselves and drive them out of there. They would lie just behind the ridge, and it would be just one ring of smoke from their guns around the entire range. We would simply lie still and let them shoot away their ammunition. When their nerve was at the proper point, they would come up and charge us. They would sit back on their horses and ride up and we would pour it into them, and they would then fall back. That was kept up all day long.

"I don't know how many wounded we had the night of the 25th. I didn't go down where Dr. Porter was at work with the hospital until some time on the 26th. There may have been about twenty wounded men, but I can't say exactly. The horses and pack animals were all corraled in a circle, all in together, by tying the reins of about a dozen horses together and fastening them to the legs of the head horses. The corral was covered by Captain Moylan's company behind the pack saddles, and on the left was Captain Weir's troop, and I think Godfrey's also. On the right was French's company, with Wallace's and McDougal's—that is, commencing at about the center of the line, and that took it around to the left until McDougal's left rested on the river. On the up-stream side was a little knoll that was higher than the ground where most of us lay, and on that ground Captain Benteen got his company in line. I do not think the command was in position to do any very hard work, at least more than they were forced to do under the circumstances, and probably the majority of them slept that night.

"I was not with Major Reno at the time we were moving back to our original position, after having advanced down toward where Captain Weir had gone. The only time I was in a position where I could hear him give an order was when we were going back to this far point where the command stopped—at least, I found a portion of it halted. As I came back I rode up near to him, and heard him say something to the effect that he was going to select his position to make his fight a little further on. We were moving up stream then.

"As to his exercising the functions of a commanding officer directing the troops, the movements and positions of the men, in the presence of great danger, he certainly did that. He was present with the command, giving orders. Certainly there was no sign of cowardice or anything of that sort.

"Referring again to the attempt made on the 26th to get a scout through to General Terry, I would state that the letter said in the first place that we had arrived at this point about such-and-such a time; that we had attacked the Indians and that we did not know where General Custer was. It described our location on the hill, and stated that we were holding the Indians in check. I am also very certain that it asked for medical aid and assistance. That is about as near as I can remember. This letter was written by Major Reno.

"At the time I saw the gray horse troop, while we were fighting in the river bottom, the men in that troop were certainly in a position to see exactly what we were doing down there. What part of the column the gray horse troop was in I cannot say. How far General Custer was in advance of the gray horse troop I cannot tell. But assuming that he was riding there with the column, he had just passed the point where I had seen the gray horse troop. He certainly must have been in a position to know exactly what was going on. I certainly believe that General Custer would be watching the progress of the fight at that time. If he saw us there—and I certainly can't help thinking that he must have seen us—then it was the last information he got concerning us.

"General Custer may have attempted to cross the river at the fording place and have been driven back, and left no particular signs, unless there were tracks where the horses came down, or else where someone had been wounded, or there had been dead horses; but I don't know of any dead horses or bodies or anything that indicated a fight, although he may have gone in there. The first evidence I found showing where General Custer's command had been engaged with the Indians was in coming up over the field where those dead bodies were found. There were just a few in that vicinity, here and there. It must have been about two miles from Major Reno's position on the hill. It may have been a little more than that.

"As to whether Captain Benteen's command could have united with Reno in the timbered place we occupied in the river bottom, it would depend. At the time we left the timber the Indians turned from us. Now if we had remained there and Captain Benteen had started to come in there, what force the Indians would have put against us is a problem— and the Indians are the only ones who know anything about that. When Benteen came up, he came to us from up stream, on the right hand bank. From what I understand of the direction in which he came, he would have joined us probably on that trail by which Major Reno went into the woods. I suppose of course the firing would have attracted him, and he would have come in, unless he had different orders. Whether the Indians would have had force enough to have attacked him as soon as they saw him coming, and prevented him from uniting with us, I cannot say. If they had sent men enough down there, they might have sent him into the timber and prevented him from uniting with us on the hill. If Benteen had joined Reno in the river bottom with the pack train and all the extra ammunition, they could certainly have held the bottom for some time. Of course the presence of our troops as near as we were to the village, would necessarily have kept a force of Indians in our front to fight us; they could not leave the village while we were there.

"As far as forming a junction with Custer—by going through the village in that direction—I don't believe that either Custer or Reno either could have done that—that is, that either command could have joined the other by charging through the village.

"Custer must have been in action before Major Reno and Captain Benteen united their forces.

"We started on the 28th to go down to the Custer field and bury the dead, and we went down on a trail which I supposed was General Custer's. When we got to the high hill with lots of little stones and Indian medicine bags on top of it, I went up to see what it was. I rode off the trail and circled around and came down to it where I supposed the point "B" on the map made by Lieut. McGuire is located. That point was very much cut up by pony tracks. It was evidently a watering place. Very soon after that, we went up to where I had seen two or three bodies, and we received an order from Major Reno to go away back on some bluffs, well out from the river, with the Indian scouts, and operate as a lookout while the men deployed around the field burying the dead. I was not over the field at all until the burial took place. The bodies I did see were in a gully or ravine.

"You ask my judgment as to the number of Indians that were engaged during the 25th and 26th of June, 1876, and whether they were not sufficient in numbers to have overcome both commands even if each had been separately engaged at the same time. My reply is, that I would not like to take half the warriors they had and take the command we had with us, and fight them. There must have been a great many warriors there. From the estimates of other people and what I heard the Indians estimate later, and putting everything together that I could pick up, I do not believe there were less than four thousand warriors to fight.

"Regarding the number of Indian warriors in that village, I have heard it estimated at from twenty-five hundred to twelve thousand. I think myself that there were at least fifteen

thousand men, women and children in the village, and four
thousand fighting warriors, if they all had their families with
them; but I don't think they all had their families along. I
know there were a great many wickiups at the lower part of
the village left standing, and they were quite thick along the
edge of the timber on the stream, and at the lower end of the
village.

"If there were fifteen thousand Indians in the village it
would take not less than twenty thousand ponies to move
them. I didn't see the village moving. I saw those ponies
when I was on the bluffs the night before the fight. The
Indian scouts with me described them as they stood and
looked at them. They said that there were more ponies than
they had ever seen together before in their lives, and that it
looked like an immense buffalo herd; but I could not see a
thing myself, for my eyes were bothering me terribly from
the heat, dust and loss of sleep. The Indians tried to show
me the pony herd by advising me to "look for worms crawling
in the grass." General Custer came up there, too, and he
looked but he could not make out any pony herd.

"While we were on the hill, just after Captain Benteen
had arrived, I heard firing away down stream, and I spoke
of it to Lieut. Wallace. I had just borrowed a rifle from him
and had fired a couple of shots at long range at the Indians
in the river bottom. Just as I was handing back the rifle I
heard firing, and remarked, What does that mean? It was not
like a volley, but a heavy firing—a sort of crash! crash! I do
not mean that it was necessarily the general's command
which were doing the firing; it may have been the Indians.
It was from that end of the village down in the vicinity where
Custer's body was found. I thought he was having a pretty
hot time down there, as the firing was very heavy.

"I do not know anything about the plan of the fight—if
plan there was. I merely saw the companies going into action
and I went in with them.

"When I saw the command going along the bluffs—at the

time I observed the gray horse troop—I noted, of course, that
some battalion or command was going to attack the village
—was going in or engage the other end of the Indian camp;
but how large the command was, or exactly what it was
going to do, I cannot tell.

"In regard to the guns used by the Indians against us, I
believe the longest-range rifles they had were those they had
taken from General Custer's command, with some few exceptions. There were one or two Indians on a particular point
who had very long range guns. As regards the range of the
Winchester rifles used by the Indians, it was not as great as
the carbines we carried. The Winchester carried a considerably less charge of powder than did the Springfield carbine,
the caliber of which was 45/70, while probably the Winchesters used by the Indians in that fight were the Model
1873 44/40 caliber—only a little more than half the powder
our own cartridges carried. One could shoot with reasonable
accuracy up to a thousand yards with the Springfield carbine.

"I don't believe the plains Indians, such as the Sioux, would
have been likely to have charged the troops in the timber
while mounted on their ponies. It would not have been a very
healthful place for an enemy to go in mounted while the
troops were in there. Indians will try to take advantage of
every sort of cover rather than risk their lives. Major Reno's
troops in that timber were under cover, and the Indians—
while they were out on the plains where we could see them
—they also had the advantage of timber above and below
on the stream, which they could have used as we did.

"Every Indian fights for himself. Each one has his own
method of fighting. The way they will fight depends very
largely upon their numbers and the forces of the enemy.

"In conclusion I would state that I have related this engagement of the battle of the Little Big Horn just as I experienced it and as things came under my own observation.
Probably no two men will relate the same incidents alike, as
they may have been viewed from entirely different angles."

GUN USED IN LITTLE BIG HORN FIGHT

The Old 45-70 Springfield Single Shot Carbine—Model 1873.

To all who are interested in the question as to what gun the 7th Cavalry used in the Custer fight this letter from Col. Varnum should settle the controversy:

San Francisco, May 26, 1924

"My dear Mr. Brininstool:—

Yours just received. We used the 45 caliber Springfield carbine in 1876, with 70-grain ammunition. No, Spencer carbines or rifles were not used in the regiment in my day. When I joined, in 1872, we were armed with Sharps' carbines, and some of the troops had three kinds of carbines for experimental purposes, viz: Ward-Burton, 50-caliber, Springfield, 50-caliber and Remington, 50-caliber, but in 1876 we all had Springfield 45's. I never saw but one Spencer in my life, and that was an old worthless gun that someone picked up.

"Very truly yours,
"CHAS. A. VARNUM."

Colonel Varnum was, in 1876, a lieutenant of the 7th Cavalry, and had charge of all the Indian scouts engaged by the command.

The weapons used by the Indians were vastly superior to those used by the troops in every way, being Henry repeating rifles, 44-caliber; Winchester Model 1873 repeating rifles, as well as some Sharps single-shot weapons, and many also carried bows and arrows.

Another great error made by artists and moving picture companies who have attempted to depict "Custer's last fight" on canvas and screen, is in showing the Seventh Cavalry fighting with sabers. Custer is generally shown by the movie people (who never come within a mile of the truth in their weak attempts to portray the Custer battle) as standing in the center of a devoted little band, with a huge saber in one hand and a revolver in the other.

As a matter of fact—there was not a sword or saber in the entire Seventh Cavalry on the occasion of the battle of the Little Big Horn. Not even an officer carried one. If anyone doubts this assertion he is referred to "Custer's Last Battle," the article written by Gen. E. S. Godfrey, and published in "The Century" of January, 1892. He there says: "The men were armed with carbine and revolver; *no one, not even the officer of the day, carried the saber.*"

CHAPTER 5

A THRILLING ESCAPE—
DE RUDIO AND O'NEILL.

WHEN THE FORCES UNDER MAJOR
MARCUS A. RENO made their gallant, but ineffectual attack on the Indian village strung along the Little Big Horn
River, Montana, on that fatal morning of June 25th, 1876,
some thrilling incidents occurred. None, however, of the Reno
command, underwent more marvelous adventures than Lieut.
Chas. C. De Rudio and Sergt. Thomas O'Neill, whose escape
from death at the hands of the savages was nothing short of
miraculous.

When Major Reno ordered the troops to mount and charge
through the Indian cordon and get to the high hills across
the river, this order was not generally understood, as no bugle
calls were given. Owing to the dense dust kicked up by the
Indian ponies, as their riders raced back and forth, as well as
to the smoke and general confusion, many of the troopers
did not see their companions leave, and about a dozen or
fifteen were left behind. It may have been that the horse-
holders, who remained in the timber when the skirmish line
was formed, either lost control of the animals or else turned
them loose in order to effect their own escape. In any event,
these men were unhorsed and obliged to take to the brush
to escape the Indians.

They were thus left in a most desperate plight. The majority
of the men, however, successfully eluded discovery and cap
ture, and managed to rejoin Reno on the bluffs late that night.
But Lieut. De Rudio, Sergeant O'Neill, Billy Jackson (a half-

breed scout) and Fred F. Girard (an interpreter) were not so fortunate.

These four remained together at the start, but eventually separated under most thrilling circumstances, and for more than thirty-six hours De Rudio and O'Neill were kept busy, dodging about from point to point, to elude capture. Finally, late on the night of June 26th, they managed to get across the river, after some miraculous escapes. Here they wandered about over bluffs and through ravines, for several hours before they were able to locate the Reno command. About 2 o'clock on the morning of the 27th, they heard the distant bray of a mule, and shortly thereafter were welcomed inside Reno's lines.

After serving out his enlistment, Sergt. O'Neill removed to Washington, D. C., where he was appointed a captain of the park police. During that time he wrote the story of the escape of Lieut. De Rudio and himself. From the original copy, the author has drawn the following facts of their remarkable experience:

"We marched until late on the evening of June 23d, then went into camp for the night. The following day we began the march at 4 a.m., continuing up the Rosebud, and made camp late that evening. About 10 o'clock that night, we received orders to again saddle up and make a night march. We continued on the trail until 4 a.m., when we halted and made coffee, resuming the march about 6 o'clock. After a few hours we came to the head of the Rosebud. Then we began to cross the divide between the Rosebud and Little Big Horn Rivers. Shortly after this, the command halted. Officers' call was sounded, and all the officers reported to General Custer for instructions.

"This occupied but a short time, and soon we were again in the saddle. Our scouts were kept busy in front and on the flanks of the column, reporting new signs of Indians.

"We were now marching on an Indian trail which was nearly a quarter of a mile wide in some places. Indications

Lieut. Charles C. DeRudio, Troop A, Reno Battalion, who survived thirty-six hours of exciting adventure on foot to regain the command after the retreat from the valley.

were that large bodies of savages had very recently passed in the direction we were going. When we were within about 10 miles of the Little Big Horn River and the Indian camp, Capt. F. W. Benteen was ordered out to the left and front of us with three companies of cavalry. If he saw no Indians after going as far as he thought prudent, he was to rejoin the command. As a matter of fact, he saw no signs of Indians until he got back within sight of the river, just as Reno's men had about finished their charging through to the other side of the stream.

"Within three miles or so of the river we came to a place where a small band of Indians had been camped. We evidently surprised them, as they retreated to the larger camp on the river, leaving their cooking utensils on the fires, and one tepee standing. From this point we took the gallop, finally arriving at a high bank over the river. Down the river, on the other side, and about a mile from us, we could see the Indian camp at the edge of a narrow strip of timber or brush, where there were some small cottonwood trees growing. At this point the stream ran close to the high banks. The Indian village was partly concealed from us by a bend in the river. The Indians, however, appeared at the edge of the camp in great numbers, mounted, and running around, apparently greatly excited.

"It was at this point that Gen. Custer ordered Major Reno to take his battalion of three troops to the other side of the stream and attack the camp, 'and I will support you,' were the words he used. I belonged to Major Reno's battalion, and we were marched down an old dry creek-bed which debouched into the river near by. Here we crossed the Little Big Horn, the water being about to the horses' bellies. On the opposite bank we formed in fours and took up the gallop toward the Indians. When within about seven hundred yards of them, we came left front into line of battle across the river bottom. When within about five hundred yards of the Indians they opened fire on us.

"As the Indians came out in great numbers to oppose us, and moreover as from this point we could see the extent of the village and the immense number of Indians it contained, and how impossible it appeared to be for us—about 130 or 140 men*—to attempt to charge through such a superior force, our officers decided to act on the defensive. Orders were thereupon given to 'Dismount and prepare to fight on foot.' Three troopers out of each four men dismounted, the fourth man holding the horses. Line was formed, and the horses maneuvered with the line and six or seven yards in the rear of it.

"We now began to answer the fire of the Indians, the main body of which seemed to be about a thousand yards away, but great numbers circled about within five hundred yards or less, all mounted and shooting at us. Our right rested near the brush, the left extending about two hundred yards across the plain, the men being three yards apart on the line. At this time, Custer's command was on the opposite side of the river, and the space between the two columns became greater as we advanced. When the fighting commenced, I should judge Custer and Reno were about a mile and a half apart.

"General Custer and his five companies now disappeared behind a high bluff, going in the direction of the lower end of the Indian village, and that was the last we ever saw of him or his command alive.

"From the point we now occupied we could see the extent of the village. It appeared to be over two miles in length, the tepees covering the river bottom thickly, and the camp in some places was seven or eight hundred yards wide.

"Shortly, the Indians began to close in on our left flank, which was not as well protected. Major Reno evidently realized the danger of being surrounded, or flanked, and wheeled the line, our backs being to the river and our right resting toward the village. It was discovered that at some previous

* Reno's testimony at the Court of Inquiry was that his total command numbered 112 men.

time the stream had run close to our back position, but had changed its course further away about three hundred yards, which left a deep ditch in our rear. We were ordered to lie down on the edge of this bank, keeping up a constant fire, our horses being led behind us. Twenty men under Lieut. McIntosh (of whom I was one) were ordered to deploy in skirmish line and scout the brush, in order to ascertain if the Indians could attack us from the rear. We found thick underbrush and vines and some cottonwood trees growing on this place, and at the head of it and toward the village, a very deep cut or washout. As we discovered no Indians between us and the river, the lieutenant came back and reported.

"At this time the fighting was terrific, the Indians charging up very close. They would deliver their fire, wheel their ponies and scamper to the rear to reload.

"But we observed that they were forming in greater numbers on our left, where they could deliver a flank fire. It was thought by our officers that they were forming for a charge on that end. A brisk consultation was held by the officers, who shouted back and forth from their positions on the line. It was decided to retreat to a place where they could defend themselves better, as we were losing many men and horses. The order was thereupon given by Major Reno to 'get to your horses, men.' While this order was being given and executed, the fire from the troopers slackened very materially —in fact, it practically ceased. This gave the Indians greater confidence than ever, and they pressed in on us in greatly increasing numbers. Their forces were greatly augmented by hundreds of others arriving every minute from the lower end of the village.

"Reaching our horses the command 'Mount' was given. It was to be a charge to reach the other side of the river. Pistols were drawn by each man, carbines loaded and carried in front of us on the saddles or hanging by our side from the sling-belt, ready for immediate use.

"The troopers rode out of the thicket by twos, those on

the right being expected to deliver their fire in that direction, and those on the left to attend to that side. It was about three-quarters of a mile across a perfectly level plain before we could reach a fording place. After that, there was a remarkably steep bank to climb to reach the bluffs, and in climbing this, the troops would be fully exposed to a merciless fire.

"Every man of our small command seemed to realize fully the desperate situation we were in, and what was expected of him—which was to keep up a constant fire and make every shot tell.

"As we emerged from the thicket the warwhoop burst forth from a thousand throats It was a race for life The Indians pressed in closely on each side of the column, firing into the troopers, while the troopers in turn answered this fire. It was a hand-to-hand conflict, both Indians and troopers striving to pull each other from their horses, after emptying their weapons, and both succeeding, in a great many instances. I saw six or seven of our men in the act of falling from their horses after being shot. One poor fellow close to me was shot in the body, and as he was falling to the ground, was shot again through the head. I heard the shots as they struck him.

"I now found myself in the most desperate situation I had ever faced in my life. Our men were falling; Indians were tumbling from their ponies, either killed or wounded; ponies and horses, riderless, were dashing here and there, rifles, carbines and revolvers were roaring about me, while the cheers of the troopers and the warwhoops of the Indians made everything a perfect pandemonium.

"Before I had ridden two hundred yards, my horse crumpled under me, stricken down by an Indian bullet, and I was left dismounted in the midst of the Indians. I saw my comrades leaving me far behind, and expected every minute to feel a bullet, arrow or spear in my body. For a moment I was paralyzed with fear, and did not know what to do. My first thought was to run after the command, and then the folly of such a course became apparent. Then I determined to see if I could not reach the thicket out of which we had just ridden. So I faced about and legged it in that direction, expecting every moment would be my last on earth. But the Indians seemed all intent on getting at the mounted men, and many of them passed me without seeming to take the least notice of me. Others pointed their guns at me as they swept past on the dead run; some fired at me, but missed. At those who came very close to me, I pointed my carbine. Some would drop to the other side of their mounts, lying nearly flat against the side opposite me, exposing only a foot and part of an arm. At some of these I did fire, but I saw only one fall, although as I was always considered an excellent shot in the regiment, I am sure I must have wounded some whose ponies carried them safely on.

"As I reached the thicket and dashed into concealment, I came face to face with Lieut. De Rudio. Like myself, his horse had been shot from under him, and he had had an experience similar to mine in reaching the thicket. The lieutenant was looking intently at the retreating column, doubtless wishing, like myself, that he was with it. I was overjoyed at seeing him, even under such perilous conditions. Prior to that moment I thought I was the only unfortunate left behind.

"The lieutenant then told me that there were two others left behind, like ourselves, and that they were but a few yards from us. It developed that the two men were Billy Jackson, one of our half-breed scouts, and Fred Girard, an interpreter. Lieut. De Rudio got us together and gave us some hurried instructions what to do in case the Indians made a rush on us—which we expected every minute, and we could not possibly hope to escape detection long.

"We lay in a hole or indenture in the sand, which I think must have been the river bed at one time. Some thick underbrush growing around this hole pretty effectually concealed us from the view of the savages, who were riding back and forth on the plain in front of our position, and not more than fifty or sixty feet away. They were greatly excited, and reminded me of an ant's nest when disturbed—everyone seeming intent on something, and everyone on his own business.

"The lieutenant instructed us not to fire until discovered—and we expected every second to be. We were lying on our stomachs, with our heads even with the top of the hole, on the lookout for anyone who might approach, and each watching in a different direction, when we would all four fire at them.

"The lieutenant kept his keen eyes on all points of the compass, and encouraged us to be cool. 'Men,' he said, 'we have to die sometime, and we will die like brave men; but I am in hopes we will get out of this scrape yet.'

"It was not long before several squaws came around quite close to our position. They picked up their own dead or wounded, their grief seeming most pitiable, wailing and crying. The dead bodies of our men they stripped of their clothing, and cut and mutilated them in every conceivable way with the knives which they carried. Some of their actions we could plainly see. It made me faint and sick, not knowing how soon they might be disfiguring my own body in a similar manner, and I determined to sell my life dearly in the event of discovery. Owing to our good position, we figured that we should be able to kill several of our assailants before they could dispose of us.

"I did not know what Lieut. De Rudio's own hopes were, but I know that all mine vanished, and I never expected to get out of that place alive. My whole life seemed to pass in a panorama before me, carrying me back to the old home in the East, and to friends who I had not thought of before in years. All the principal events of my life came crowding forward, one after another, so fast that for a short time I forgot the danger which surrounded me.

"An hour passed—two—three, and yet no effort was made to effect our capture, nor were we discovered. In this conceal-

Sgt. Thomas O'Neil shown in the uniform of a Washington, D. C. park policeman many years after the Custer fight. A member of the group who rejoined the command after being left behind in the Reno retreat.

ment we lay until darkness over-shadowed the plain in front of us. Then after a whispered consultation we determined to try and find the command—if any of it remained alive, of which we had grave doubts. 'Indians never fight in the night time,' the lieutenant confided in a low tone, 'and if we keep together and you men will act under my orders, I believe we will yet reach the command alive.'

"We had no idea how it had fared with Custer or Reno. We had listened to terrific firing both up and down the river, and realized that the loss must have been heavy. For myself I thought that when the firing had ceased in the direction Custer had gone, it meant that he had retreated to Major Reno's position. I think it was about 5 o'clock when we heard the last shots from Custer's direction; but Major Reno's command kept up their firing at intervals, as though they were being charged upon. But along about dark, all firing from that direction also ceased.

"We talked but little, lest we should be overheard by the Indians. But now we determined to leave our hiding place, although such a move was decidedly precarious, even after darkness had settled down. We looked about and listened intently, but could neither hear nor see anything. The moon was up, and shining through a haze, but it was not very bright, so we decided to make a break for our lives, come what might, as it was our only salvation. We did not dare remain in our present position until daybreak.

"Of course we had had nothing to eat or drink. It had been an intensely hot day, and our throats were parched. Perhaps I was more thirsty than the others, owing to the fact that while with the command on the skirmish line, I had caught my foot while maneuvering around, tripping and falling on my nose, which made it bleed profusely. Not being able to give it attention at the time, the blood had run down my throat and almost choked me. It seemed as if I should die of thirst before I could reach water.

"When we emerged from the thicket, Girard and Jackson were mounted on ponies they had concealed in the brush. The lieutenant and I were on foot. We advanced but a short distance when a ghastly sight met our eyes. We were on the ground where our command had met the Indians in their retreat. The savages had rushed upon them, killing several of the men, who were lying there, stripped of their clothing, and cut and hacked with the knives of the squaws. We did not pause here many seconds. All the men were beyond any aid from us. We followed along in the trail as well as we could in the uncertain light, the route being well marked by the dead bodies of either troopers or their horses.

"We had advanced not more than half way toward the river, when we met—or would have met, had they not sidled off to our right about one hundred yards—a party of mounted savages, eight or ten in number. Lieut. De Rudio and I tried to hide ourselves on the opposite side of the ponies ridden by Girard and Jackson, thinking we might be taken for some of their own people. Evidently the Indians were suspicious, as they ran away from us in the opposite direction—for which, it is needless to say, we were devoutly thankful.

"Quickening our pace, we soon reached the river at the point where the command had jumped their horses into the stream in their wild retreat. We scanned the opposite bank for some trace of the spot where they had climbed the precipitous bluff, but could discern nothing but a black, steep bank, towering high. A short distance away there also seemed to be a level piece of flat river-bottom of about fifty yards' extent.

"The lieutenant whispered to me to lower myself into the water to ascertain its depth. Holding to some bushes at the edge of the bank, I slid in. I went nearly up to my neck at the first plunge, and the current was so swift it almost swept me off my feet. I climbed hastily out with the assistance of the lieutenant. But he was not satisfied until he had tried it himself. I held him while he slipped into the stream. But he decided it was impossible for us to cross at this place.

"It was the first chance we had had of getting a drink of water for many long, weary hours, so I took off my large slouch hat, the crown of which would hold about a gallon, filled it from the stream and passed it around. Each man drank until he was satisfied, and we all declared it was the sweetest water we had ever tasted.

"The night was slipping away, and we cautiously explored

the bank of the swift-running stream for a ford. Owing to the fact that the melting snows in the mountains at that season of the year sent all streams in that section almost out of banks, it looked like a hazardous undertaking.

"In the rear, and down the river, we could see and hear great circles of the Indians holding a war dance around burning piles of wood and brush. The flames lighted· the spot about them, and the forms of the Indians could be distinctly seen, jumping about and flourishing weapons. I never will forget the weird appearance of those savages, as their yells and whoops echoed up and down the valley plainly. The only musical accompaniment was a sort of 'huh-ha, huh-ha!' We afterward learned that they had the heads of three of our comrades, and that these men were partly burned in the fires by these red devils.* It looked as if even the squaws were taking part in the exciting dances.

"From the excitement, it was quite apparent to us that the Indians had had a successful day of it. As we had not heard anything further from our comrades since dark, we thought probably they had taken advantage of the night to retreat still further. One thing we did know—our only hope of safety was in getting on the other side of the river.

"We continued our march upstream slowly and cautiously, trying in vain to find a fording-spot, but were unsuccessful. We then decided to return to the place where the command had crossed early in the afternoon when making the first attack on the village.

"In this conclusion we came to a spot where it seemed likely we could cross the stream. I waded in and found the current less swift, the water reaching but a little above my knees. The others followed, and we crossed what we supposed was the main stream, but we afterward discovered we were on an island. The river divided a short distance above, and ran on each side of this strip of land, which was of con-

---

* The Sioux have always maintained that they took no prisoners at the battle of the Little Big Horn.

siderable extent, being nearly a mile long and several hundred yards wide. It was dotted with thick clumps of bullberry bushes, some of them covering as much as twenty square yards. There were also some young cottonwood trees on this island, and some tall, rank grass which reached to our waists. We crossed the island diagonally, supposing we were really on the other bank, but suddenly we came to the river again. This confused us very much. In riding to the attack in the afternoon we had not observed this island, and we wondered if we might not have become turned around and lost our direction. We tried again to cross the main stream, but it was useless, as we saw nothing on the other side but steep bluffs which we could not possibly climb.

"As we were moving cautiously about, we came to one of these thick clumps of bullberry bushes, and a startled voice suddenly hailed us. The deep, guttural tones were those of an Indian, and Girard and Jackson wheeled their ponies like lightning and galloped away in the direction from which we had approached. That was the last we saw of them until we met them in camp the following night.

"Lieut. De Rudio and I were some ten yards apart when the challenge came. I saw him kneeling down in the tall grass, and followed suit as quickly as possible. Had we run away, there was a clear space of nearly a hundred yards which we would have to cross before we could get under cover of one of the brush clumps. The Indians most assuredly would have fired on us. Hearing nothing further after Jackson and Girard galloped away, the Indians evidently thought something was wrong, as they jumped their horses into the river with the greatest haste and confusion. To accelerate their flight, Lieut. De Rudio fired two shots from his revolver in quick succession. I had my carbine pointed in their direction, and I sent a bullet after them. While I was reloading, the lieutenant sent another shot after them. By this time they were across the river. I had not seen any of them, only heard the noise and clatter, but the lieutenant, who was nearer the river, said he could see six or seven Indians, who appeared to be on picket on the point at the fork of the river where it divided to form the island.

"As I was about to fire a second shot, De Rudio called out, 'O'Neill, they are all gone.' Possibly the Indians were somewhat drowsy after their hard day's fight, and maybe we caught them napping. I think it must have been about two o'clock at this time. We retreated backward a few hundred yards. From there we wandered about on the island, unable to understand how we were surrounded by water as well as Indians.

"After this experience we were afraid to go up to the ford of the afternoon, for fear of running into more Indian pickets. After walking back and forth along the main part of the stream, in a vain attempt to find a ford, I became so tired and utterly worn out that I exclaimed, 'Lieutenant, please let us sit down. My boots are full of water, and my clothing all dripping, and I want to wring them out.' So we sat down in a clump of brush, and I took off some of my clothes, my boots and stockings. I had just finished wringing my saturated clothing, and began to put them on again, when we were once more startled by the clatter of horse's hoofs and the sound of voices. The morning was dawning on us before we realized it was growing so late. The Indians were coming past in front of us and along the river bank to begin another attack on Reno's command. The lieutenant had pulled on his boots and I was tugging at mine. He arose and looked out. A column of mounted men were passing us about two or three hundred yards away. Calling to me in a low tone, he excitedly said, 'O'Neill, I believe it is the command.' By this time I had my boots on and joined De Rudio. I could see horsemen, but in the uncertain gray of approaching dawn I could not distinguish who they were. They were riding in great numbers, and were near enough so we could distinguish the sound of voices only. Some of them had ascended the bluff through a cut or washout in the bank, which heretofore we had not observed.

"The lieutenant observed one man dressed in a buckskin

suit, whom he took to be Capt. Tom Custer, as he had worn such an outfit on this expedition. De Rudio whispered excitedly, 'That surely is Tom Custer!' Some of the horsemen were climbing the steep banks on the other side of the river; some were just at the top and could overlook the island we were on. The rider whom we took to be Tom Custer was just going up the cut. I thought it surely was Captain Custer, and was nearly overjoyed at the prospect of soon being with my comrades once more. At the same time, Lieut. De Rudio stepped boldly out on the river bank and shouted, 'Hey! Tom Custer! Tom Custer!' The riders stopped and looked in our direction, and then in an instant the warwhoop sounded and a volley of at least fifty shots were fired at us! How we escaped being hit is a miracle, for the bullets cut the brush about us in every direction! The riders were all Sioux Indians dressed in some of the uniforms they had taken we later learned—from Custer's men in the battle the previous afternoon, and were riding Seventh Cavalry horses which they had captured.

"Our escape on this occasion was simply miraculous! None of the Indians made any attempt to cross the river after us. We jumped into the bushes on the opposite side from where we had been standing, and stooping low, ran toward another clump, bending over so that only our backs could be seen above the grass. In this way we reached another thick clump of brush, and just as we were going around it we ran plump into another party of mounted Indians! In fact, we were so close that we almost ran over each other. There were six or seven Indians in the party, and our sudden appearance took them by surprise and frightened their ponies to such an extent that the animals all reared and began to plunge about. Evidently this party was not looking for us in that direction, although some of the savages on the hill were shouting to their companions down below, doubtless warning them to be on the lookout for us.

"I had my carbine at a ready. The lieutenant had carried his pistol in his hand for hours, and he immediately opened

Billy Jackson, half-breed scout, who with Lt. DeRudio, Sgt. O'Neil and Fred Girard was left behind when Reno retreated from the valley, but joined Reno's command later.

fire. I also commenced shooting at them. The Indian ponies were rearing, snorting and plunging about to such an extent that their riders had all they could do to stay on the backs of their animals without using their guns. And to this we owed our lives. While they were in this confusion we poured eight shots into them. Two of the riders, I am sure, fell, and

I saw three ponies gallop away riderless. I think we must have wounded others who managed to cling to their ponies.

"This was a most one-sided encounter. We had the advantage of being on the ground and could deliver a rapid and effective fire. We stood shoulder to shoulder. I did not even throw my carbine to my shoulder—the Indians were so close—but just pointed it in their direction and pulled the trigger. Though I scarcely expected to remain alive five minutes longer, I felt the greatest satisfaction at having inflicted so much injury to the enemy in the short space of time allowed us.

"I have often wondered if those Indians who did manage to get out of range alive did not consider us two demons whom they ran against in the gray of that June morning, to inflict so much damage among them in such a short space of time. The lieutenant was a quick and accurate revolver shot. He fired five shots, and I am sure he hit the mark every time, while I fired three shots with my carbine. The Indians only fired a single shot at us, which went wild of the mark. De Rudio then shouted to me to run. The last thing I saw of those Indians, two or three of them were on the ground, and several ponies were rearing over each other.

"In our flight, and about a hundred and fifty yards from the spot of this last encounter, we came to a place of all places on the little island which was an ideal spot to make a defense and have the advantage of covering. Some time previously, several cottonwood trees had been cut down at this particular point, leaving stumps about three feet high. A freshet had later occurred, washing many fallen logs against these stumps, and there they had remained, forming a small angle, and making a perfect breastwork from which to fire. Lieut. De Rudio's quick eye caught the place, and he exclaimed, 'Quick, O'Neill, get in here!' He jumped in among the fallen logs and I after him. We wormed our way still deeper into the mass of debris, and found that we were perfectly protected by the logs. Before any Indians could get at us, it would be necessary for them to cross an open space of nearly one hundred yards, and besides, would have to climb over our barricade to reach us.

"We here shook hands with each other, declaring we could not run a step further. If we had to die—as it certainly seemed—we would die there fighting. I took off my cartridge belt, and found that I had just twenty-five rounds left for the carbine and twelve for the pistol. As the lieutenant was the better pistol shot, I gave him mine in addition to his own, and the ammunition for them, while I retained the carbine.

"About the time we landed in this retreat, we heard fierce musketry on the hills, apparently about a mile distant. The Indians had again attacked Reno's command. We could hear our comrades responding beautifully. We could also hear the Indian chiefs calling to their men down in the river bottom. Several shots were fired in our direction, but we laid low and did not respond.

"All this time we were momentarily expecting the Indians to make a rush on us, and we were looking in every direction for them. The ground behind us sloped down to the river, which was about two hundred yards away, and there was a clear space all about us of nearly a hundred yards. The grass was tall, and we kept a sharp lookout, lest some of the Indians crawl up on our position. We figured that in the event of a charge, we ought to be able to kill five or six of them anyway. I do not think they knew exactly where we were, although several of their bullets struck the logs behind which we were lying. Occasionally we could see them by twos, threes and fives, but not any closer than two hundred and fifty yards at any time; so we laid low and never fired a shot because we did not care to draw their fire.

"The lieutenant cautioned me: 'When they come to the clearing, and seem to be looking for us, you take dead aim at the foremost, and then keep up the fire while they are coming toward us, but don't shoot until you are dead-sure of your aim.' At target practice I could hit an object the size of my hat nearly every time at two hundred yards. I was nervous no longer. I had become so desperate that it seemed to quiet my nerves, and I am sure I was as steady as at any time in my life and could do as good shooting. We scarcely expected to get out of this place alive, but it seemed our duty, so the lieutenant said, to defend ourselves as long as possible, and to the best of our ability. There was no use surrendering, as it only meant death by the most horrible form of torture.

"About this time a second charge was made against the troops on the hill, and again the Indians were repulsed. Then a desultory firing was kept up by the savages. As we later learned, the Indians picked off a great many men during the intervals between the charges.

"It was now about 9 o'clock in the morning of the 26th, and we were wondering how long the Indians were going to delay the time when they would come to hunt us out. We conversed in a low tone. The lieutenant said, 'O'Neill, I believe they are afraid to come after us; they do not know exactly where we are, and they know they will lose more than they can get. That lesson we taught them a while ago may be our salvation.'

"Then De Rudio added:

" 'O'Neill, are you married?' " 'No, sir,' I replied.

" 'Well,' was the response, 'I would not care so much if I were alone, but what will my wife and three young children do if I get killed? That's what is worrying me.'

"About this time we heard the sound of voices and the tramp of horses close at hand. Looking cautiously out, we could see great bands of the squaws and children passing on the bottom, up the river, toward the mountains. The squaws were riding like the men, carrying their babies on their backs. Children six years of age and upward rode ponies, and all such were mounted. Their cooking utensils and provisions were all packed on travois. Other ponies were being led or were driven along. We were glad we were not lying where they could see us as they passed. The squaws seemed quite merry, as they were singing and 'ke-ing,' laughing and shouting to each other. I judge that it took them an hour or more to pass. Sometimes there were bunches of them a couple of hundred yards wide. They did not march in any regular order. Finally it appeared that all had passed us.

"Although we could not now see an Indian any place, yet we knew they were on the bluffs over us, as an occasional charge was made on the command. Our hopes now began to revive considerably. We trusted that the command would be able to drive them away, not realizing how badly the troops had been crippled, and how they had to act on the defensive.

"One hour after another gradually wore away, until it became about 3 o'clock in the afternoon. I think it was about that time the Indians made the last charge against the command, and it seemed to be a most desperate one and more fierce than any preceding it, judging by the musketry fire and whooping and yelling on the part of the Indians and the cheers from the troopers.

"We later learned that the position held by Reno was on top of the highest bluff, while the ground sloped gradually away, with several washouts or deep cuts running in all directions from it. The troopers were formed in line all around the top of this bluff, and in order to reach them, the Indians were obliged to climb the steep sides. In the last charge, some of the savages managed to gain the top of the bluff before they were killed. The troops counter-charged them, and the loss among the Indians was so severe that they made no further attempts to gain the bluff. Had they once broken the line, not a man would have been left to tell the tale.

"By 5 o'clock the shooting seemed to have entirely ceased. Neither could we see any further signs of Indians. I finally asked the lieutenant if I might crawl out and take a look around. He told me to do so, and I crawled out to make a little reconnoiter. On the high bank on the other side of the river I saw one solitary Indian, mounted, seemingly on picket. I now moved to a spot where there was a little more shrubbery growing and very cautiously stood up for a look. On our side of the river, and only about three hundred yards from us, I counted fifteen Indians sitting in a circle, seemingly smoking and talking among themselves. They were near the bank of the main channel of the river. After a glance about I stooped down, and carefully and slowly crawled back to the lieutenant and reported what I had seen.

"We now renewed our vigilance, feeling sure that an organized effort would be made to locate us before the Indians left. As we heard no further shooting, nor any signs from the command, we concluded they had retreated and that the main body of Indians had followed them up, leaving a few to guard the spot where we had last been seen.

"Now it was again getting near sundown and darkness would soon be coming on. Our hope of getting away now began to rise again rapidly. I became so nervous that I could not contain myself, and for the first time during the day began to feel afraid. Everything was deathly silent around us. I often imagined I saw the forms of Indians creeping up on us, and was nearly ready to fire as the dusk of night came on.

"It was now, as much as at any previous time, that Lieut. De Rudio showed himself to be one of the coolest and bravest men I ever saw. He repeatedly quieted me by his sound advice and reassuring manner, saying, 'O'Neill, I know we will get out of this all right if you will just be patient a little while longer. From our experience last night I am certain the Indians will not shoot at night if we chance to run into them. We now know how to get across the river, and if we do not find the command, we will follow our trail back to the Yellowstone River, traveling at night and hiding by day. We can pick up some scraps to eat in our old camps, or maybe we can shoot a deer or an antelope. I am sure we can reach the 'Far West' (our supply steamer) in five days; but I am in hopes of finding the command on the other side of the river, and then we will be all right.'

"We had had nothing to eat in almost forty hours, and

nothing to drink all that hot summer day. Our throats were nearly parched. I did not feel at all hungry, however. Night came on about 9 o'clock, and we then left our snug retreat and crept through the long grass to the water's edge. After looking cautiously about, we waded into the stream and crossed in safety to the other side and climbed up the steep banks. Nothing of life was to be seen or heard; not a sound, except the wind sighing through the rank grass and sagebrush.

"We now wrung out our wet clothes and dried ourselves as much as possible. We were, as we thought, about a mile from Reno's supposed position, and as we did not see any further signs of Indians, we walked along in that direction. Occasionally we would lay down and listen, but could hear nothing. The great valley seemed absolutely deserted. We had thought that if the command still held the place where we supposed it to be, we ought to hear some sign of life, and came to the conclusion at last that the troops must have retreated.

"Our next decision was to follow the trail down to the Rosebud, and thence to the Yellowstone. We knew the general direction. We decided to cross the divide as soon as possible to the Rosebud and when daylight came to hide in the brush until night, then resume our march until we came to a place of safety.

"We began our march along a dry creek and continued on a mile or so until we came to quite a high knoll looming up in front of us. We then concluded to climb to the top and see if we could locate any campfires anywhere. When we reached the top we looked about in every direction, but no fires were to be seen.

"We were just about to take up our march, very much disheartened, when we heard a mule braying in the direction Reno's command had held. That was the sweetest music I believe I ever listened to. It luckily changed our plans very materially. We figured that the mule surely must belong to the command, so we concluded to search for them, come what might. It was a dangerous undertaking at best. If we

The bend in the Little Big Horn river where Reno made the initial
attack on the Indian Village.

were certain it was our men we could assuredly go up within
hailing distance and call to them, but we had not forgotten
our thrilling experience of the early morning in hailing
strangers, and determined to take no such chances. If we
crawled up on the command some picket might see us and
shoot us, thinking we were Indians.

"We walked some distance further in the direction from
which the braying of the mule had come, stopping every few
yards to listen. At last we came near enough to hear the sound
of voices, but could not distinguish whether they were our
men or not. Now our predicament was perilous in the extreme. We crawled along on the ground on our stomachs,
hitching along a few inches at a time, expecting every
moment to be detected and shot at. We still heard the sound
of voices. Sometimes we would think they were Indians,
while again we thought they sounded familiar. At last we
heard someone exclaim in a loud voice, 'Bring that horse
here' I recognized the voice of Sergeant McVey of A Troop,
whereupon I called out to him. 'Mac, don't shoot on us!' It is
O'Neill and Lieut. De Rudio!' Several voices thereupon

shouted, 'Come on in!' which we did in double-quick time. We were in the hands of our comrades at last!

"Needless to say, we had much to relate that night before we snatched a little sleep. We discovered that Jackson and Girard had come into camp but a short time prior to ourselves. It seems that after they had run away and left us, they abandoned their ponies and concealed themselves in some thick brush all the next day. Luckily for them, the Indians did not pass close to them, they being outside the line of march. After dark, like ourselves, they found the camp. Jackson was a half-breed Indian scout—a very young man, but brave and cool.

"The Indians had all retreated that evening up the river toward the mountains. General Terry and his command came up about 11 o'clock the next morning, and it was learned that General Custer and every man of his command had been killed about three miles from our position.

"Often when I begin to think of all we went through during those trying thirty-six hours of mental torture there in the river bottom, dodging the Indians, I wonder if it is possible that it all did actually happen, or if it was some terrible nightmare."

*   *   *

In connection with the entrance into the Reno entrenchments of De Rudio and O'Neill, the author received the following interesting communication from Col. Chas. A. Varnum of San Francisco, the first officer of the Seventh Cavalry to welcome the fugitives inside the lines:

"Dear Mr. Brininstool:

"I have been pretty busy since I received your letter or would have answered sooner. You know, of course, that on the evening of June 26th, we moved our position to some extent. The up-stream flank of our position became the downstream flank, and we extended it toward the river and fortified it some. We also got our horses and mules down to water, a few at a time. I was up and busy till midnight or past. Everything was quiet. My pack-mule was lost and I had no baggage. In looking for something to make myself comfortable I found De Rudio's bedding-roll. I thought I might as well use it. I had just got well fixed for a nap when I heard a picket challenge and De Rudio answered: 'It is me—Lieut. De Rudio and Sergt. O'Neill.' I was some distance down from the bluff when I heard the challenge and answer. I ran up the slope calling to De Rudio to wait till I got there, as he would fall into gullies if he tried to come to my voice where I was. As I arrived at the crest near the gully, I stumbled over something and fell over a dead Indian. Then I ran on and called to De Rudio to come to me, which he did, and embraced me and was very much excited. I took him to his bed and got him something to eat.

"In 1898, on Decoration Day, I visited the field with a party from Sheridan, Wyoming, where I was buying horses. I found the monument marking where Dr. De Wolf and Lieut. Hodgson fell, and from there told members of the party what to look for as I went on, and my memory was verified by their finding traces of what I described.

"I was standing where I thought I found that Indian's body and spoke of it, and how I happened to be there, etc., when a newspaper man said, 'What is this?' Small round stones had been laid in a square about two feet each way, and then built up with other small stones, forming a sort of pyramid about four inches high. Sticks stuck in the ground with red cloth bundles, medicine bags tied to them and some other ornaments were there, and I said at once, 'That is that Indian's monument.' This Indian was scalped by interpreter Fred Girard, and the scalp was given to a newspaper man in Chicago when we were there at the Reno investigating board, or Court of Inquiry; at least, Girard told me so when we were in Chicago at that time. I never knew O'Neill's first name. He was a G Troop man I think."

After the remnant of the 7th Cavalry was encamped on the Yellowstone River a few weeks following the Little Big

Horn fight, Lieut. De Rudio, in a letter to a friend, in re-counting the thrilling experience of himself and Sergt. O'Neill, wrote:

"I should do injustice to my feelings if I were to omit to mention the fidelity and bravery of Sergt. O'Neill. He faithfully obeyed me and stood by me like a brother. I shall never cease to remember him and his service to me during our dangerous companionship. This brave soldier is highly thought of by his company commander, and of course will ever be by me and mine."

CHAPTER 6

WAS MAJOR MARCUS A. RENO A COWARD IN CUSTER FIGHT?

FOR MANY YEARS the general public has been led to believe that Major Marcus A. Reno played the part of a coward in the battle of the Little Big Horn, June 25, 1876. People who are not well posted on this remarkable engagement have come to believe that Reno left Custer to his fate, entrenched himself on the bluffs across the river, and was afraid to go to Custer's relief. Let us investigate this alleged misconduct of Major Reno's and see whether these charges have any foundation whatever.

Without going into full details of the battle, let us begin at the point where Custer and Reno separated, which was some few miles from where the actual fighting began. Custer ordered Reno to attack the upper end of the great Indian village with the three companies assigned him—Companies M, A and G, *promising him the full support of his (Custer's) own battalion of five companies.*

Reno did as ordered. His three companies consisted of exactly 112 men, many of them green recruits who had enlisted that spring; who never had seen a hostile Indian until that morning, were not experienced horsemen and were poor shots. After Reno had reached a point where he could view the extent and size of the village, he saw at once that he was "up against it," and that he was outnumbered appallingly. Custer had ordered him to "charge the village." But when Reno noted that this would mean the immediate sacrifice of his command, he wisely and prudently refrained from doing anything of the kind. He started the engagement, but soon noting that the Indians were closing in on him from all sides, front and rear, he withdrew to a stand of timber where the horses of the command had been left when his men started for the firing line. In a very few moments, Major Reno saw that he was in a veritable hornet's nest, from which he must immediately withdraw unless he met utter annihilation. Further, *Custer had not come to his support, as promised.*

The major decided that the high hills on the opposite side of the Little Big Horn River, about one mile distant, was the best place to make a stand. In the excitement and roar of battle, the order to mount and get to the hills was not generally understood, and a dozen or fifteen men were left behind, either because their mounts escaped from the horseholders or were hurriedly taken by others.

Just about this time, Custer began his attack four miles down stream and on the opposite side of the river from where Reno began the battle. This drew the attention of many hundreds of the Indians, who at once left off attacking Reno and rushed to the assistance of their red brothers at the other end of the village. However, there were fully a thousand of the savages left to harass Reno's charge for the hills, although they did not follow up the advantage they gained on the retreat from the timber to the edge of the river. In this movement Reno lost some twenty-nine men.

Gaining the high hills across the river, Reno was shortly joined by Capt. F. W. Benteen, whose command of three companies had been ordered "off to the left" by Custer; but as Benteen met with no Indians, he gradually worked back into the trail made by Reno in advancing to the battle. Here he met Reno's excited battalion fighting its way across the river, and at once joined him on the hill. There the two commands fought until the afternoon of June 26th, successfully keeping the savage hordes from overwhelming them, all this time wondering what had become of Custer, little dreaming that he had been annihilated to a man the previous afternoon.

Major M. A. Reno, commanding Troops, A. G. and M, whose attack on the Indian village was repulsed and who years later was exonerated by a Court of Inquiry of the charge of failing to go to Custer's aid.

The advance up the river of the troops of Generals Terry and Gibbon—whom Custer had been warned to wait for, but for reasons of his own failed to obey these instructions—was noted by the savages, and they accordingly left off attacking Reno's command and prepared for a hurried flight, departing in one immense body, but gradually breaking up into small parties and scattering. It is stated that this great Indian village consisted of about 15,000 men, women and children, and that they had a pony herd of 20,000 animals.

Between 1876 and 1879, much talk was indulged in by the press and the general public about the battle of the Little Big Horn, which finally assumed such proportions, and was of such bitter criticism against Major Reno, that the latter demanded a Court of Inquiry to investigate his conduct in the battle.

This was held in Chicago in January, 1879. Twenty-three witnesses were examined—officers of the 7th Cavalry, scouts, teamsters, packers and two or three non-commissioned officers. With the exception of two packers, all the witnesses came out in defense of Major Reno. The two packers testified that Reno was drunk and assaulted one of them. Major Reno and Capt. Benteen both testified that they had continually to drive skulkers out from the packs. Several witnesses were placed on the stand after the two packers had testified. These all declared that Major Reno was not drunk nor showed any sign of having taken liquor; that at no time he played the part of a coward or anything of the sort, but that he did his full duty as an officer and a soldier during the engagement.

Now, if the testimony of these officers and others is correct—and there is no reason for suspecting it to be otherwise—Major Marcus A. Reno, 7th Cavalry, was not only NOT a coward and was NOT drunk, either on the 25th or 26th days of June, 1876, while the battle of the Little Big Horn was in progress, but it would further appear that for seventy-six years he has been a greatly maligned man and

Captain George D. Wallace, who as a First Lieut. was acting engineer officer of Reno Battalion. Killed in 1890 at Ghost Dance War of Sioux.

soldier. Major Reno won a brilliant record in the Civil War for his bravery and skill in handling troops. The author is well aware that Reno was dismissed from the army about 1880—it is said he engaged in a fist fight in a billiard room—but that has nothing whatever to do with his conduct at the battle of the Little Big Horn. In that alone are we interested, so far as this chapter is concerned.

It happens that among the data which the author has been collecting for some fifty years on the Custer fight, is the complete stenographic report of the Reno Court of Inquiry, comprising nearly two hundred columns of testimony. The author has gone carefully through this and segregated all which bears on the conduct of Major Reno. As this report is official, it is a document which cannot be disputed or lightly passed over, and must be accepted as the truth—unless we foolishly brand the witnesses as liars. Some quotations from this may serve to alter the opinions of those who, perhaps, have been critics of Major Reno's conduct on the occasion of this greatest of Indian fights on the American continent.

Lieut. George D. Wallace testified as follows:

"Major Reno's conduct was all that could be expected of anyone. The troops could not have been handled any better. * * * I think Reno did the only thing possible under the circumstances. If we had remained in the timber, all would have been killed. It was his duty to take care of the command, and use his best judgment and discretion. * * * I can recall no act of Major Reno's during those two days that exhibited any lack of courage as an officer or soldier that I can find fault with, nor any lack of military skill."

Lieut. Charles A. Varnum said in his testimony:

"As to Major Reno's conduct—certainly there was no sign of cowardice or anything of that sort. * * * If Reno thought he could not hold the timber and saw no troops coming, it was for him to use his own judgment and leave it for a place he could defend better. * * * The position in the timber was as good as any on the left bank, but I don't think that he (Reno) had men enough to hold it and keep the Indians out of it. * * * We could not have united with Custer except by going through the village to him, or his coming through to us. Neither force could have done that. * * * Certainly there was no sign of cowardice or anything of that sort. * * * If 1000 Indians had attacked Reno on his way from the timber to the river, he never would have got to the hill."

Dr. H. R. Porter, surgeon, with Reno's command, testified:

"I heard the adjutant give an order to Major Reno about one o'clock, June 25th. The adjutant told him that the Indians were just ahead, and General Custer directed him to charge them. *He said Custer would support him.* Reno asked if the general were coming along, and he said, 'Yes.' "

Capt. Myles Moylan testified:

"I am perfectly satisfied that Custer knew about our movement. Whether he followed us on the trail toward the crossing I don't know. I only knew by what Major Reno's adjutant told me *that he would be supported by Custer.* * * * The object of leaving the timber was, if possible, to save the command. * * * If we had stayed 30 minutes longer in the timber unsupported, I doubt whether we could have gotten out with as many as we did. We could not have successfully resisted the force of Indians if they had followed us to the river. We had not sufficient ammunition. The command was not, however, actually driven from the timber. * * * Major Reno gave his orders during the advance to the bottom as coolly as any man under the circumstances. During the afternoon of the 25th he seemed perfectly cool. * * * I saw nothing in Major Reno which betrayed evidence of cowardice. There was a certain amount of excitement visible in his face, as in that of anybody else, but no trace of cowardice. * * * In my judgment if he had continued to charge down that valley, he would have been there yet. In my judgment the command, without assistance, would have been annihilated in the timber. If the Indians had followed and closed in on the retreat to the bluffs, the same result would have followed."

George Herendeen, citizen scout and interpreter, testified:

"About a mile and a half from the village I heard General Custer tell Major Reno to lead out *and he would be with him.* Those were the words I understood him to use."

Lieut. Luther R. Hare testified as follows:

"There were probably a thousand Indians opposing Reno in the bottom. (NOTE—Reno had just 112 men in his com-

Little Big Horn river at the site where Reno crossed to attack the Indian village.

mand, according to his own testimony.) If all the Indians had followed us they would have got us all. * * * If the Indians had charged the timber we could not have lasted long. We could have stood them off for perhaps thirty minutes. * * * Whether such an attack on the flank as Custer would have made would have supported Reno, would depend entirely on what disposition the Indians made. As it was, *it was no support at all and did not amount to anything.* The results of the battle show that. * * * Major Reno stayed in the timber *till all hope of support from Custer had vanished.* I think the reason we left was because if we had stayed much longer— say 20 minutes—we could not have gotten out at all. * * * If the command had been pursued by the 1000 Indians who were about us, we would all have been killed. It would not have lasted ten minutes. * * * My impression of the retreat from the timber was that Major Reno thought we would be shut up there, and the best way to get out was to charge out. * * * I can only estimate his (Reno's) conduct by the way it turned out. I think his action saved what was left of the regiment. His conduct was always good. He seemed to be very cool at all times. * * * Of course Reno could form no estimate of his duties, based on any action of Benteen, unless he knew those orders.

* * * I saw Reno but once in the timber. * * * The disposition of the troops in the timber was a very good one. * * * If Reno had continued to advance mounted, I don't think he would have got a man through. The column would not have lasted five minutes. His dismounting and deploying was all that saved us. * * * I can't think Major Reno lost much time (after reaching the hill) in moving in Custer's direction. His column moved altogether about a mile or so. * * * I saw no evidence of cowardice on Reno's part. The command was under good control, and the disposition as good as possible under the circumstances. * * * Reno could not have seen the Indians in the coulee before he halted and deployed. I could not see them till they came out, and I was in a better position to see than he was. * * * If Gen. Custer saw us deploying, he could also have easily seen that there were five times as many Indians as we had men. In my opinion if Major Reno could get away as he did, General Custer could, by leaving his dead and wounded, have gotten away also."

Testimony of Lieut. Chas. De Rudio:

"As soon as we cleared the woods, Reno called the battalion into line and moved at a gallop. He was ahead of us about fifteen yards. He was continually checking the men and keeping the horses in good order. * * * The line remained (after deploying) about ten minutes, during which time I saw Reno encouraging the men. He stood there and directed the fire. * * * I think Major Reno had more Indians around him the evening of the 25th than were in the attack on Custer. * * * I saw no indication of cowardice on Reno's part, nor any want of skill in the handling and disposition of the men. When he halted and dismounted I said, 'Good for you,' because I saw that if we had gone five hundred yards further we would have been butchered. * * * The effect of sighting Benteen's column was to check the Indians' pursuit of Reno."

Sergt. F. A. Culbertson testified:

"If the skirmish line had not been retired, or had been held there three minutes longer, I don't think anyone would have gotten off the line. I don't think Major Reno could have held the timber but a very few minutes. My estimate of the number of Indians about his position on the skirmish line and in the timber, is about 1000 to 1200. During the 25th and 26th I saw Major Reno several times in positions of great danger. * * * I saw no evidence of cowardice on the part of Major Reno at any time."

Testimony of Trumpeter John Martin:

"I saw Major Reno when we took position, and again that night at 12 p. m., when he sent an order to sound reveille at 2. a. m. Major Reno was in the center of the corral at reveille, and afterwards was around the skirmish line examining the position."

Testimony of Capt. F. W. Benteen:

"I showed Reno the order I had from Cooke, and asked him if he knew where General Custer was. He said he did not; that he had been sent to charge those Indians on the plain, and that General Custer's instructions to him, through Lieut. Cooke, were that he (Custer) *would support him* (Reno) *with the whole outfit.* * * * Reno was just as cool as he is now. * * * A movement could have been made down the river in the direction Custer had gone, but we would all have been there yet. * * * The Indians had picinic parties as large as a regiment standing around in the bottom looking on; there was no place to put them. Fully 2000 were around us, waiting for a place to shoot from. * * * I think his (Reno's) conduct was all right. I saw him every fifteen or thirty minutes those two days and during the night of the 25th was with him nearly the whole time. * * * I might have joined Reno in the timber, but would not have attempted it without first getting the pack train; but my losses would have been much greater. * * * There was not a foot of unoccupied ground in that country—there were Indians everywhere, from twelve feet to 1200 yards away. * * * I saw no evidence of cowardice on Reno's part. I found it necessary at one time to caution him about exposing himself. I told him to be careful how he stood around in front of the point, as volleys were coming constantly. * * * When I received my order from Custer to separate myself from the command, I had no instructions to unite at any time with Reno or anyone else. *There was no plan at all.* * * * I was separated from Reno fifteen miles when at the greatest distance. * * * Reno could not have expected me to join him. There were no orders to do so. * * * When I left, I did not know that Reno had any command; the division had not been made yet, and I don't think Reno knew anything about it at the time I left. When I passed him he asked me where I was going, and I told him I was going to the left, with instructions to pitch into anything I came across. The next time I saw Reno was on the hill. * * * *It was the belief of the officers on the hill during the night of the 25th that General Custer had gone to General Terry, and that we were abandoned to our fate.* * * * When I left, Reno had no command that I know of. Reno had no reason to think I was near or was following the same trail. I scarcely knew myself what I had to do. He had no right to expect any assistance whatever from me. * * * If there had been any plan of battle, enough of that plan would have been communicated to me so that I would have known what to do under certain circumstances. Not having done that, I do not believe there was any plan. * * * And if I found them (the Indians) the distance would have been so great that we would have been wiped out before he could get to us. * * * It would have taken me an hour and a quarter to bring up the packs after I got the Martin order. * * * The three orders I got from Custer did not indicate that he expected me to cooperate in any attack on the village. * * * But I am convinced that when the order brought by Martin reached me, General Custer and his whole command were dead. It was about 3 o'clock. * * * From the orders I started out with, he (Custer) could not possibly have known where to find me within ten or fifteen miles. My going back was providential or accidental or whatever you may be pleased to term it * * * and I got there as soon as I could. * * * From my orders I might have gone twenty miles without finding a valley; still, I was to go on to the first valley, and if I did not find any Indians, I was to go on to the next valley. *Those were the exact words of my order.* No interpretation at all. I was at least to go on to the second valley. I understood it as a rather senseless order. We knew there were 8000 or 10,000 Indians on the trail we were following, and it was scarcely worth while hunting up any more. * * * *Why I was sent to the left I don't know.* It was not my business to reason why. I went. * * * If I had carried my orders out I would have been at least twenty-five miles away. I don't know where I would have been. As it was, I was certainly too far to cooperate with Custer when he wanted me. * * * His plan of attack was * * * known only to himself and not to Major Reno. * * * The reason we moved down stream after I joined Reno was the presence of about 900 Indians on the other side, who seemed pretty vigorous and well-armed. I have never expressed an opinion adverse to Major Reno's conduct as an officer."

Testimony of Lieut. W. S. Edgerly:

"Major Reno's orders were to move down the valley and attack anything he came to; those were the orders I heard. Major Reno was not present when Benteen got his orders. * * * He (Reno) did everything that was necessary. * * * I saw Reno walk across the line as I saw other officers, and he seemed cool. * * * Major Reno exercised the functions of a commanding officer so far as I know. * * * I do not pretend to give the history of all Major Reno did—only my own personal knowledge. The nature of the fight was such that no special directions from him were necessary. I saw no evidence of cowardice on his part. I distinguish excitement from fear, most emphatically * * * In the charge suggested by Capt. Benteen, Major Reno accompanied the troops; Capt. Benteen did not. * * * I believe Custer's command were all killed within 20 minutes to a half hour from the time the Indians first attacked them."

Lieut. Edgerly (recalled):

"I saw Major Reno on the night of the 25th about 9 o'clock. He came along toward where I was from the direction of Capt. Benteen's line. *He was perfectly sober. No evidence that he had been drinking at all.* I saw him again at 2 o'clock, *and he was perfectly sober then.* I never heard the faintest suspicion of intoxication until I came to Chicago this time. If he had been intoxicated the officers would not have permitted him to exercise command."

Capt. Benteen (recalled):

"I may say I was with Major Reno all the time the night of the 25th. I saw him every fifteen to twenty minutes till 3 a. m. I laid down in his bed. *He was as sober as he is now. He is entirely sober now and was then. There was no time during the 25th or 26th when there was any indication of drunkenness on the part of Major Reno.* He could not have been staggering and stammering without my knowing it. * * * I know nothing about any altercation with a packer except by hearsay. I know they robbed the packs and robbed me, and I also know there was not whiskey enough in the whole command to make him drunk."

Testimony of Capt. E. S. Godfrey:

"I do not think Major Reno exhibited cowardice—rather, nervous timidity. * * * There was an impression among the men that Custer had been repulsed and had abandoned them. I had no such impression however."

Testimony of Capt. E. C. Mathey:

"I was in charge of the pack-train from June 22nd to the 28th. * * * We had 160 mules. I had about 70 men and four or five citizen packers. * * * I received no orders from

Custer, Reno or Benteen on that march; only from Capt. McDougall. * * * I heard Major Reno say (on the hill) that we must try to find Custer, and something about going in the direction Custer had gone. * * * When Major Reno first came up he was somewhat excited, as any man would be under such circumstances. It was not long since he came out of the fight, and that would be the natural condition for a man to be in. I did not think to question his courage, and saw no act to indicate lack of courage or cowardice. * * * *I saw no drunkenness on his part, and never heard any intimation of it until last spring."*

Testimony of Capt. Thomas McDougall:

"I was commanding the rear guard, in rear of the packs. * * * I think it was about 4 o'clock when we reached Reno. * * * At the time Major Reno asked me to walk around with him, the fire was not ceasing—the bullets were flying fast. * * * As to Major Reno's conduct—when I found him he seemed perfectly cool; and nothing to say, and during the day I did not see him till he asked me to go around with him. He was perfectly cool then; he was as brave as any man there; they were all brave; no officer or man showed the white feather. * * * I think Major Reno would make as stubborn a fight as any man; men are different. Some are dashing, and others have a quiet way of going through. I think he did as well as anyone could do. * * * Reno had about 280 men, I think, after the forces joined."

Lieut. Wallace (recalled):

"I kept the itinerary. * * * I estimate the commencement of Reno's fight in the timber at 2:30 o'clock. Adjutant Cooke's order to Reno was given about 2 o'clock, nine or ten miles from the place of division into battalions. I neither saw nor heard Custer give any order in person to Reno. * * * *I am positive that General Custer gave no order in person to Major Reno.* * * * Benteen got his order and moved to the left almost immediately after the separation—about two hours before the order to Reno."

Testimony of Major Reno:

"I was second in command, but was never consulted at all. * * * About 10 o'clock Lieut. Cooke came to me and said, 'The general directs that you take specific command of Companies M, A and G.' I turned and said, 'Is that all?' He replied 'Yes.' * * * I moved forward to the head of the column on an order from Lieut. Cooke, and shortly after, Lieut. Cooke came to me and said, 'General Custer directs you to take as rapid a gait as you think prudent and charge the village afterwards *and you will be supported by the whole outfit.*' * * * I took a trot and proceeded to carry out my orders. * * * My first thought was to make a charge with two companies and hold the third as a rallying point, but when I saw the number of Indians, I sent my adjutant to bring the third company on the line. * * * I saw I could not successfully make an offensive charge; their numbers had thrown me on the defensive. * * * I dismounted by giving the order to the company officers. * * * We were on the skirmish line under hot fire for 15 to 20 minutes. * * * It was plain to me that the Indians were using the woods as much as I was, and were scattering and creeping up to me. * * * After going down to the river and seeing the situation I knew I could not stay there *unless I stayed forever.* The regiment was scattered, or someone would have brought me an order, or aid. * * * At the time I was in the timber I had not the remotest idea where either the pack train or Benteen's column was. There was no plan communicated to us; if one existed the subordinate command did not know of it. * * * I had made up my mind to go through those people (the Indians) and get to the hill, and get the regiment together, so as to have a chance to save those who got through. There was no use of staying in the timber, where I could assist no one. I acted on my best judgment, and think events proved I was right. * * * My opinion is that 600 or 700 men (Indians) were there, *and I had but 112 men.* I thought it was my duty as a military movement, and I took the responsibility. * * *

Two views of Little Big Horn at the point where Reno crossed in the retreat. Top shows almost inaccessible steep bluffs looking East. Bottom, looking South, toward the Reno crossing. Brininstool photos 1913 and 1938.

I felt sure that some of us would go up; we were bound to. Some would get hit, and I would lose part of my command. I was willing to risk that in order to save the lives of the others from the desperate situation we were in. * * * The Indians had Winchesters, and the column made a big target, and they were pumping their bullets into it. I did not regard the movement as a triumphant march, nor did I regard it as a retreat. When I reached the hill I thought it was as good a position as I could get in the time I had, and immediately put the command in skirmish line through the company commanders. * * * At the time I left the timber I did not see Benteen's command, nor had I the remotest reason to expect him to unite with me. * * * I selected the position (on the hill); it appeared to be the best I could get. I knew I would have all I could do to take care of myself. * * * We hardly had time to dispose of the horses and get the men on the line before we were attacked in large numbers. * * * There was no protection whatever, except the greasewood—which was no protection whatever. * * * There was not the slightest suspicion or belief that Custer had been destroyed. It was supposed he could take care of himself as well as we could. He had nearly as many men as I had—more than I had when I opened the fight. * * * I stated in my official report that I estimated the number of attacking Indians at about 2500. I think now that estimate is below the mark. I think they were all there on the hill. * * * Nothing that came to my attention on the 25th or 26th led me to suspect that Custer had been destroyed. * * * On the 25th I went around the line and found a great many skulkers in the packs and drove them out. I did this several times. * * * I never had any intimation that Benteen was to support me. I did not even know where he was. * * * My effort to communicate with Custer the night of the 25th was as much for my benefit as his. * * * I made an effort on the 26th to communicate with General Terry with a Crow scout. He took the note and left the lines, but came back shortly. I do not know what became of the note. I finally got one to Gen. Terry on the 27th. * * * When I say that no plan was communicated to me, I mean to the regiment. I do not think there was any plan. * * * My relations with General Custer were friendly enough, and if my own brother had been in that column I could not have done any more than I did. * * * I consider that I obeyed orders. I did not charge the village, but I went far enough to discover that it was impossible. Of course ten men could be ordered to charge a million. * * * I then knew nothing of the topography, but it afterward developed that had I gone 300 yards further, the command would have been thrown into a ditch ten yards wide and three or four feet deep. The Indians were in it, and the command never would have got that far. By the time they had got within a few yards, most of the saddles would have been emptied and the horses killed. * * * I did everything I could to assist and cooperate with General Custer—as much as if he were my own brother. I feel that I did everything possible, short of sacrificing my command. * * * There was no communication to me that Custer's command had been sighted from the timber. * * * When I retreated from the bottom I had no idea where Custer was. I knew he was not on the side where the village was, and if there was any chance for him to see me, it was on this hill."

* * *

In view of the fact that Major Reno has, in the eyes of the general public, been blamed for "not going to the rescue of Custer," all this mass of testimony is likely to show WHY certain phases of the Little Big Horn fight were not carried out according to what MAY have been Custer's battle plan —if he had any. It does not appear from the testimony that Custer DID have any—not, at least, until he sent his hasty message by Trumpeter Martin to Benteen to "come on." But Benteen was miles away when that message reached him, and was in no position whatever to assist Custer—or Reno, either, until he joined the latter on the hill. Then Reno had to wait until the pack-train arrived with extra ammunition before making any move in Custer's direction. Reno's men had exhausted most of their cartridges in the fight in the river bottom, and it would not have been a diplomatic move to have tried to join Custer with no ammunition with which to assist him. And if Reno HAD left immediately when he got on the hill, the Indians at that end of the field might easily have gobbled the pack-train (with all the reserve ammunition, 24,000 rounds) if they saw it coming, which could hardly have been defended by the small number of troops with McDougall, who had it in charge. It is very doubtful if even 500 cavalrymen could have charged one mile through that Indian village, which was nearly four miles long and from a quarter to a half-mile wide.

The author is also well aware of the fact that Major Reno's private life has been assailed time and again. That, however, has no place in any criticism of his conduct in the Little Big Horn fight, and is, in the eyes of the author, an underhanded and despicable way of trying to "get back" at an officer whose bravery and skill in handling troops had never before been questioned As to the charges of cowardice which have time and again, both in private and in public, been hurled at Major Reno, the testimony of his own officers who fought at his side, should be sufficient evidence of his ability and military skill on that occasion. Major Reno won several brevets and a brilliant record in the Civil War for his bravery and proficiency in handling troops.

Further evidence that Major Reno's conduct at the battle of the Little Big Horn must have been such as call for no criticism from the officers and men under him, is shown in the following incident which took place just one week after the battle, while the Seventh Cavalry was lying in camp on the Yellowstone River:

A petition was circulated and signed by 235 members of the Seventh Cavalry—practically the entire remnant of the regiment—and sent to Gen. Sherman, at Washington, to be presented to Pres. Grant and Congress, asking that Major Marcus A. Reno be promoted to lieutenant-colonel of the regiment, vice Custer killed, and that Capt. F. W. Benteen be made major, vice Reno promoted. As the author owns a photostat copy of the original petition, there certainly is no "joker" in it. Here is the petition in its entirety:

"Camp near Big Horn, on Yellowstone River, July 4th, 1876.
"To His Excellency,
The President
And the Honorable Representatives
    of the United States.
"Gentlemen:

"We, the enlisted men, the survivors of the battle on the heights of the Little Big Horn River, on the 25th and 26th of June, 1876, of the Seventh Regiment of Cavalry, who subscribe our names to this petition, most earnestly solicit the President and Representatives of our country, that the vacancies among the commissioned officers of our Regiment, made by the slaughter of our brave, heroic, now lamented, Lieut.-Col. George A. Custer, and the other noble dead commissioned officers of our Regiment, who fell close by him on that bloody field, daring the savage demons to the last, be filled by the officers of the Regiment only. That Major M. A. Reno be our lieutenant-colonel, vice Custer killed; Capt. F. W. Benteen our major, vice Reno promoted. The other vacancies to be filled by officers of the regiment by seniority. Your petitioners know this is contrary to the established rule of promotion, but prayerfully solicit a deviation from the usual rule in this case, as it will be conferring a bravely-fought-for and a justly-merited promotion on officers who, by their bravery, coolness and decision on the 25th and 26th of June, 1876, saved the lives of every man now living of the Seventh Cavalry who participated in the battle, one of the most bloody on record, and one that would have ended with the loss of life of every officer and enlisted man on the field, *only for the position taken by Major Reno,* which we held with bitter tenacity against fearful odds, to the last.

"To support this assertion—had our position been taken one hundred yards back from the brink of the heights overlooking the river, we would have been entirely cut off from water; and from behind those heights, the Indian demons would have swarmed in hundreds, picking off our men by detail, and before mid-day, June 26th, not an officer or enlisted man of our Regiment would have been left to tell of our dreadful fate, as we would then have been completely surrounded.

"With the prayerful hope that our petition be granted, we have the honor to forward it through our Commanding Officer.
                                "Yours respectfully."

This petition bears the signatures of 235 members of the regiment, and was forwarded to General Sherman who did not present it to the President or to Congress, for reasons mentioned in General Sherman's reply, as follows:

"Headquarters Army of the U. S.
Washington, D. C., Aug. 5th, 1876.

"The judicious skillful conduct of Major Reno and Captain Benteen is appreciated, but the promotions caused by General Custer's death have been made by the President and confirmed by the Senate; therefore this petition cannot be granted. When the Sioux Campaign is over, I shall be most happy to recognize the valuable services of both officers and men by granting favors or recommending actual promotion.

"Promotion on the field of battle was Napoleon's favorite method of stimulating his officers and soldiers to deeds of heroism, but it is impossible in our service because commissions can only be granted by the President, on the advice and consent of the Senate, and except in original vacancies, promotion in a regiment is generally, if not always, made on the rule of seniority.

"W. T. SHERMAN,
General."

* * *

Some twenty-six years ago, while putting the finishing touches to his most excellent and truthfully-written volume, "The Story of the Little Big Horn," before its publication, in 1926, Col. W. A. Graham, then Judge Advocate U. S. A. held spirited correspondence with many old Indian fighters. To one, who in common with Gen. Nelson A. Miles had severely criticised Major Reno's conduct during the fight in the valley, referring to Reno as a "cowardly poltroon," Col. Graham wrote a reply, a copy of which came into my hands, and which I have his permission to publish. That "critic" was Major Robert G. Carter, retired, Fourth Cavalry. Col. Graham has lately told me over the telephone that this letter *expresses the opinion he then held, and still holds.*

Because the letter is so impartial and judicial an analysis of the whole situation, and so clearly demonstrates the unfairness and injustice of certain so-called "historians" who have sought to cover up the fatal errors of General Custer, which led to his defeat, by making Reno a scapegoat, I am publishing Col. Graham's letter written in 1925, and offer it herewith, with these comments, which are entirely my own, as a valuable contribution to the military history of "Custer's last fight."

The Author.

COLONEL GRAHAM'S LETTER

"March 18, 1925

Dear Major Robt. G. Carter:

"I cannot agree with you about Reno. Nor do I believe, if you will take the time to make a careful and comprehensive study of the fight in the valley, that you yourself would hold to the views you have expressed.

"I do not know whether you have read the testimony taken by the Reno Court of Inquiry, held at Chicago in 1879, but if you have, you cannot reach the conviction you now hold without discrediting the sworn statements of every military witness, whether called by the prosecution or the defense, who recount what occurred in the valley. These were Wallace, Hare, Varnum, Moylan and DeRudio of the officers, and Sergeants Culbertson and Davern of the enlisted men.

"In all their testimony you cannot find one word in criticism of Reno's action in halting and deploying in skirmish line, instead of charging headlong into the village. On the contrary, you will find only commendation and unanimous agreement that had he not done as he did, his little force (112 men) would have been swallowed up and exterminated in five minutes.

"And you will find no criticism, but only approval of his action in getting out of the timber; and unanimous opinion that had he remained there, without support, (which he might have done a short time longer), his command would have been completely wiped out.

"I am not ready to agree that Reno was a 'cowardly poltroon' because he did what all these officers say was the only thing he could have done with the knowledge he had of the situation; and, which they all agree, saved what was left of the regiment.

"I do not doubt that Reno was alarmed; that he was frightened and lost his head during the retreat. But that fact does not justify any such charge against him. If every officer who gets alarmed and frightened during an action is a 'cowardly poltroon,' the army is full of them; always has been, and always will be.

"The test—if one wishes to be fair and impartial—should be—not, was he scared? nor, might he not have done something else? but did he do what, under the circumstances which confronted him, he ought to have done? I think he did, up to the time that his column reached the river in retreat. And I believe you will think so, too, if you will study the situation with care, and with an open mind.

"You would not say that Wallace and Hare and Varnum and Moylan and DeRudio were all 'cowardly poltroons,' I feel sure. Yet, to be consistent, you must say either that or that they wilfully and deliberately perjured themselves at Chicago in 1879. And you would not say that, either.

"The truth is—and I think you will recognize it when you think it over—that most of the criticism and condemnation of Reno comes from men who were not there with him in the valley, and whose ideas upon that matter were based on hearsay—not always too accurate; and upon the natural disdain that arose from his passing of the buck to Benteen, as soon as the latter came up.

"I hold no brief for Reno; but I believe in giving even the devil his due; *and it is not necessary to attack and condemn Reno in order to account for what happened to Custer.* (Italics are Col. G's)

"Don't forget that Reno's 112 were opposed in the valley by not more than 25 per cent of the Indians at any time. There were never to exceed 800 or 900 of them. The rest—fully 2,500 or 3,000, were attacking Custer before Reno's retreat got under way. There was no hope for Custer from the moment he abandoned his intention to support Reno from the rear. His command was doomed as soon as it rode down the river. If he, with *five* companies, was unable to even reach the river, what chance had Reno with *three* companies to charge through the camp? (Italics Col. G's) The idea is absurd. There were enough Indians there to defeat the whole Seventh Cavalry, just as Crook been defeated the week before (June 17th) at the Rosebud fight, forty or fifty miles south.

"Was Crook a 'cowardly poltroon' because he, realizing that the Indians were too strong for his force—much larger than the Seventh Cavalry, (Crook had over 1100 against Custer's 650 men) and not divided into far-separated detachments—withdrew?

"I don't think you can compare Forsyth's Beecher Island fight with the Little Big Horn fight at all. Forsyth's men were all picked frontiersmen (not soldiers) while the Seventh was from thirty to forty per cent raw recruits, who had never been in the field before. Forsyth, moreover, was entirely alone, cornered, and had to fight to the death, whether or no. Reno *could* get out, and had a chance at least to rejoin the rest of the regiment. The two situations are in no sense comparable.

"Now, Major, put yourself in Reno's place for a minute. Just forget all you know of what happened *afterward,* and confine your estimate to the situation as it had developed up to the time he made his retreat. (Italics Col. G's) What are the facts?

"Custer's order was: *'Take as rapid a gait as you think prudent and charge afterwards; and the whole outfit will support you.'* That's the only order he ever got. He starts, reaches the river, and sends word *twice* to Custer that 'the enemy is in force in my front.' Nothing comes back from Custer. Reno has every reason to believe that Custer is following him in support. He gets down the valley two miles from his crossing; he finds himself confronted by a force of Indians which outnumbers him ten to one. He can see that the village is an immense one, and that there are hordes of Indians in the distance. His scouts, who form his left flank, run, as soon as the Sioux attack. His left flank is in the air, and Sioux by hundreds are massing there and to his rear.

"I concede that he might have gone on, just as the Light Brigade went on at Balaklava. But the promised support was not coming, as everyone could see. To go on meant that in less than a minute he would be in the midst of a thousand warriors, which you aptly describe as 'the finest light cavalry in the world.' They were not only ready for him, but inviting him to continue his advance. His little command wouldn't have lasted five minutes if he had gone a thousand yards further. It would have been utter lunacy to have gone on.

"When he halted, remember, Custer was on his way down the river, on the other side. He was not attacked for a good half hour after Reno halted and dismounted. If Reno had charged into the village, his command would have been wiped out and gone, the better part of a half hour before Custer reached the point where the Sioux met him. His failure to charge, therefore, could not, and did not, have any bearing whatever on what happened to Custer. Its only result was to prevent the annihilation of his (Reno's) own battalion.

Crow King, prominent leader of the Sioux in the Custer battle, and one of Gall's chief lieutenants.

"What did he do next?

"He formed a skirmish line, dismounted, and that line advanced a hundred yards or more, and until the nearest tepees were within range, for many of his bullets reached them. As soon as he did this, the Indians massed against his left flank, and came into the timber, where Reno had put his horses, from right flank and rear.

"What did he do then?

"He took G Troop off the line and put it in the timber to protect the horses, and Moylan (A Troop) extended to the right to fill the gap, and this extension made the line so weak that the left flank was crushed in, and he was forced to change front, and bring the line in to the edge of the timber.

"So far, certainly, he has done nothing that indicates cowardice and poltroonery. He has preserved his command from utterly useless *and senseless sacrifice,* and has it in a position where the support, which Custer had promised, can reach it. I call that good leadership so far. Can you find any flaw in it? I think not.

"How long did he stay out in the open, in skirmish line?

"You know how long military movements take. Figure it out. Could it have taken less than fifteen or twenty minutes to do the things he did? He did all these things—not one right after another as if on a schedule, but as the necessity for them developed. You have had long experience in handling troops. I have had a little myself. But we both know that situations do not develop, nor are troop movements made, in an instant.

"What next?

"He is on the bench now, his men along the edge of the timber, as far as they will reach. So far, only one casualty. He finds that he has not enough men to cover the position and keep the Indians out of the timber. If he puts his men at the long intervals, necessary to line the edge of the timber, they will be so far apart as to be beyond supporting distance—and also beyond control of his officers. The Indians are creeping up along the front; they are slipping into the woods on the right, and from the rear. He is being fired on from all sides, *and Custer's promised support still does not come* (Italics Col. G's.)

"I grant you that Forsyth, with his picked and experienced men, might have held that timber as long as their ammunition lasted, and that *they* would not have wasted ammunition. But do you think it was possible to exercise any great fire-control—always a difficult thing, even with the best troops—over a command that was forty per cent raw recruits, every one of whom was probably scared stiff.

"All the time—and don't lose sight of this—Reno and his officers and men expected to see Custer come charging through from the rear. They had no reason to believe that he would *not* do what his order promised. They had no reason to be very sparing of ammunition, so far as they knew; and there would have been no need of it had Custer supported the attack.

"How long was Reno in the timber?

"It is hard to tell; but at least as long as he was on the plain. And long enough to become convinced (from the fact that in every direction from which support would come, the country was full of Indians) *that Custer was not coming!*

"He (Reno) made up his mind to get out and go where he had a chance to save his command, and to connect with other parts of the regiment. For this, you condemn him!

"Well, let's see: If he had stayed there half an hour longer (if not wiped out by that time) Benteen's command would have come along, following Custer's trail (not Reno's) and might, or might not, have discovered where he was. But don't overlook the fact that Reno *didn't know* that Benteen was coming; and Benteen, on the other hand, didn't know that Reno was across the river in the timber.

"By the time Benteen could have crossed the river and gotten to where Reno was, IF he had stayed there, it would have been at least as late in the afternoon as when Benteen did join him on the hill, or after 4:00 o'clock; probably later, as Benteen would have had to fight his way through.

"By the time that the remnants of Benteen's battalion had joined him, (conceding that he could have cut his way through) he must have used much of his ammunition, lost some horses, and had some casualties. Upon joining Reno (after 4 PM,) the two together might have made a charge into the village, leaving their wounded in the timber.

"Suppose they had done so. Custer was already hotly engaged, and had been for some time, and was at least three miles away on the other side of the river! The combined force of Reno and Benteen *might* have created sufficient diversion in Custer's favor to have drawn from him a part of the Indian force. Whether it could have been done soon enough to have saved any considerable part of Custers' command, is problematical, and I think rather doubtful. I think most of Custer's command was dead by the time it was possible for Benteen to have joined Reno in the timber (conceding for the sake of speculation that he would have tried to do so).

"You say in your comments that you do not think it possible to have done anything for Custer after Benteen and Reno united on the hill. How, then, would it have been possible to do anything more, had Reno remained in the timber, and Benteen had joined him there, after fighting his way through? The time element, to say nothing of others, is more unfavorable to the chance in the latter case than in the former.

"No, Major, I don't think it was 'in the cards,' however played, to have saved Custer's command. From the time he divided the regiment and separated the various detachments so widely, without any plan for co-operation, what happened was bound to happen. The enemy was too strong—too cohesive—too confident —too well equipped. The Seventh Cavalry could not have beaten them. Why not admit it?

"Supposing, however, that Benteen had joined Reno in the timber, and the two together had charged into the village. They had at least *two miles of village* to go through before reaching a point anywhere near Custer, *whose whereabouts they did not know, and could not have known.* (Italics Col. G's)

"It is within the bounds of possibility, I grant you, that the Indians *might* have left what remained of Custer's command, if any, to oppose them. And what was then left of Custer's command (if they had any horses, ammunition or spirit left) *might* have crossed the river and tried to fight through to the south. What chance would either force have had to fight through to the other?

"And in the meantime, what would have become of the pack-train which had ALL of the reserve ammunition? (24,000 rounds)

"But Reno didn't stay in the timber—so all this speculation is beside the point. I have merely called to your attention some grave objections to your assumption that IF he had remained there, and IF Benteen had joined him there, and IF together they had charged the village, it *might* have saved Custer's battalion.

"When Reno decided to get out and recross the river, both you and General X seem to be under the belief that he made a break, and that officers and men followed, helter skelter, each man for himself. But this is very far from the fact, unless again all the military witnesses at Chicago deliberately perjured themselves.

Wallace, Hare, Varnum and Moylan all describe what was done —how the word was passed to get to the horses—how the companies were formed in the clearing—how the Indians who had gotten into the timber fired into them point blank, killing Bloody Knife at Reno's side, and mortally wounding another; how they broke from the timber and formed on the plain in column of fours, and with pistols drawn, cut their way to the river. It's all in that testimony and perfectly clear, if you read it with an *unbiased mind*.

"And I am free to say, that in my opinion, based upon the most careful and painstaking study, with no reason in the world to be biased one way or the other, Reno, up to the moment that Bloody Knife was shot down at his side, and the Sioux fired a volley point-blank into his troops, had done only what a capable commander·should have done in the circumstances.

"At that point, however, he became excited and lost his head. He broke out of the woods, instead of waiting to collect all of his men—many of whom, belonging to G Troop were scattered through the timber; and once out, the companies were hastily formed into columns, and the retreat began.

"And it was just as I have described it. The head of the column reached the river in very good order, but along the length, what with the Indians firing into it, it became a rout, a panic, at the rear.

"And what happened to Reno's column on this retreat gives you a very fair picture of what would have happened to Benteen's, had he tried to cut his way through to Reno in the timber (supposing Reno to have remained there.)

"The *character* of the retreat is the only thing that can rightly be charged against Reno. And even that, the evidence showed, was intended by him, and understood by everybody, to be a charge, to cut through the surrounding enemy and gain contact with the regiment.

"The most that can be fairly charged against Reno is that he became excited and lost his head when this charge or retreat began; that he failed to cover his crossing, and temporarily lost control of his men. That much is true. But to blame him for the disaster to Custer is not only unfair and unnecessary, but, in the light of the demonstrated and demonstrable facts, most unjust.

"Sincerely yours,
(Signed) W. A. Graham.

To Major Robert G. Carter (Retd)

CHAPTER 7

THE STORY OF TRUMPETER MARTIN.

THE MAN WHO CARRIED CUSTER'S LAST MESSAGE for reinforcements was John Martin, orderly trumpeter to the general on June 25, 1876—this, in spite of the fact that probably a dozen men have appeared on the horizon claiming the same distinction. They were all fakers, pure and simple. To Trumpeter Martin, and to him alone went that promience.

John Martin died in Brooklyn, N. Y., December 24, 1922, and in his demise there passed a man who played a conspicuous part in the celebrated battle of the Little Big Horn; and John Martin was probably the last man of all the members of the Seventh Cavalry—except those who were killed with Custer—to see the general alive.

Pages have been written and much speculation has been indulged in as to why Custer received no reinforcements in his dire hour of need on that sagebrush-covered hill, where he and a handful of his dauntless troopers perished to a man in the greatest Indian battle in all the annals of our Western frontier. Major Reno has been blamed for "not going to Custer's relief," but nothing is said as to why Custer failed to go to Reno's relief, after ordering him to make the initial attack and promising him the full support of his (Custer's) five companies of troops. Custer's defeat was due to no negligence whatever on the part of Major Reno or any other officer of the Seventh Cavalry. They did exactly as Custer ordered them to do—save that Major Reno, with prudent

Trumpeter John Martin, who carried Custer's last message to Benteen (written by Lt. Cooke, adjutant) and the last man to see Custer alive.

judgment, refused to sacrifice his own command by carrying out an order which was as absolutely impossible to perform as if Custer had ordered him to capture the Indian village single-handed!

To what, therefore, was Custer's defeat due? The author is well aware that he is now treading on ticklish ground. Nevertheless, after an exhaustive study, covering over sixty years, of the battle of the Little Big Horn; after personal interviews with men who fought with the Reno battalion;

after personally visiting the battlefield many times and going carefully over the ground; and after reading the complete testimony of the Reno Court of Inquiry, covering nearly 200 columns, and perusing everything written on the subject which was available, the question "Why was Custer defeated?" resolves itself—in the mind of the author, at least, to this:

It was due to his own lack of knowledge of the superior strength, organization and arms of the Sioux; his own lack of knowledge of the lay of the land, and above all, his neglecting to scout the country thoroughly and march further south, as ordered, while awaiting the arrival of Generals Terry and Gibbon with the other troops of the expedition, and finally, separating his regiment into three battalions all beyond supporting distance of each other, and attacking the Indians with wearied and played-out horses and men.

Custer's highest estimate of the number of Indians he would find in that village along the Little Big Horn, was 800. His own Crow and 'Ree Indian scouts warned him that he would find many times that number. "Mitch" Bouyer, a half-breed in charge of these Indian scouts as interpreter, told Custer he "would find Indians enough to keep him busy two or three days." Charley Reynolds, Custer's chief of scouts, and a plainsman of great fame, skill and renown, was greatly perturbed by the reports of the Indian scouts, and remained silent and reserved the night before the battle, as if anticipating the terrible fate in store for him the following day.

Custer had been instructed by Gen. Alfred Terry, the commanding officer of the expedition, to follow the Indian trail which Major Reno had discovered a few days before. But that if it led in the direction of the Little Big Horn—as it was thought almost certain that it would—he was *not to follow it directly, but to continue on further south, and thus give Generals Terry and Gibbon time to arrive on the ground with their infantry, artillery and few companies of cavalry*. Then, and not until then, Custer was to swing about and march north while Terry and Gibbon were marching south. They thus expected to entrap the Indians between the two commands, and persuade the red men to go back to their reservations or give them battle. Indeed, it turned out later—according to the reports of some of the leading chiefs in the fight, that had Custer waited until the other troops arrived, a battle doubtless would have been avoided.

Gen. Terry knew the impetuous, dashing make-up of Custer. He had tried to persuade him to take a battery of Gatling guns and some of the Second Cavalry to augment his own forces, but Custer had declined this tender. He said that he could whip any body of Indians he might run across, with the Seventh Cavalry alone, and that the Gatling guns would impede his progress.

Gen. Terry warned Custer that the commands of Gibbon and himself could not possibly reach the scene of action until June 26th at the most, and that he was to so time his marching as to reach the valley of the Little Big Horn not sooner than that date.

But here was Custer—twenty-four hours ahead of the date he had been instructed to appear; a whole day in advance of the specified time he was expected to reach the valley of the Little Big Horn. Custer waited for nobody. With his characteristic impetuosity and dashing, daring manner, he clung to the Indian trail like a hound to the scent of a fox. He made forced marches, wearing out both men and animals, and without rest for trooper or beast, arrived on the ground a whole day ahead of the time designated.

The Indian village was strung along the Little Big Horn River for a distance of nearly four miles, and contained nearly 5,000 fighting warriors, and nearly 10,000 old men, women and children in addition. It was the largest assemblage of Indians ever found in one camp on the American continent. For weeks the young bucks had been slipping away from their reservations, by twos and threes, and joining the hostile ranks of Sitting Bull, Gall, Crazy Horse and Crow King. Custer was not aware of this.

Fifteen miles from the scene of action, Custer made his first division of the regiment. To Capt. Benteen he gave three companies, with orders to "move to the left and pitch into anything you come across." To Major Reno he also gave three companies, with orders to "move forward at as fast a gait as you think prudent, charge the village *and we will support you.*"

Benteen moved to the left. In his rear—came the pack train, carrying all the reserve ammunition—24,000 rounds. Reno made his attack—but Custer did not support him. He and Reno moved forward together down a small tributary of the Little Big Horn, and when Reno crossed the river to attack the village, Custer apparently changed his plans—if plans he had—and with his five companies, swung to the right, over bluffs and ravines, with the evident intention of attacking the village at its lower end. He never reached that point.

Benteen marched for many miles as ordered—to the left. No signs of Indians were discovered, and the lay of the land gradually forced him back into the trail made by Reno. He came in sight of Reno's command just as the latter was cutting its way through a thousand yelling, whooping, victorious savages—not in time to be of any assistance until Reno's shattered remnants, exhausted and "all in," had crossed the river and gained the bluffs on the other side of the stream.

But how about Custer, anyway? Let John Martin himself tell the story. John Martin was the last man to see Custer alive of those who accompanied him into the fight. He was the orderly trumpeter for Custer that fatal day. For many years he was living in Brooklyn, N. Y., in retirement from service. He served in the United States Army continuously from 1874 to 1904, when he was retired as a sergeant. A fine old soldier, he, with a record of long and honorable

Photo at the Custer Monument on the 10th anniversary (1886) of the Custer fight. Left to right—Corp. Hall; unidentified; Capt. Godfrey; Capt. Benteen; Dr. Porter; Capt. McDougall; Pvt. Aspinwall and Scout White Swan, who was seriously wounded in the fight.

service, and he gave two stalwart sons to the American Army as well. He was an Italian by birth. Here is what Martin said in an interview granted to a friend of the author shortly before his death:

"The general (Custer) seemed to be in a big hurry. After we had gone about a mile or two (after the separation of the regiment) we came to a big hill that overlooked the valley, and we rode around the base of it and halted. Then the general took me with him and we rode to the top of the hill, where we could see the village in the valley on the other side of the river.

"We didn't see anything of Reno's column when we were on the hill. I am sure the general didn't see them at all, because he looked around with his glasses, and all he said was: 'We have got them this time.'

"Then the general and I rode back to where the troops were, and he talked a minute with the adjutant, telling him what he had seen. We rode on, pretty fast, until we came to a big ravine that led in the direction of the river, and the general pointed down there and then called me. This was about a mile down the river from where he went up on the hill, and we had been going at a trot and gallop all the way. It must have been three miles from where we left Reno's trail.

"The general said to me: 'Orderly, I want you to take a message to Col. Benteen. Ride as fast as you can and tell him to hurry. Tell him it's a big village, and I want him to be quick and to bring the ammunition packs.'

"He didn't stop at all when he was telling me this, and I just said to him: 'Yes, sir;' and checked my horse, when the adjutant said: 'Wait, orderly, I'll give you a message,' and he stopped and wrote it in a big hurry in a little book and then tore out the leaf and gave it to me.

"And he then told me: 'Now, orderly, ride as fast as you can to Col. Benteen. Take the same trail we came down. If you have time, and there is no danger, come back, but otherwise stay with your company.'

"In a few minutes I was back on the hill where the general and I had looked at the village. From here I could see Reno's battalion in action. It had not been more than ten or fifteen minutes since the general and I were on the hill, and then we had seen no Indians. But now there were lots of them riding around and shooting at Reno's men, who were dismounted and in skirmish line. I didn't stop to watch the fight. I had to get on to Col. Benteen, but the last I saw of Reno's men they were fighting in the valley, and their line was falling back.

"I continued on, and shortly I saw Col. Benteen's command coming. Soon I met him. I saluted and handed the message to him. He said: 'Where's the general now?' I told him what the general said—that it was a big village and to hurry. I then joined my company with Benteen."

This was the famous message to Benteen for help. It was worded as follows: "Benteen, come on—big village—be quick—bring packs. P.S.—Bring packs."

But Benteen was not able to carry out his orders. It was an utter impossibility for him to have done so. By that time Custer was beyond all aid. His part in the fight lasted, according to the best authorities, from twenty minutes to half an hour. Benteen was just able to reach Reno, and shortly their respective commands were surrounded by thousands of exultant, blood-thirsty and victorious Sioux. Go to Custer? They might as well have tried to reach the North Pole! There were—by actual measurement—just four miles and one hundred and sixty yards* of hills, gullies and ravines to cross, between Custer's position and that occupied by Reno and Benteen, with thousands of savages between the two commands. Reno did make an advance toward Custer's position. He went about one mile, and was driven back again with the swiftness of a tornado by the overwhelming odds against him.

---

* This is the official measurement made by Lieut. McGuire, of the Engineer Corps, two days after the battle.

Nobody knew the fate of Custer until Terry and Gibbon approached from the north on the morning of June 27th, and the Custer field was discovered by Lieut. James H. Bradley, in charge of the Indian scouts, who was riding three miles in advance of the command. Terry and Gibbon relieved Reno and brought away all that was left of the Seventh Cavalry.

But there were no *Custer* "survivors." Of the Reno survivors there are quite a few, and John Martin, orderly trumpeter for Custer, was one of them. He was the last man to see his beloved general alive—the bearer of his last, urgent message for help—help which it was too late to give.

CHAPTER 8

SIBLEY AND THE SIOUX.

"LIEUTENANT SIBLEY will select twenty-five men from the various companies of the Second Cavalry, and with Frank Grouard and Big Bat as guides, will make a scout to the northwest in an endeavor to locate the hostiles."

Such were the orders of General George Crook to Lieutenant Frederick W. Sibley at Crook's camp on Goose Creek, Wyoming, July 5th, 1876.

Custer and five companies of the Seventh Cavalry had been annihilated on the Little Big Horn June 25th—as yet unknown to Crook. Crook, with twice the force of the entire Seventh Cavalry, had been practically defeated on the Rosebud River, June 17th—this unknown to the shattered remnant of the Seventh Cavalry far to the north. It had been a bitter lesson to Crook. Including his Crow and Shoshone allies, his casualties at the battle of the Rosebud numbered 9 killed, 35 wounded, and he had been obliged to retire to his base on Goose Creek, and await supplies and reenforcements.

Several weeks of enforced idleness had been spent by his command. Daily it had been expected that he would receive supplies and more troops from Fort Fetterman; but these had not arrived, and General Crook was becoming impatient and restless.

There had been much speculation among the troops as to why Crook did not follow up the trail of the Indians after the Rosebud fight on June 17th. Doubtless, however, Crook felt that his command was greatly outnumbered, and he did not care to take any chances. Three weeks had now passed; no reenforcements had arrived; the hostile Sioux had scattered and Crook could only speculate as to their whereabouts. He did not know that one week after his own disastrous battle on the Rosebud, Custer, with five troops of the Seventh, had been wiped out to a man on the Little Big Horn, a brief two days' journey distant from his own camp, nor did he receive this news until the tenth of July.

Hence, Crook's reason for sending Lieutenant Sibley on a scouting trip. Meantime, doubtless the expected reenforcements would arrive from Fetterman, and with the return of the scouting party, with the hostiles located, Crook expected to be able to start on the trail, surprise their village, if possible, and give them battle again.

Lieutenant Sibley was expected to carefully reconnoiter the country to the northwest, along the base of the Big Horn Mountains, and if he located the hostile camp, to return post haste to Crook's camp with all possible information. Sibley was young, but courageous, full of energy, and Crook felt that he was particularly capable for the work in hand. The utmost caution would be necessary to avoid discovery, which might thwart the plans of the commanding officer. It was well known that the Indians must be somewhere within the radius of the country to be scouted over—indeed, a scout had been made by another officer but two days previously, and several war parties of the Sioux had been sighted.

Lieutenant Sibley's instruction were to select his men and be ready to leave camp at noon the following day, July 6th. The personnel of the party, exclusive of the troops and scouts, included but two others—John Becker, a packer, who had had some experience as a guide in those parts, and John F. Finerty, war correspondent of the *Chicago Times,* well and favorably known to every old army officer of the frontier days as the "fighting Irish pencil-pusher."

Finerty was a character. He was as brave as a lion, a good shot and horseman, and had reckless disregard for his life

Lieut F. W. Sibley, in command of the Sibley scouting party.

when on the firing line. He was a general favorite with both officers and men, while the scouts looked upon him as "one of their own."

"Make a note of it, Finerty!" "Big Bat" would yell at the scribe, when something of unusual news value broke loose. And Finerty always did!

A word as to the scouts. Frank Grouard was at that time regarded as one of the greatest scouts and frontiersmen in all the west. His father had been a missionary; his mother was a native of the South Sea Islands. Grouard had served as a mail-carrier around old Fort Hall and in the upper Missouri River country. On one of his trips he was captured by a war party of Sioux, who, observing his dark skin, concluded he was an Indian, and had spared his life. Grouard remained with the Sioux for several years, becoming very proficient in their language, and, to all intents and purposes, one of the tribe. However, at the outbreak of the Sioux war of 1876, he decamped, joining the forces of General Crook as a scout, and rendering most valuable services. Indeed, so well was he regarded by Crook, that the latter is said to have remarked, "I would rather lose a third of my command than Frank Grouard."

Baptiste Pourier was equally proficient as a scout and frontiersman, having spent his entire life among the Indians of the Plains tribes. He had played an important part in the famous "Hayfield fight" near old Fort C. F. Smith, in August, 1866, wherein nineteen men, fighting inside a corral constructed of lattice willow work, successfully withstood the attacks of over two thousand of Chief Red Cloud's most able warriors, killing and wounding so many that the Sioux finally gave up and retired. Pourier was regarded by General Crook as one of his most reliable and trustworthy scouts. He was universally known as "Big Bat."

Finerty, the newspaper correspondent, had quite a stormy session with General Crook before the latter would consent that he accompany the scouting party.

"Young man," warned the general, "don't you realize that this is a very dangerous mission on which I am sending Lieutenant Sibley? You are liable to lose your hair, and I don't care to be responsible for the safety of your return."

"Never mind that, general," retorted Finerty. "I'll assume all the responsibility. I'm out here with your command to report what takes place, and I've stuck around camp so long now that I'm liable to dry-rot if I don't get into a little excitement soon."

General Crook shrugged his shoulders.

"So you didn't get excitement enough in that Rosebud fight less than a month ago, eh? Well, if that's the way you look at it, go ahead, but I warn you right now that you may get into more trouble than you perhaps anticipate."

"What kind of an epitaph shall I write for you, Finerty?" jokingly inquired General Crook's aide, Captain John Bourke.

"You'll be wishing you were back in Chicago, perhaps, before another twenty-four hours," volunteered Sibley. "However, I'm mighty glad you are going, just the same. Captain Wells, what do you think about it?"

Grim Captain Wells shook his head. Then, turning to his orderly, commanded: "Orderly, bring Mr. Finerty a hundred rounds of Troop E ammunition."

No pack animals were to be taken. Each man was to take a double supply of ammunition and rations for several days, all to be carried on the horses ridden by the command.

"Remember, Finerty, we'll be starting at noon tomorrow, and will muster beyond the creek," explained Lieutenant Sibley. "Be on hand promptly."

"Don't you think it's a mistake to start out in broad daylight, lieutenant?" queried Finerty.

"Maybe so, but General Crook is very anxious to get some positive information as to the whereabouts of the Sioux," was the reply, "and I am of the opinion that the sooner we start, the quicker we'll locate the hostiles. We expect to march only about thirteen miles tomorrow afternoon. There's a good

John F. Finerty, correspondent for Chicago Times, known as "The fighting Irish Pencil Pusher."

place to camp further up on Goose Creek, and we'll remain there until about sundown, let the horses graze, get supper, and then make a night march until about 2 in the morning before camping."

Promptly at noon the following day, the little party assembled. Lieutenant Sibley was cautioned to move carefully, and the scouts, Grouard and "Big Bat," likewise enjoined to employ all the skill at their command while on this scout. The little command left camp with General Crook's best wishes and the God-speed of all who witnessed their departure.

The Goose Creek stopping point was reached shortly after

a two hours' ride. Here a halt was ordered. When the shadows again began to lengthen, Frank Grouard, as chief scout, advised Lieutenant Sibley that the strictest watchfulness must be maintained, the command must march as silently as possible, with no loud talking. With this caution enjoined, the little party mounted.

Just as the advance was about to be ordered, Big Bat, who was observed to be keenly scanning a small ravine at one side of the trail, exclaimed:

"There's a man on horseback down there watching us."

"Where?" exclaimed Lieutenant Sibley, spurring his horse to Bat's side.

"Right there in that shallow ravine. Look! There he goes now. Did you see him, Frank?" turning to Grouard who had promptly ridden up.

"There he is again!" exclaimed Bat, pointing excitedly ahead.

There certainly was something—either a horseman or a wild animal. Grouard promptly spurred ahead, peering keenly through the gathering gloom; but the object, whatever it was, fled like the wind and disappeared into the depths of the ravine.

"What was it, Frank?" asked Lieutenant Sibley, as the scout rode back.

"Dunno. Too dark to make out. Maybe an elk—or maybe one of Sitting Bull's braves watching us."

"An Jnjun as sure as you're born!" ejaculated Bat.

"Maybe, but I'm not so sure," replied Grouard. "But you can bet we're on ticklish ground from this point on, and we can't be too careful."

"Don't forget to make a note of that, Finerty," cautioned Big Bat with a chuckle.

Cautiously the command moved forward over the trail. Strict silence was the watchword; smoking was forbidden, lest the sharp eye of some watchful Sioux detect the flare of the tell-tale match.

The party was now marching over the old Fort C. F. Smith trail, the scouts and Lieutenant Sibley ahead of the command a hundred feet. From every point of vantage Frank Grouard kept a sharp lookout ahead, scanning each ridge.

About 8 o'clock the full moon rose behind them, rendering every object as clear and distinct as though it were daylight. Like a troop of phantoms the Sibley party looked, marching through a solitude which, for grandeur and beauty of scenery could not have been surpassed, with the lofty Big Horn Mountains looming up on the left flank. In silence as undisturbed as possible, save for the occasional grinding of the iron-shod hoofs of the horses over the pebbles in the little mountain water-courses, the command marched, until, at 2 o'clock Frank Grouard advised a halt among some small grass-covered bluffs.

"Reckon we'll be safe here till daylight," he remarked to the lieutenant.

"Let the men half lariat their horses," were the orders of Sibley, "and sergeant, post your men on the high points hereabouts. We'll take no chances of surprises, even though Grouard thinks we are in a good position."

Some of the men snatched fitful naps. Most of them were too excited, however, to sleep. Finerty made some entries in his note book, the moon shining so brightly that his writing was plainly discernible. Lieutenant Sibley remained awake, watchful.

There were no disturbances through the night. Early in the morning the command was again in the saddle, pressing ahead cautiously in the direction the scouts believed the Indian village to be located. As usual, Grouard and Big Bat, with Lieutenant Sibley, rode in advance.

Reaching a point some miles from the late bivouac, and not far from the Little Big Horn River, whose shining waters could be seen ahead, Grouard turned to Sibley.

"Wait here until I go up on that little knoll and take a look," he advised.

Sibley signaled to the command, which at once halted. Grouard rode toward the knoll, slipping from his animal slightly below the crest, while Sibley order the command to dismount until the scout returned.

The lieutenant watched every movement of the intrepid Grouard with peculiar interest. He knew the command was likely to encounter Indians at any minute.

The scout crept cautiously to the top of the knoll, field glasses in hand. Removing his broad-rimmed sombrero, he raised himself carefully and took one look, instantly ducking down again, and quickly turning and motioning Big Bat to join him.

Bat, also leaving his horse below the crest, joined Grouard, and both scouts then keenly scanned the country again. Something was wrong, Sibley conjectured, for the two scouts were excitedly talking to each other, pausing every now and then to use their field glasses.

Suddenly both, bending low, ran for their horses and came galloping back to Sibley.

"Quick, lieutenant, we've not a second to lose! mount your men and follow me, for your lives!" cried Grouard.

"But what —"

"No time to talk now," snapped Grouard. "Follow me as fast as you can and we'll talk afterward."

Wondering, but without further questioning, Sibley ordered the command to follow. Grouard and Big Bat lashed their horses into a run, heading for some bluffs of red sandstone which formed the footstool of the mountain chain. Over rocky ledges and slippery boulders Grouard and Big Bat led the command, until five minutes later, a bluff of sufficient size had been reached to conceal the horses of the party on its westerly side.

"Don't let the men dismount," cautioned Grouard, "but you, lieutenant, come with Bat and myself for a minute."

Up into the rocks clambered Grouard like a goat, Big Bat and Sibley at his heels.

"What on earth is the matter, Frank?" breathlessly exclaimed Sibley when a sheltered spot had been reached. "What did you and Bat see over there—Indians?"

"Yes, and plenty of them," was the reply. "We've surely run into a hornet's nest this time. Whew! What if our trail is discovered? Look! What did I tell you?" and Grouard pointed toward the bluffs to the north.

Even as he spoke, groups of mounted Indians appeared in dozens, and their numbers increased every second. The savages scattered out, Indian fashion, and seemed to cover the bluffs. It was a war party—no doubt about that!

"We'll have to do some quick figuring if we get out of here alive," exclaimed Grouard. "What do you think, Bat?" turning to the older scout.

Big Bat shook his head. "It don't look good to me," he coolly remarked. "Of course a miss is as good as a mile, but—"

"Well, it all depends on whether they strike our trail or not," interrupted Grouard. "It don't seem likely that they will. If they don't we are yet comparatively safe. If they do—"

Breathlessly the three watched the movements of the war party, as its right wing swung around and approached the ground over which the command had but recently ridden. Surely no keen-eyed Indian out on the warpath would overlook their trail.

Nor did they. Suddenly a redskin wearing a blue blanket, reined in his pony and scanned the ground sharply. Then he began to ride his pony in a circle.

"By hokey!" exclaimed Lieutenant Sibley. "Now we are in for it! That fellow has discovered our trail, as sure as shooting!"

"Yes," chimed in Grouard, "and he'll have the whole bunch after us in the shake of a buck's tail."

"What do you suggest, Frank?" queried Sibley excitedly.

"Let's git while the gittin's good, I say," broke in Big Bat. "I ain't quite ready to leave my hair in a Sioux lodge."

"That's about the size of it, lieutenant," nodded Grouard. "Get to the horses first and take to the mountains—it's the only chance we have. We'll have to cross the range and make for Crook's camp on the other side. Come on, quick!"

Back to their horses hastened Sibley and the scouts.

"Men," spoke the lieutenant, in as calm a voice as he could muster, "we're in a tight place. The Indians have discovered our trail, and we may have to do some tall fighting. Grouard has a plan, which we shall try to carry out. If we can make an honorable escape all together, we will do it. But if worst comes to worst, and retreat proves impossible, let no man surrender. Die in your tracks, for the Sioux will show no mercy to any who are captured."

"And make a note of that, Finerty," added Big Bat, with a sickly grin.

"Come on," sharply ordered Grouard. "No lagging now. Every man of you keep tight at my heels."

Without further talk the whole party followed the two scouts up the rough side of the mountain, which at that particular point was seemingly almost inaccessible. As the command worked its way laboriously up over the rocks, until it reached a point where the country below could be overlooked, they observed that the Indians, now less than a mile distant, had halted, and appeared to be watching their movements and consulting together.

Grouard and Big Bat led the men along as fast as the horses could travel. Half an hour later an old Sioux hunting trail was struck, on the first ridge of the mountains.

"This trail," announced Grouard, "leads to the snowy range. I hunted in that region when I was living with the Indians, and if we can reach there without being overtaken or cut off, our chances are pretty fair."

"Then let's make time while we can," advised Sibley.

The trail at this point being fairly good, he ordered a trot. "No lagging now," he sharply commanded. "Remember, the life of every man in this command is at stake!"

Frank Grouard, son of a missionary, one of the greatest scouts of the West, who had lived for years with the Sioux Indians before joining Custer as a scout.

"What a whale of a story this is going to make!" exclaimed Finerty. "I wonder if we'll have a brush with the reds before we strike camp?"

"You may never live to write your 'whale of a story,'" drily observed Big Bat, "Make a note of *that*, too, Fineity."

For over two hours the party proceeded, now at a trot, now at a gallop, as the nature of the ground afforded. Eight or ten miles had been safely passed without any evident sign of pursuit. Now the horses began to show signs of fatigue. Many of the men were becoming exhausted from hunger and thirst.

"Do you think it's safe to halt a bit, rest and graze the horses and get a bite, Frank?" Sibley looked questionably at the scout.

Grouard hesitated. The horses needed a little rest, that was certain. The men could stand the hunger and thirst, but it was their animals on which depended their escape.

"Well, we ain't seen any of them following so far," finally remarked Grouard. "Maybe it will be safe to stop for twenty minutes or so, but I'm rather leery of it myself. Still, we can try it."

The grazing was good, and in five minutes the horses of the command were eagerly cropping the abundant herbage. Under the shady trees the men threw themselves. Some made coffee. Remarks were freely passed that "we've got them Injuns distanced all right."

At the end of half an hour, Grouard, who had ridden ahead to scan the country, returned.

"Better saddle up and get a-going," he advised. We ain't out of this pickle yet by a long shot, and I'm not so sure we ain't made a mistake in stopping at all."

Just as the command was about to mount, John Becker, the packer, accompanied by a trooper, who had lingered somewhat in the rear, came dashing up.

"Indians!" they shouted.

Glancing hastily about, Grouard, Bat and Sibley saw a party of the savages riding rapidly along the right flank, and at no great distance from them.

"Forward!" shouted Sibley, and the command dashed ahead on the trail.

"Keep well to the left—close to the woods," yelled Grouard. "We're liable to run into an ambush! We had no business to stop back there. I knew—"

His sentence was cut short by a ringing volley poured in upon the command from the rocks and trees on the right, and about two hundred yards distant. Three or four horses in the command were struck, but not a man was injured.

"Fall back into that patch of timber!" shouted Grouard. "It's our only chance! Quick! We've not a second to lose!"

Every horse was wheeled toward the timber on the left. Finerty's animal had been struck by a bullet. It stumbled from the shock and all but went down, but recovering its feet almost instantly, bore its rider in safety to the edge of the timber.

The Indian fire was very rapid, but, providentially it lacked the necessary accuracy to damage the command. The horses, frightened by the firing, needed no urging toward a place of shelter.

Reaching the timber, the troopers hastily dismounted at its edge. Here Lieutenant Sibley ordered a dozen of the best shots to open fire on the enemy with a view of confining them to their ambuscade until his own party could get under cover.

A few rattling volleys had the desired effect. Meantime such of the horses as could keep their feet, were tied to trees near the edge of the woods, and at that point Lieutenant Sibley formed his men into a semi-circular skirmish line, and the firing on both sides soon became hot and rapid.

Fortunately for the troopers, there was plenty of fallen timber, admirably suited as breastworks, behind which they were well protected.

"Keep cool men," cautioned Lieutenant Sibley, "and don't waste your lead. Make every shot count if possible!"

Meantime the horses were the only real sufferers, and apparently the Indian fire was so directed as to kill off the animals, whereby all means of retreat, save on foot, would be cut off, and the Indians doubtless expected the troopers would then be at their mercy.

Occasionally the Indian leader could be detected, dressed in what appeared to be a white buckskin suit, while his gorgeous war bonnet trailed the ground. He directed the movements of his warriors in a skilful manner.

"I know that Indian," volunteered Grouard, "and I'll bet he has recognized me. His name is White Antelope, and he's a leading Cheyenne chief. There's Cheyennes along here with him and these Sioux. You remember him, don't you, Bat?"

Big Bat nodded. "I reckoned it was White Antelope all the time. He's a reg'lar rip-snorter of a fighter, and we've got to git him sure. If we can knock him out, if may discourage the rest of his gang."

Not a man in the party had been struck by a bullet, despite the fact that they rattled against the tree trunks and down timber like hail stones on a barn roof.

Meantime Grouard, whose keen eyes were taking in every detail, observed that the Indian horde was increasing. The enemy swarmed out on the open slopes of the hills until it appeared that there were hundreds of them.

The firing on both sides had been heavy. Presently Lieutenant Sibley noticed that the Indians had slackened their fire considerably, and he turned to Grouard.

"Why are they letting up, Frank?"

"I'll guarantee they are getting ready for a charge," replied the scout. "Better tell the men to get ready for it. I don't like that silence. It means mischief."

Word was quickly passed along the skirmish line, and every man, lying low, gripped his weapon in anticipation of a thrilling moment.

It soon came. Suddenly the war whoop echoed through the timber, and scores of the savages leaped from their concealment behind the rocks, and, led by the chief came dashing forward.

"Steady, men!" shouted the lieutenant. "Don't fire until I give the word. Frank, you and Bat attend to that chief. Ready, men—*NOW*—!"

A crashing volley shot out from behind the trees and logs. Great gaps were made in the ranks of the savages. White Antelope fell, riddled through and through. Those of his followers who survived, fled back to the shelter of the rocks, with wild yells of rage.

"Good work, men!" shouted Sibley. "A few more doses like that, and they'll learn we are able to hold our own."

"White Antelope won't lead any more charges, anyhow," observed Grouard, refilling the magazine of his Winchester.

"Don't furgit to make a note of that, Finerty," called Big Bat. "That'll liven up your story a little bit."

But Grouard realized, far better than any of the others, unless it were Big Bat, that the sound of battle would hurry scores of keen-eared Sioux and Cheyennes to the spot. Something must be done, or the command would never get out of their predicament alive.

"No use talking," the scout finally exclaimed to Lieutenant Sibley, "we're up against it, good and proper. Those fellows are receiving reenforcements every minute. This firing can be heard for miles, and it's going to bring every Sioux and Cheyenne in this section of the country down upon us."

"What can we do?" anxiously inquired Sibley. "We can't charge them. They're so well sheltered behind those rocks that they'd clean us out in a couple of volleys. The horses are about all down, and we can't make a running fight. We can't lie here and be picked off eventually, and we haven't enough ammunition for any prolonged fight."

"Hark!" The scout lifted a warning hand. "They've recognized me at last; they're calling out my Indian name. Listen!"

From the rocks came a loud voice in the Sioux tongue. "Standing Bear, do you think there are no men but yours in this country? We have got you trapped at last."

"Looks like it," muttered the scout to himself. Then aloud: "They say they'd give a heap to lift my scalp—and they're likely to get it if we stick around here much longer."

The Indian yell was getting stronger, and the Indian bullets

"Big Bat" Baptiste Pourier, civilian scout, regarded by General Crook as the best scout of his day.

were hitting closer every moment. A disabling wound at that time would have been worse than death. "No surrender" was the word passed from man to man along the little skirmish line. Every man of the puny force felt that he would rather blow his own brains out than fall alive into the hands of the infuriated savages—more enraged than ever over the death of their leader. Not a man of the command expected to leave the spot alive. The members of the Sibley scouting party who saw the skull and cross-bones as clearly as that grim emblem seemed portrayed on that 7th day of July, 1876, felt indeed that no subsequent glimpse of grim mortality could hold any greater terrors for them.

One thing was in their favor. None of the command had thus far been struck by an Indian bullet. But Grouard knew —and so did Big Bat and Lieutenant Sibley, that every member of the party was staring death in the face, and that the eternal shadows seemed fast closing around them. It was the indefatigable Grouard—ever resourceful and keen in strategic Indian warfare—who finally suggested to Sibley:

"Lieutenant, the Indians are occupying the passes to the east, west and north of us. We can't possibly make a getaway on horseback. There's an opening on the south which doesn't seem to be occupied by the Indians, and we're got to take advantage of it right away. This position is untenable at the distance we are from Crook's camp. We can't possibly send a man through for relief, and even if we could, we couldn't hold out till a rescue party arrived. The Indians are being reenforced every minute—I can tell that by their yells of encouragement to each other."

"Frank's advice is good," urged Big Bat. "He knows what he's talkin' about, and if you don't follow it, you'll have to take the responsibility of what happens."

Sibley nodded. "I suppose you are right about it. We must get out of here or we'll stay here for good. I'll pass the word for the men to get all their ammunition from their saddlebags first. We'll leave the horses and trust to luck on foot."

Not a second was to be lost if the command were to get away at all. There was nothing to gain, but everything to lose by remaining in their perilous position, to be starved out, smoked out or picked off one by one.

After Grouard and Big Bat had convinced Lieutenant Sibley that a retreat on foot was the only possible chance of saving the lives of the command, the troopers acted with understandable promptness.

"Have the men fire several scattering volleys," advised Grouard. "That will give the Indians the idea that we are still in the same position. The Indians will see that our horses are yet here, and I don't reckon they'd ever think of our trying to escape on foot."

Accordingly a heavy fire was again opened by the troopers, while they silently passed their brave young lieutenant, who was determined to see that every man under his command was in the line of retreat before he himself stirred. As Grouard led them rapidly through the timber, a few scattering shots were fired after which the men rushed and stumbled along through bushes and over rocks, boulders and fallen timber, into the more uneven portion of the rugged mountain fastness. Grouard hurried them through a barricade into which no horseman could penetrate, over the roughest and most inaccessible ground he could select.

Finally a branch of the Tongue River was reached, and as the almost-exhausted men paused to catch breath and drink from the icy-cold stream, they heard in the distance a half-dozen ringing volleys in succession—doubtless the final fire of the Indians before they charged the late position of the troopers, with the expectation of getting their scalps. Their disappointment at finding the birds had flown, leaving their horses behind, can well be imagined.

"Well, I guess we're safe again for a while at least," remarked Grouard, as he surveyed the panting, exhausted troopers, "but they won't give up the pursuit so easy, so let's waste no time in putting more distance between us."

But the command had escaped one danger only to encounter another. Fully fifty miles of lofty mountains, heavily-timbered forests, roaring mountain streams and deep canyons still lay between them and Crook's camp, with hundreds of Indians to be guarded against running into. There was not a morsel of food in the command, as their ammunition had been accounted more necessary than the rations in their saddle-bags, and they could not carry both. They must hang to their rifles and ammunition at whatever cost. Not a man in the command, save Frank Grouard and Big Bat, had ever been in that country, and to these two intrepid scouts must be entrusted the safety of the entire command.

But the brave and dauntless Grouard, ably seconded by Big Bat, conducted the wearied men through that mountain wilderness with a skill which was little short of uncanny. Grouard kept the command on the move, through a bewildering fastness, with his watchful eye ever alert for signs of pursuit, while the men marched and scrambled over impediments which would have been impossible but for the thought that hundreds of blood-thirsty pursuers might overtake them.

Not until midnight would Grouard consent that a halt be made. But there is a limit to human endurance, and that point had now been reached. Bivouacking under the lee of immense overhanging rocks, on the very summit of one of the loftiest peaks of the Big Horn range, a furious mountain storm descended upon the command, which was both spectacular and terrifying. The temperature dropped to the freezing point; the wind roared a perfect gale; trees were uprooted and fell by the hundred, and their noise as they snapped or were uprooted, resembled rapid discharges of field artillery. All the men were dressed in summer campaign clothing and they were soaked by the rain and chilled to the bone by the fury of the elements.

Needless to say, there was no sleeping in the command. Almost before daylight, Grouard had the men again on the move. Shortly thereafter they reached the edge of a tremendous canyon which led into a branch of the Tongue River. This canyon, Grouard said, must be descended in some manner.

"I can't make it!" groaned one young trooper. "Look at them feet—boots all slit to nothing. I'm all in. Let the Injuns have me if they want me, but I'm not going down that steep canyon right now!"

"Well, them is my own sentiments," nodded another. "Only you can make that cup o' coffee two cups."

Grouard was scanning the canyon wall. "The rest of you wait here a few minutes," he said. "There ought to be an easier way of getting down to the river."

Ten minutes later the scout reappeared. "I've found a game trail that seems fairly easy to follow," he announced. "Let's try it."

An hour later the famished and exhausted troopers came into a little open valley on the left bank of the stream, down which Grouard led them as fast as he could walk. It was taking an awful risk, for if discovered by any very considerable war party, the little command could only halt and fight to the death.

But fortune smiled upon them. They waded the stream to the right bank without any interference. Then Grouard spoke:

"We must be about twenty-five miles from camp now, lieutenant. Out there in front, toward the east, lies the plain through which Tongue River flows; but it's full of game, and where there's game in this country you'll find Indians. We can't possibly go that way and hope to escape without a fight —and your men are in no condition for that."

"What's the next best move?" wearily questioned Sibley.

"We've got to climb this precipice on this side of the canyon. It's a tough job, but it's the only chance without running an awful risk—and I've brought your men this far without running an awful risk and without losing a single one by Indian bullets, and I'd like to get them into camp with their hair still on their heads. Are you fellows all game?"

Some objections were offered by the more exhausted of the men. The majority, however, were in favor of Grouard's plan.

"All right; we'll rest here for one hour and then tackle it," he announced.

The wearied troopers threw themselves on the ground, but it seemed scarcely five minutes before the tired members of the command were aroused by Sibley.

"Come, men," he exclaimed, "now let's see what you are

made of. Grouard says it's only about an hour's climb, and once we gain the crest we can see the point, only about twenty miles away, where camp and good grub in plenty awaits us. So buck up, and let nobody lag behind. Keep going. You'll have something to talk about for the rest of your lives after you get back to camp."

Led by the tireless Grouard the ascent of the canyon wall was begun. In an hour's time, just as the scout had predicted, the command stood on the crest, although by this time the men were half-dead from fatigue, famine and thirst. Game had been encountered, but no shooting had been allowed. Grouard said it would undoubtedly bring Indians to the scene to investigate.

Then down into the eastern foothills Grouard led the staggering troopers, without allowing them a respite. Here a dive into a deep valley was made to obtain water—the only refreshment they had on the entire trip after abandoning the horses. Hardly allowing them time to slake their thirst, Grouard again hurried the command up into the hills.

Scarcely had the timber belt been entered, when the scout dropped to the ground, excitedly exclaiming, "Down, down— quick! Every man of you!" at the same time pointing to the north.

"Injuns ag'in, by cracky!" exclaimed Big Bat. "Looks like the varmints are everywhere hereabouts."

Wheeling around the base of the point of the mountain which the command had doubled but a short time before, appeared another strong war-party of the Sioux, riding in open order. They did not appear to be in any hurry and rode leisurely.

"Whew!" exclaimed Sibley, mopping his face, "We didn't get under cover any too quick that time!"

"Well, I've told you we are in constant danger," said Grouard, with just a bit of sarcasm in his voice.

"Do you suppose that bunch will make trouble for us?" anxiously inquired Sibley.

Grouard shook his head.

"Looks to me like it was merely the advance guard of a bigger party. If they don't ride high enough up into the hills to discover our trail, we are perhaps safe. But let's get a good position here among the rocks, and be ready for the worst."

Quickly Lieutenant Sibley gave his orders, placing the men in a position where they could command a good view of the approaching war party, yet well sheltered behind the rocks and boulders. Not a man of the command felt, at that moment, any inclination to try and get away. Hunger, fatigue and exposure had left them in such a weakened condition that a fight would have resulted in the annihilation of the entire party.

But fortunately the Sioux did not discover them, nor advance high enough into the hills to stumble onto their trail. The savages passed along within easy rifle range, blissfully unconscious that two dozen good scalps were within their grasp if they chose to fight for them. But the troopers laid low, and thankfully watched the Indians disappear around a range of low foothills.

Then outraged Nature asserted her rights, and the men, thoroughly exhausted, fell asleep. None but the seemingly tireless Grouard, and the vigilant Big Bat kept watch.

At dark the men were awakened. They were now famished, gaunt, weak, desperate; yet twenty miles of perilous country remained to be traversed, every foot fraught with danger. Grouard was for again taking to the mountain route, but Lieutenant Sibley himself would not agree to it.

"No use, Frank, we never could make it," he remarked with a shake of his head, glancing at his tattered command, all but on the verge of utter collapse.

Grouard smiled. "Well, I'm not overly anxious to try the mountains any more myself. Of course it's safer, but—"

Thereupon the jaded men took their lives in their hands and struck across the plains for Crook's camp. Big Goose Creek was reached in safety at 3 o'clock in the morning. The

Chief Two Moon, Northern Cheyenne leader in the Custer battle.

waters were as cold as snow from the upper ranges could make them; the stream had to be forded, and it was more than waist-deep.

"Lieutenant," wearily exclaimed Sergeant Cornwell, "I just don't want to tackle that ford. I can't swim a stroke anyhow, and I'm too darned weak to get into that strong current. Let me hide out in the brush on this side till you can reach camp and send out a horse by somebody."

"Them's my sentiments to a T," echoed Private Collins. "I'm just all in, and I don't care a hang whether the Injuns get me or not."

In vain did Lieutenant Sibley alternately threaten and coax the two jaded troopers to "Keep a-going." Here were two of his best men, either of whom could face bullets, tomahawks or Indian arrows without flinching, yet they could not be induced by any manner of means, to cross Big Goose Creek.

"All right, you bull-headed fools!" stormed Sibley, "I'm not going to sacrifice the rest of this command for a couple idiots like you fellows, so stay here and lose your hair, if that's your decision."

"Come on, lieutenant," argued Grouard, "if those dubs want to risk losing their hair, let 'em stay here. We ain't out of danger yet."

Reluctantly Lieutenant Sibley gave the order. The main camp was yet twelve or fifteen miles distant, and the men were thoroughly "used up;" their boots were in bad shape from clambering over rocks and rough ground. Finerty stated that it took them four hours to make six miles, so absolutely "done up" were the troopers, unused to "foot-work." They were gaunt and half-starved. Shortly, the command ran across two troopers of the Second Cavalry who had obtained permission to go on a hunt, not knowing the danger from Indian hordes. Lieutenant Sibley sent them into camp for horses and rations, while the troopers threw themselves on the ground to await the arrival of the horses and provisions.

One of the captains, with an assistant, appeared with led horses and some cooked provisions, to which the hungry troopers did full justice. Shortly thereafter the two men who had been left in the underbrush of Big Goose Creek were picked up, and the command reached the main camp on the 9th of July.

Grouard and Big Bat were warmly praised for their efficient work in bringing the command back without the loss of a man, while Lieutenant Sibley was commended for his coolness and sound common sense, and for taking the advice of the two intrepid scouts.

The "Sibley Scout" has, in all the annals of the Indian fighting of the West, been regarded as one of the most thrilling and dangerous ever made.

CHAPTER 9

THEODORE W. GOLDIN'S EXPERIENCE IN CUSTER BATTLE WATER DETAIL.

At the battle of the Little Big Horn, in southeastern Montana, June 25-26, 1876, commonly known as "Custer's Last Fight," Theodore W. Goldin served with Troop G, under Major Marcus A. Reno. He has not attempted to give the details of the fight in the river bottom between the three troops under Major Reno and the Sioux Indians in which he took part, but relates a most interesting account of what he experienced in the fight on the bluffs after the disastrous battle along the river. This is the true story of the "water detail." It differs quite materially from other spectacular accounts told by other troopers who made the trip to the river to get water for the wounded. In a letter from Mr. Goldin to the author, he states: "According to others who claim to have been members of other water parties on June 26, 1876, our trip lacks practically every spectacular, sanguinary element possessed by the others. Of course I might have drawn on my imagination and interspersed some sharp fighting and many hair-breadth escapes; but I preferred sticking to the actual facts and telling the story as it has remained in my memory all these years."

Modestly related, but teeming with interest, is the story of Trooper Goldin, who won the coveted Medal of Honor for the daring act which he and the other members of the detail he accompanied performed (they also were given the Medal of Honor) in their heroic attempt to relieve their wounded comrades, suffering and dying from thirst and wounds under a pitiless burning sun on those sagebrush-covered bluffs above the Little Big Horn river seventy-six years ago. It is a most valuable contribution to the history of this most disastrous battle in American Indian warfare and should be carefully preserved by every student of frontier history.

—The Author

"I HAVE BEEN ASKED MANY TIMES to relate the experience of the party I happened to accompany to the river to procure water for the wounded men of Major Reno's command on the second day of the battle of the Little Big Horn.

"Compared with the stories told by men who claimed (and doubtless rightly so) to have made the same trips, always led me to think that both the trips our party made were so prosaic, so lacking in the elements of sensation and heroism, as to be almost without interest.

"I think we may safely start on the theory that there were not twenty canteens of water in either Reno's or Benteen's squadrons.

"Our march on June 24th had been through a country where little but alkali water was to be found. Then came our brief halt, and the cooking of supper—each man for himself; and the little water we did have was largely used for this purpose.

"Following this came that grueling night march, with not a sign of water until we halted, before daybreak of the 25th, at the foot of the Rosebud divide, a high ridge separating the valley of the Rosebud from that of the Big and Little Big Horn rivers. We found some water here, out of which coffee was made, but when issued we found it so strongly alkaline that we could not drink it. Even the horses, thirsty as they must have been, turned away from the water.

"When the march was resumed, some hours later, and we crossed the divide and came into the valley of what was later known as Reno Creek, its rough, broken slopes stretching away to the timber in our front, fully twelve or fifteen miles distant, which we were told bordered the Little Horn (or Little Big Horn), our advance—at least, that of Reno's squadron—had no opportunity of either filling our canteens or watering our horses, had water been available.

"Nor was opportunity offered the men as they crossed the Little Big Horn, save for a very brief halt to allow the horses

Theodore W. Goldin, Medal of Honor trooper of Troop G, Reno Battalion.
a member of the water detail. Photo taken in 1916.

to drink. At this time some of the men managed to fill, or partially fill, their canteens with water roiled up by the plunging horses.

"After Benteen's squadron had joined Reno, and the pack-train and rear guard came up (the latter nearly an hour after Benteen's arrival, which afforded Reno's men an opportunity to replenish their depleted stock of ammunition), an advance was made, headed by Captain Weir and D Troop, and followed in fairly good order by the remainder of the troops, the pack-train bringing up the rear. A considerable number of the men were on foot, their horses having been either shot or stampeded in the fight in the river bottom at the time of Reno's first attack.

"I recall one particular movement, noted at the time, and to which, many years later, Benteen referred in a letter to me, and again in a personal conversation with him at his home in Atlanta, Georgia, after his retirement. It was as follows:

"Every time Benteen's troop reached an eminence of any height, he brought them 'front into line,' and the men cheered and waved their hats. Benteen, telling me this, said he had it done in the hopes of attracting the attention of Custer and his command, that they might know where we were, and that we were trying to reach him.

"As a fact, I believe undisputed, Custer had by this time been wiped out, as Captain Weir had not advanced any great distance down a considerable arroyo, when he encountered and engaged large bodies of Indians, seemingly flushed with a victory we could not then understand.

"The story of this encounter and the subsequent retreat of the entire command, has been so often, and so much better related than I can tell it, that I will not attempt any description of it. Suffice it to say, that keeping up a running fight for a mile or more, the Indians appeared almost momentarily in larger numbers, and became more and more aggressive.

"This retreat was made with the one thought of finding some place that would afford a slight shelter for men and animals, and which could be defended with some prospects of success.

"Finally, after falling back beyond, yet not entirely out of rifle range of a high bluff that reared its head above the many smaller ones around it, Benteen came to Lieutenant Wallace and grimly remarked:

" 'Well, Wallace, this looks like the best place we have passed. No use going any further. Deploy your troop, the right resting there (pointing with his hand) and stand 'em off. I'll send you help, and tell you more about it when I find out myself.'

"In obedience to this order, G Troop was deployed and opened on the Indians as opportunity offered. We were shortly afterward reinforced by K Troop, which had been covering our backward movement, and later, and during the night or early the following morning, B Troop, under Captain Mc-Dougall took its position on our left, his deployed line extending to a point which commanded a considerable view of the land toward the river, as well as some deep arroyos leading upward from the river below, and not far from the point where Reno crossed when he left the valley after his supply of ammunition was much depleted, and he had failed to receive the support he had been led to expect.

"It was now quite late in the afternoon, but the fighting was kept up, the Indians surrounding us on every side, and waging an almost constant and relentless fire.

"I cannot give accurately the position of the other troops, aside from those in our immediate vicinity, as we were kept entirely too busy to do much sight-seeing or pay many social calls. I recall, however, that Captain Benteen, with H Troop, occupied a rather isolated and exposed position, on what might be called the right of our line. This position, although a difficult one to hold, gave him command of a considerable bit of country, and a slope leading toward the river, at the edge of which several considerable ravines seemed to converge.

"We had mighty little opportunity to dig in and entrench ourselves, and made use of such natural cover as we could find, as the fighting was fast and furious every minute of the time.

"When we made our final stand, horses and mules were placed in almost a circle at a point that seemed to offer the most protection; and within this protection the hospital was located, and it was not long before Dr. Porter, our only remaining surgeon, had his hands more than full, as the wounded men came drifting in from all parts of the lines.

"In those early days we had no such hospital service as the army of today enjoys. There were no attendants, trained in their work, but the less severely wounded rendered such assistance as they could to Dr. Porter.*

"Operations and dressings were of the crudest; there was no water to cleanse wounds; no anesthetics to alleviate pain, but hour after hour he worked, seeking as best he could to stifle the pain and suffering.

"Night finally came on, and save for occasional scattered shots, the firing ceased; but any unusual movement inside our lines was sure to bring a fusillade of shots from every direction. There was no thought of sleep, and officers and men, side by side, with tin plates, tin cups, knives or whatever else came to hand, spent the hours in digging in and preparing for the battle we knew was sure to come with the early morning light. It came with a vengeance, and with it, added casualties in both dead and wounded.

"Some time during the latter part of the morning, a little group gathered together in the shelter of the corral, having come in with wounded comrades, and were now awaiting a lull in the fighting to rejoin their troops.

---

* Of the tireless devotion and heroic work done by Dr. H. R. Porter, but 26 years of age at that time, enough cannot be said. Dr. Lord and Dr. DeWolf had both been killed earlier in the fight, and Porter was the only surviving surgeon. For five or six days and nights he did not have his clothes off, nor get a wink of sleep, having all the wounded to care for aboard the "Far West" on its trip down the Missouri.

"From where they crouched they could hear the moaning of sorely-stricken comrades, interrupted by incessant calls for water. Water! Yes, but how was it to be obtained? Here we were on the bluffs, several hundred feet above the rushing current of the river; and, so far as we knew, every foot of that distance was under the watchful eye of a cunning foe. To reach the stream seemed an impossibility; and yet we were thinking of nothing else but the possibility of answering those piteous calls which again and again came to our ears.

"Just at this time, Captain Benteen passed, and overhearing a bit of conversation, paused, and after listening a moment, said:

" 'Men, I haven't seen a shot fired nor seen an Indian in that ravine between McDougall's line and mine. I don't know whether you can make it or not, but it looks like the only chance. If you try, give me a signal, and McDougall and I will give you all the help we can by a rapid fire barrage.'

"He passed on toward McDougall's line. For a moment no one spoke, and then Mike Madden, the saddler of K Troop, said, 'Say, fellers, we're a-taking' about ninety-eight chances right here. What's the matter wid makin' it ninety-nine, and tryin' to git thim fellers some wather?"

"In a moment the little group separated, coming together a few minutes later, each man with as many canteens as he thought he could bring up that steep trail. Some one had an inspiration and came lugging a small camp kettle.

"At this late date, fifty-six years after the occurrence, I will not pretend to give the names of all who were in the little party; but I recall Madden and another man of K Troop, Dwyer, Campbell and myself from G Troop, and I think one, or possibly two, from Troop B.

"There was no officer with us, no one really in command, and the only thing savoring of a command was Madden's 'Come on, fellers, lave us run!' as he took a hitch in his trousers and dashed across a little open space to a point where the ravine sheltered us from sight.

"We all made the rush in safety, save little Campbell, of G Troop, who went down with a ball in his shoulder, just a few feet from the shelter of the ravine. One or two of the men halted and turned back to his assistance, but he pluckily called out, 'Go on, boys; I can make it back some way.'

"Once in the shelter of the ravine, which we saw was deep and crooked, we instinctively strung out into something like skirmish formation, every man on the alert, carbines at a ready and Madden in the lead. Our descent was necessarily slow, as we cautiously scouted every turn in the tortuous ravine. We finally reached the bottom without encountering the enemy or seeing any signs, save an occasional pony track crossing from some side ravine, and even these seemed many hours old.

"Once at the bottom of the hill, we took stock of the situation. We noticed over a bit to our right a projection reaching out from the bluff to a point near the river, and which apparently promised protection from every direction save right across the river. We observed many Indians moving about on the other side, but it was evident we had not been discovered.

"Seeking such shelter as we could find, we held a hurried council, and decided that our best plan was for a couple of the men to take the camp kettle, make a dash for the river, fill it and get back under cover and transfer the water to the canteens in greater safety.

"Two by two the men took their turns at this hazardous work; but to our surprise not a shot was fired at us, and in a short time the canteens were filled, and after a steep climb we regained the shelter of the hospital, and the water was turned over to those in charge and we rejoined our commands.

"Later in the day, along about the middle of the afternoon I should judge, word was passed down the line asking if the men who were in the former party would chance it again, as water was much needed. To a man, practically the same party assembled at the corral, and, with possibly one or two additions, made a rush for the ravine, and cautiously, although a

The gully used by the water detail to reach the river. Looking west from near Reno Hill.

bit emboldened by our first experience, scouted our way to the place we had found so convenient on our previous trip. Bringing the hidden camp kettle into use again, we adopted the same plans used before so successfully, and finally had all the canteens but three or four filled.

"At this point, Madden turned to the group, saying:

" 'Fellers, there's no use a-goin' back wid any impties; thim b'yes will need ivery danged dhrop av wather we kin git.'

"Then grasping the camp kettle, he turned to Dwyer of G Troop, who had been his pardner in the previous journeys, and said:

" 'Come on, Patsy, l'ave us thry it wanst more,' and in an instant they were off.

"They made the run successfully, filled the kettle and dashed for safety. They were almost within the shelter of the point, when a withering volley was fired from the bushes on the opposite side, and poor Madden went down. So close was he to safety, that when he fell his head and the upper part of his body were inside the shelter.

"Dwyer seemed to be unhit, but the old camp kettle was spouting water from half a dozen bullet holes. Dwyer staggered into cover with the kettle, and while most of us sprang to cover and returned the fire, which, to our surprise was not continued, Dwyer and another of the party sought to save what they could of the precious fluid, and others drew Madden to safety.

"A hasty examination disclosed that Madden's leg was broken twice between the ankle and knee. For a few moments we crouched under cover, expecting further attack, but as none came, we concluded that the first volley was from a passing party moving down the valley, and as only Madden and Dwyer were in sight, doubtless concluded they were not worth bothering over.

"Now came the problem of getting Madden up the hill and into the hospital. It seemed as though we were already burdened with all we could manage. Madden came to the rescue (as he thought) with the remark, 'I'll tell yez phwat to do; 'lave me me carbine wid some shells, and yez g'wan up wid th' wather. Th' b'yes will be lookin' fer it, and then yez can come back afther me; and if any av thim red divils come, I'll be gittin' some av thim whoile they're a-gittin' me.'

"That suggestion was not to be considered, and after a brief council, one of the men took an extra gun or two, others divided the surplus canteens between them, and two of the men raised Madden to their shoulders. Mercifully to him, he fainted, and was spared, in part, the agonizing pain of that terrible return journey. The trail was rough and steep, and bearers had to be changed every little while; but finally—just how I cannot tell to this day—we made the hospital and turned both water and the wounded Madden over to the surgeon.

"Some time later, and after the Indians had left us and were disappearing up the valley, I had occasion to visit the hospital. There I found Madden stretched out on a blanket, a saddle for a pillow, his face white and drawn with pain, even under the coating of dust and powder smoke, his leg amputated at the knee. I learned later that the operation had been performed without the use of an anesthetic, and General

Godfrey tells us that after the operation the surgeon gave Madden a stiff horn of brandy. Swallowing it, Mike smacked his lips and feebly exclaimed:

" 'Docther, give me another wan av thim and cut off me other leg!'

"I cannot vouch for this story, but have no reason to doubt the word of his troop commander.

"When I found Madden I asked how he was feeling, and he replied weakly, 'I'm f'alin 'moighty bad, me b'y.' I tried to condole with him, but he came back at me instantly with the remark:

" 'Av coorse it's bad loosin' th' leg, but it isn't th' pain that's makin' me feel bad; it's in me hear-r-rt. Fer many a year I've been a-ridin' and a-fightin' under the Old Flag and wid th' old outfit, and 'tis many a foine shindy we've had, too, but now I'm nothin' but a poor, damned wan-legged sojer, and 'tis no more ridin' and foightin' I'll be doin'. That's what hurts. Do yez know, me b'y, if it wuz only for hearin' th' sigh av satisfaction av thim poor felleys whin they twishted their lips around th' mouths of thim old canteens, I'm be damn near willin' to go back and give thim a chanst at th' other fut.'

"I have understood that other parties made this trip for water, and according to the stories I have heard and read, their experiences were more sanguinary than ours. Of these trips I do not pretend to write, as I know nothing about them.

"I have often talked with some of the fellows who were in our party, and the sentiment almost unanimously expressed was that we could have done no less than we did and retain our self-respect. There were others—hundreds perhaps—who could have taken the same chances we did, had the opportunity offered. I have always felt that most, if not all of us, regarded the possibilities of leaving that hill alive mighty slim, and one chance, more or less, did not change the situation materially.

"In that hospital were wounded comrades—buddies and

friends with whom we had fought, scouted and hunted for many moons. They were calling piteously for water, and I feel that any man who wouldn't have taken the chances we did, was unworthy to wear the uniform of a soldier."

CHAPTER 10

 TWO MODEST HEROES OF THE
CUSTER EXPEDITION.

IN ALL THE ACCOUNTS which have been written of the battle of the Little Big Horn, but little mention ever has been made of the prominent parts taken by two modest heroes of Custer's last campaign, Dr. H. R. Porter, a civilian surgeon who accompanied the command, and Capt. Grant Marsh, of the steamer "Fur West," the boat chartered by the government to carry supplies for the expedition to the head of navigation.

Dr. Porter was detailed to accompany Major Reno's battalion, after Custer had divided his forces. When Reno made his charge out of the timber for the high hills across the Little Big Horn River, several men were left behind in the excitement and confusion. Dr. Porter was one of this number.

He was administering to a dying soldier in a little clump of bushes, after the command had worked back into the timber along the stream. Charley Reynolds, Custer's beloved scout, had just been shot dead, after shouting a warning to Dr. Porter that the Indians were shooting at him. The doctor's orderly had departed, and he was totally unarmed. The main command had passed on the run, and the surgeon was left alone, with all escape seemingly cut off.

The din of battle was sounding all about him—the whoops of the victorious savages, the crack of carbines and the shouts of the charging cavalrymen. The trooper to whom Dr. Porter was administering, had given his last gasp, and then the surgeon realized the extreme danger of his own position. Bullets were cutting the brush all about him, and the alarm of death was sounding on every hand.

In some unaccountable manner Dr. Porter managed to reach the river bank, leading his horse, unharmed. Indians dashed past within ten feet of him, but paid no attention to him, whether because he was unnoticed in the smoke and dust clouds or because the savages were too intent on reaching the front, where the mass of the troopers were.

The doctor's horse was a powerful black animal, which, frightened by the firing and the yells of the Indians, plunged and reared as if mad. The doctor realized that if he lost his hold on the bridle rein, his chances of escape were absolutely gone, and that death would be his portion if the horse broke away before he could get into the saddle.

Leap after leap did the surgeon make to gain his seat on the animal's back, but the horse was so badly frightened that it reared and plunged from side to side, evading his efforts for some time. Finally, by one supreme effort, Dr. Porter managed to get one foot in the stirrup. Away flew his charger like the wind, the rider gained the full seat, and, leaning low across the animal's neck, ran a gauntlet where the chance of escape was but a thousand to one.

The black charger with its low-lying rider was quickly detected as it fairly flew toward the river, and a storm of leaden hail fell about them. Dr. Porter had absolutely no control of his mount, but the animal was bearing him toward his friends and safety. It was only a half mile at the most to the river crossing, and the frenzied animal reached that point in safety, dashing madly into the stream, and though a rain of rifle balls was showered about the pair, the animal splashed through, rushed up the opposite bank and gained the Reno command. Horse and rider were saved. It was destiny.

Throughout the afternoon of June 25th, as well as all that night and during the 26th, Dr. Porter was conspicuous for his utter disregard of hostile bullets. There was no other surgeon. Dr. De Wolf, another physician who had accom-

Dr. H. R. Porter, only surviving surgeon of Reno's command. At the age of 26, he had the responsibility of caring for the 52 wounded evacuated on the "Far West."

panied the Reno command, had been killed while climbing the bluffs in the retreat from the river bottom. Dr. Porter was but 26 years of age, yet he performed all his tasks with the coolness and courage of a seasoned Indian campaigner, working in such a heroic manner as to call forth the admiration of the entire command.

When General Terry and General Gibbon arrived on the field, early on the morning of June 27th, there were fifty-two wounded men in the Reno command to be carried many miles on hand-litters down to the steamer "Far West" lying at the mouth of the Little Big Horn. From there they were to be carried as fast as steam could urge the boat, to Bismarck, nearly one thousand miles away, down rivers filled with treacherous sand bars and innumerable snags and other dangerous obstacles.

Captain Grant Marsh—the gamest, nerviest pilot that ever ran a boat on the Missouri River—had already performed an exploit unequaled in the history of steamboating in the West, when he pushed his noted craft up to the mouth of the Little Big Horn, to be as near Custer as possible with supplies and extra ammunition. The news of Custer's defeat had already been brought to the boat by "Curley," one of the Crow scouts loaned to Custer by General Gibbon. "Curley" had succeeded in escaping from the battlefield (doubtless before the actual fighting began).

Captain Marsh, therefore, was well prepared to accommodate the wounded men as far as the size of his boat would allow. Grass had been cut along the river bank and thickly strewn over the deck to serve as a mattress, and heavy tarpaulins were laid over this. The wounded troopers were then tenderly carried aboard and laid out in rows, and Dr. Porter was detailed to accompany them on the down-river trip to Bismarck, although he had been working without sleep ever since the battle.

"The "Far West" was in a strange land and on an unknown river, for it must be understood that that section of the country in 1876 was as unknown as the heart of Africa. The Little Big Horn River was scarcely more than a creek, full of dangerous turns and curves, and Captain Marsh keenly felt the great responsibility which rested upon his broad shoulders. The utmost skill would be required to carry these gallant wounded heroes to their destination without accident. The steamboat had been fully "wooded up," and everything was ready for the long race with death.

Before the order came to cast off the lines, General Terry was closeted with Captain Marsh for some moments in the latter's cabin. The general instructed the veteran steamboat captain to use all the skill at his command, as there were treacherous rivers to navigate the entire distance. First, there was the Little Big Horn to traverse down to the Big Horn itself; thence, the course would be down the Big Horn to the Yellowstone; thence, down the Yellowstone into the Missouri. It was indeed a long and circuitous route which had to be followed. General Terry told Captain Marsh that every wounded man on his boat "was the victim of a blunder—a sad, terrible blunder."

It was about daylight on the 30th of June when Captain Marsh was ready to start with his precious cargo. His engineer was George Foulk, a veteran at the levers, and the pilots were Dave Campbell and Captain Marsh himself, with Mate Ben Thompson as second in command. All these men deserve the utmost praise and commendation for the skill and knowledge of navigation they displayed on that remarkable run.

When the boat had started down stream, Captain Marsh gave orders to keep up a full head of steam—"to the very limit of safety." It was fifty-three miles to the mouth of the Big Horn where it emptied into the Yellowstone, and Captain Marsh was kept busy dodging in and out among the numerous islands which infested the Big Horn, and as he had been over the route but once before (on the up trip) to such a point, it required all the skill at his command to keep the boat in the channel of the narrow stream.

Grant Marsh, commander of the steamboat "Far West."

However, late in the afternoon the steamer safely reached the Yellowstone and tied up to the bank where General Gibbon's wagon train was parked. Here the boat was obliged to lay until late in the afternoon of July 3d to ferry Gibbon's command over to the opposite bank of the river, that officer's column not arriving until July 2d.

By this time fourteen of the wounded men had so far recovered as to be able to be carried ashore and remain with Gibbon's command. It was about 900 miles from this point to the destination of the "Far West."

About 5 o'clock on the afternoon of July 3d, the steamboat headed down the Yellowstone. Under ordinary conditions no craft ever traveled at night on this stream, because of the snags and sandbars which they were likely to encounter, and because of the ever-shifting channel of both the Yellowstone and the Missouri; but there was to be no tying up at dark with Captain Marsh on this trip.

It so happened that the Yellowstone was carrying a good volume of water, but, nevertheless, it was no child's play to drive a steamboat at twenty miles an hour down a channel, which was perilous enough in the daytime and under ordinary conditions. The boat was rushed through the water under a full head of steam, and on some occasions was so crowded for speed that the steam-gauge reached the danger mark.

Captain Marsh and Dave Campbell took turn about at the wheel in four-hour shifts. Down below in the engine room, sooty and begrimed firemen fed wood into the fireboxes until the boat quivered from stem to stern under the force with which she was driven through the water, while the shriek of the "Far West's" whistle re-echoed between the cliffs, sending herds of deer, elk and buffalo on wild stampedes. Occasionally the bottom of the boat came in contact with a rock just below the surface, or struck a projecting snag, with such force as to throw the deck-hands off their feet. Sometimes the nose of the little craft would seemingly be on the point of burying itself in the bank, when a lucky turn of the wheel would bring the boat about so that her sides would scrape along the bank of the stream. It was a wild race with death, and Captain Marsh was taking every possible chance in order to get his cargo of human lives into the hands of doctors and nurses in the least possible time.

Meantime, Dr. Porter was having his hands full, walking

Steamboat "Far West," the supply boat of the Custer Expedition. A noted craft, used to carry Reno's 52 wounded to Fort Lincoln from the mouth of the Little Big Horn.

up and down between the rows of wounded troopers, soothing a suffering man here or ministering to a groaning trooper there. He worked without interruption and without rest, and only one man died on the trip.

Finally the "Far West" raced out into the broader Missouri River. At Fort Buford a stop of but a moment was made to land a wounded Indian scout. The boat put off again before questions were half answered by the excited people who crowded to the boat and begged for news of the awful disaster. Down the Missouri spun the "Far West" once more until Fort Stevenson was reached, where a brief halt was made. At this point Captain Marsh draped the derrick and jack-staff of the boat in black, under orders from General Terry, in honor of the dead and wounded.

This was on the afternoon of July 5th, and at 11 o'clock that night, the "Far West" bumped against the wharf at Bismarck, after a trip of nearly one thousand miles in just fifty-four hours, having established a record never before or since equalled by any other craft in the history of steamboating on the Missouri River or any of its tributaries.

Hardly had the "Far West" touched the wharf before officers and men were running up the streets to arouse the sleeping populace. The news of the appalling disaster fell like a thunderbolt among them. The news could hardly be believed. A. C. Lounsberry, editor of the Bismarck "Tribune," was aroused from his sleep, with J. M. Carnahan, the only telegrapher in the little frontier city. With Captain Marsh, Dr. Porter, Colonel Smith and others, they hurried to the telegraph office, where Carnahan sat down to the key and scarcely raised himself from his chair for over twenty-two hours. The remarkable piece of telegraphy done by this modest "knight of the key," was one of such magnitude as to call for the highest commendation. Lounsberry wrote his story as given to him by Dr. Porter and others, and Carnahan clicked it over the wires to the New York "Herald" as fast as it was handed him. More than 15,000 words were transmitted, and it cost the "Herald" over $3000 in telegraph tolls—but it was worth it! Stories like the Custer battle did not materialize every day in the week!*

To the tireless efforts of Dr. Porter and Captain Grant Marsh, the highest possible credit and commendation should be given. Both men passed away several years ago, but they will ever be remembered by those who know and realize the value of their courage and bravery.

---

* While the Bismarck Tribune has always contended that it sent the first news east of the Custer disaster, Andrew J. Fisk, whose story is related in Chapter 12, in correspondence with the author several years ago, took issue with the claims of the Tribune. Mr. Fisk has since died. The reader must form his own conclusions after reading both stories.

CHAPTER 11

WAS THERE A CUSTER SURVIVOR?

DID ANY HUMAN BEING ESCAPE DEATH of those who accompanied the five troops of the Seventh Cavalry, under personal command of Gen. George A. Custer, in the fatal battle of the Little Big Horn?

For seventy-five years this has been a greatly discussed question. Time and again men have come into the limelight to claim that they were with the Custer forces, and that they alone escaped death. To the knowledge of the writer, fourteen men have, at various times since that remarkable engagement with the Sioux, claimed that they accompanied the Custer command when it went into action, and each claimant stated that he, and he alone, escaped from the battlefield alive.

None of them, however, have been able to prove their claims, and their stories are without foundation. One Alfred Chapman had for years claimed that he was Custer's guide, was on his way to join the command and only reached the vicinity in time to watch the battle through a spy-glass a mile away, from behind the sagebrush, and that he there saw the Custer command killed to a man!

The writer, through various authentic sources, including the War Department, proved in a public statement to the Hunter-Trader-Trapper magazine (for whom it was written by the author), that the man was an impostor, and the editor of the magazine invited him to come forth and back up his assertions, which he never did. It was shown that no man by his name served with the Seventh Cavalry in any capacity whatever, much less chief guide of the expedition, which distinction belonged to Charley Reynolds, whose courage, skill and frontiersmanship had been tried to the core by Custer on numerous previous occasions. Many officers, who served with the Reno command, became interested in the discussion. Records were searched, but the name of Alfred Chapman could not be found—not even as a mule whacker! None of the officers of the Seventh Cavalry ever heard of the man, and Mrs. Custer herself, in a personal letter to the author, thanked him for unmasking the impostor and branding his claims as preposterous and absolutely false.

When General Custer partly divided his forces, he personally took command of Troops C, E, I, F and L. It consisted of about 220 officers and enlisted men. Of this entire command none was ever seen alive again, with the single exception of "Curley," one of the Crow Indian scouts who had been loaned to Custer by General Gibbon, on June 22d, when Custer left the main body of troops. It has always been alleged that Curley escaped from the battle in the dust, smoke and general confusion, by disguising himself in a Sioux blanket. This claim is absured. The Sioux were not overlooking anybody on that particular day, and if Curley ever did make such claims, they can be taken with several grains of salt. Curley's get-away was obviously made before the actual fighting commenced.

But did any white man—soldier, officer or civilian scout or packer,—escape alive?

During the early part of 1921, the author received a most interesting letter from Gen. E. S. Godfrey, then residing at Cookstown, N. J., who, in 1876, was a lieutenant in the Seventh Cavalry, and who accompanied Benteen's command when Custer separated the regiment. The movements of both Benteen's and Reno's battalions are familiar to most students of the Custer battle. Reno attacked the upper end of the great Indian encampment, which, it was later learned, contained

The author, left, shown with the Crow Indian scout Curley at the latter's cabin along the Little Big Horn. Photo taken in 1913.

nearly 15,000 men, women and children, of which, it has been variously estimated, from 3500 to 5000 were fighting warriors.

Reno's command consisted of just 112 men. He went into the battle confidently, and with the promise of the support of Custer and his five troops of cavalry. He received no support whatever from Custer, who left him in an attempt to reach the lower end of the village and attack it at that point, without giving Major Reno any notice of the move. Reno fought gamely until he saw that he was being surrounded by over a thousand of the savages, when he ordered his men to mount, charge through the Indians and gain the high bluffs across the river, a mile distant, and there make a stand where there was a better chance of success than in the thick timber and underbrush along the river. On the bluffs Reno was joined by Benteen's battalion.

In this movement, Major Reno lost twenty-nine men. Captain Godfrey was with the Reno forces on the hill all through the fighting of June 25th and throughout the following day, until at the approach of the commands of Generals Terry and Gibbon, the Indians struck camp, drew off and scattered. The Custer and Reno dead were buried on June 27th (as decently as was possible with the few implements at hand) and the wounded, fifty-two in number, were brought down to the steamboat "Far West," lying at the junction of the Big and Little Horn, a few miles north of the battleground, and carried down to Bismárck, Dakota, and Fort Lincoln, opposite Bismarck.

In his letter to the author, Gen. Godfrey stated that in connection with the escape of anyone in Gen. Custer's command, he wished to make of record the following:

"About the last of July or the first of August, 1876, Gen. Terry moved his command from Pease Bottom down the Yellowstone River, opposite, and just above, the mouth of the Rosebud. Here some infantry troops were ferried to the south bank of the stream.

Lieut. H. M. Harrington, Troop C. Despite extensive search, his body was never located or identified.

"Soon after, I heard a rumor that they had found a dead horse that was fully equipped, except bridle, and that it was a Seventh Cavalry horse. I went to the steamer at once to investigate. I crossed to the south bank of the stream and found the horse. It was impossible to determine if it was a sorrel or light bay animal. Halter, lariat, saddle, saddle-blanket and saddle bags were intact; and strapped to the cantle was the small grain bag with which the Seventh Cavalry had provided itself. The oats in the bag had not been disturbed. The saddle bags were empty. I was told that when first discovered, the carbine of the rider was there. The horse had been shot in the forehead, which must have been fatal on the spot.

"While I was examining the equipments for some identification, the steamer whistled for the return trip, and I had to leave and get back to camp. The next day I returned to continue my investigation, but found that the horse had been stripped. The animal was lying on its left side, and where the body touched the soil was so decomposed that the brands could not be identified. Endeavors to locate the taken equipment were in vain, and I never learned any thing further, either of horse or rider.

"Here was the one chance that I know of where a man may have escaped the fate of his comrades. I have met several who claim to have escaped, and have heard of many others, but never one who identified himself by this incident.

"Respectfully,
(Signed) "E. S. GODFREY.

"Cookstown, N. J., May 2, 1921."

General Godfrey further added in his letter:
"In the last few months, only four more 'living survivors of Custer's command' have cropped out."

In compiling the list of killed of the Custer command, every officer was accounted for with the exception of Lieutenants Harrington, Porter and Sturgis, whose bodies never were found, at least, not recognized. Nothing was ever learned of their fate, and while it has always been supposed that they were killed, but possibly not identified, yet, it is not beyond reason that all or one of them may have escaped, badly wounded, to die in some out-of-the-way place. Some writers have insisted that they were doubtless captured alive and tortured to death that night in the Indian village, which was flushed with its bloody victory over Custer. The Sioux, however, always have maintained that they took no prisoners on the occasion of the Little Big Horn fight.

Who rode the solitary animal found dead by Captain Godfrey a few weeks after the Custer fight, on the lonely banks of the Yellowstone River, which carried Seventh Cavalry equipment? Was its rider one of Custer's men, and who was he?

CHAPTER 12

A GREAT NEWSPAPER "SCOOP."

ONE OF THE GREATEST NEWSPAPER "SCOOPS" or "beats" ever made in modern journalism occurred on July 4th, 1876, at Helena, Montana, when Andrew J. Fisk, at that time Associated Press correspondent and general newspaper writer, first gave to the world the fate of General George A. Custer and all of his immediate command, who were wiped out on the banks of the Little Big Horn River, Montana, on June 25th of the Centennial year, by the Sioux and allied tribes under Chiefs Gall, Crow King, Crazy Horse and Two Moons.

News gathering seventy-five years ago had not been brought down to as fine a point as at the present day. There were no telephones, automobiles, bicycles or other means of rapid transit, and news dissemination by telegraph, even, was almost in its infancy. The West was a comparative wilderness, teeming with Indians, outlaws and tough characters in general; railroads were few and the country bordering on Montana and Wyoming was but sparsely settled.

Nine days had elapsed from the time Custer met his fate before the information was spread broadcast through the medium of the press, and a longer time doubtless would have elapsed but for the pluck and grit of a rancher on the Yellowstone River named Horace Countryman, himself an old Indian fighter and scout of the early days. Countryman rode 180 miles with but one change of horses to reach Helena and spread the tidings of Custer's fate.

At that time Countryman lived at Stillwater, an old stage station on the Yellowstone. To Countryman's ranch arrived "Muggins" Taylor, a scout from the battlefield on the Little Big Horn. Taylor was completely exhausted and unable to proceed until the next day, having barely escaped with his life after leaving the battlefield. He was discovered and pursued by a band of Indians, and but for the fact that he managed to guide his horse to the junction of the Big and Little Horn Rivers, where the supply steamer, "Far West," was waiting for orders from General Terry, in command of the expedition, Taylor would have been overhauled and killed, as his horse was completely winded when soldiers on the boat caught sight of him dashing toward them, firing his revolver to attract attention, while in close pursuit came a bunch of Sioux Indians, who drew up and retired into the hills upon seeing that their quarry was in safe hands.

Noting Taylor's exhausted condition upon his arrival at Stillwater, Countryman volunteered to bring the news to Bozeman, where he supposed he would be able to find a government wire and rush the news to Washington.

But when Countryman, on a foam-flecked horse, dashed into Bozeman, he found the government wire down and useless. There was nothing to do but continue on to Helena. Securing a fresh mount, Countryman scurried away, and arrived in Helena about noon on the Fourth of July, "all in" and fairly fainting from the exhaustion of his long ride.

On legal holidays, in those times, newspaper editors were not so eager to spread their pages before their readers, consequently the force of the Helena *Herald* was out "celebrating" the day and the office was closed.

It was about 12 o'clock, noon, that Andrew J. Fisk left his home and went down town to see if there was anything of news importance to wire the Associated Press. Idly sitting in his office, talking with some friends, he was suddenly startled by the appearance of a dusty, begrimed rancher, who fairly tumbled from his saddle in front of the *Herald* building, stag-

gered up the steps and reeled into Fisk's office. It was Horace
Countryman. As he dropped into a chair, Fisk sprang to his
side, exclaiming:

"Countryman, old friend, what in God's name is the
matter? What has happened?"

Countryman could but gasp in reply: "Custer's command
all wiped out on the Little Big Horn by the Sioux!"

Fisk was horror-struck, but grasping immediately the vital
importance of the news he said: "Have you told anybody
about it, except we folks here in this office?"

"Not a soul," whispered Countryman, with a shake of the
head.

"Boys," exclaimed Fisk, turning to his friends, "not a word
of this on the street to anybody. This is the biggest scoop
of the year!" Then turning to Countryman, he added:

"Come into my private office and give me the details as
you have them."

A brief conversation ensued, then Fisk said: "You stay
here and I'll go out to a restaurant and get you a bite, and
also see if I can't scare up enough of the force to get out
an extra."

Fisk hurried across the street, and quickly returned with
coffee and sandwiches. Then he rushed back, from one
saloon to another, and in a short time managed to round up a
sufficient number of the composing room force of the *Herald*
to answer his purpose. These men hastily began to distribute
type and get ready to spread a piece of news that was cal-
culated to make all Helena gasp with dismay and horror.

Fisk then hurried into his own private office, where Countryman had revived himself with food, and then closing and
locking the door, the newspaper man began to take down
in long-hand the thrilling recitals of the battle as conveyed to
Countryman by "Muggins" Taylor, the scout. Countryman
dictated rapidly and fluently.

"There was one sentence in particular that struck me for-
cibly," said Fisk, in recounting the story. "It was this.

" 'Curley, the Crow scout, and the only person in the battle who escaped to bring the news, said the firing was very rapid, and sounded like the snapping of the threads in the tearing of a blanket.' "

As fast as Fisk was able to dash off his copy he hurried the pages up to the composing room, where the foreman separated them into "takes" which the compositors rapidly turned into type. Fisk was so excited that he forgot all about his duty to the Associated Press, and then became mindful of the fact that he was not even a member of the staff of the *Herald.* By the time the *Herald* extra was on the street, it came over Fisk that the important part of his duty was not yet accomplished, and he made a bee-line for the Western Union Telegraph office, where the manager, W. E. Frederick, dropped everything he was sending over the wires and gave Fisk a clear wire to Washington to spread the tidings in the East.

On the night of July 4th, Fisk began to be besieged by telegrams from Eastern newspapers, begging further news from the front. James Gordon Bennett of the New York *Herald,* soon after midnight, wired Fisk authority to employ scouts and get them to the front with all possible dispatch.

Other papers wired for "just a little longer story," and Fisk thereupon wired the Associated Press that he had already given out all the information which had been received, and that it was an utter impossibility to get further news from the battlefield by way of Helena, and that doubtless the next dispatch would come from Bismarck, Dakota.

It was not until nearly midnight of the 5th, however, that news from the battlefield arrived in Bismarck and official notification was sent to the government.

To Andrew J. Fisk, therefore, went the credit of having given to the public the first news of the greatest tragedy of Indian warfare on the Plains—due to the pluck and endurance of Horace Countryman."

See footnote end of Chapter 10.

CHAPTER 13

HOW CUSTER BATTLEFIELD WAS DISCOVERED.

FOR SEVENTY-FIVE YEARS much speculation has been indulged in and many stories have appeared as to the actual conditions which existed on the Custer battlefield, when the remains of the Custer command were discovered, early on the morning of June 27th, two days after the battle. Many writers have stated that all the bodies were most fiendishly and shockingly mutilated, scalped and otherwise disfigured; other reports are that all the bodies were stripped; yet others, that the remains of the gallant Custer himself were not respected by the Sioux, while many writers have contended that Custer's body was in no wise disfigured because of the fact that the Indians respected his bravery.

The author is in possession of a copy of a letter written for and printed in the Helena *Herald,* under date of July 25, 1876,—just four weeks following the fight. It was written by Lieut. James H. Bradley of the Seventh Infantry, chief of scouts for General Gibbon, the latter having expected to meet Custer and the Seventh Cavalry about June 26th on the Little Big Horn River and assist in the battle which was confidently looked for between the Sioux and the combined forces of Terry, Custer and Gibbon.

Custer, however, did not await the arrival of Terry and Gibbon. He appeared, ready for the conflict twenty-four hours ahead of the time he had been expected. His approach having been discovered by the Sioux, he either had to at-

tack or see the Indians slip from his grasp. He chose to attack. Capt. Benteen was ordered to the left, into country
which precluded him from the fight until Reno was corraled
upon the hill. Major Reno was ordered to attack the upper
end of the great Indian village, in which he was promised the
support of Custer and his force. This he did not get. Custer
may have expected to assist Reno, but such a plan—if plan
Custer had—was not carried out. Custer could not reach a
ford where he could cross the river and attack the lower end
of the village, until he had gone down stream nearly four
miles on the east bank of the river. Reno, meantime, struck
the upper end of the camp, but seeing at once that he had
got into a hornet's nest, and that a charge through the village
from his end of it, would mean the utter annihilation of his
command, he did the only thing that could be done under the
circumstances—ordered a retreat across the river to the
high bluffs, where his command would have some show for
their lives—which they would not have had by remaining
in the timber along the river.

By this time Custer had been annihilated—or was being
wiped out about the time Reno's men were straggling up the
bluffs. After the Custer command had been completely
destroyed, the Indians returned again to the attack on Reno.
But the troopers put up such a stubborn resistance that the
Sioux withdrew on the afternoon of June 26th, noting the
dust cloud indicating the advance of Generals Terry and
Gibbon from the north.

Meantime the Reno contingent were all wondering what
had become of Custer. It was generally supposed that he had
been obliged to retreat, and had doubtless joined Gibbon.
Therefore, when the commands of Terry and Gibbon appeared it was supposed that Custer would be with them. That
he had been defeated was the last thing on earth the Reno
command had any thought of.

Lieut. James H. Bradley had accompanied the command of
Gen. Gibbon as his chief of scouts. Under date of July 25,

1876, written in camp on the Yellowstone River, Lieut. Bradley sent to the Helena *Herald* the following interesting communication. It sets at rest all disputes as to the condition of Custer and his command when found, and is a most valuable

Lieut. James H. Bradley, 7th Infantry, who discovered the Custer field and gave the first news to General Terry.

document regarding the actual condition on the Custer battlefield, seen by the real discoverer of the disaster.

"In the presence of so great disaster as that which overtook the regular troops on the Little Horn, and the consequent excited state of the public mind, and its eagerness to get hold of every detail, however minute, of that unfortunate affair, it is to be expected that many stories of a sensational character, having no foundation in truth, would obtain with the public. Of such a character is that now going the rounds of the press to the effect that the Sioux removed Custer's heart from his body and danced around it—a story related upon the authority of one Rain-in-the-Face, a Sioux chief who participated in the fight, and afterward returned to his agency.

"Of the same character also is the sweeping statement as to the general shocking mutilation of the bodies of the soldiers who fell on that occasion. The bare truth is painful enough to the relatives and friends of these unfortunate men, without the cruel gratuitous exaggeration of their grief that must come from the belief that they had been horribly mutilated after death. It therefore seems to me worth while that these stories should receive emphatic contradiction, and being in a position to make such denial, I address you this letter with that object.

"In my capacity as commander of the scouts accompanying Gen. Gibbon's column, I was usually in the advance of all his movements, and chanced to be upon the morning of June 27th, when the column was moving upon the supposed Indian village in the Little Big Horn valley. I was scouting the hills some two or three miles to the left of the column, upon the opposite bank of the river from that traversed by the column itself, when the body of a horse attracted our attention to the field of Custer's fight, and hastening in that direction the appalling sight was revealed to us of his entire command in the embrace of death. *This was the first discovery of the field,* and the first hasty count made of the slain resulted in the finding of 197 bodies reported to Gen. Terry.

"Later in the day I was sent to guide Col. Benteen, of the Seventh Cavalry, to the field, and was a witness of his recognition of the remains of Custer. Two other officers of that regiment also were present, and joined in their identification, and as all had known him well in life, they could not be mistaken, and the body *was wholly unmutilated.* Even the wounds that caused his death were scarcely discovered (though the body was entirely naked) so much so that when I afterward asked the gentlemen whom I accompanied whether they had observed his wounds, they were forced to say they had not.

"Probably never did a hero who had fallen upon the field of battle appear so much to have died a natural death. His expression was rather that of a man who had fallen asleep and enjoyed peaceful dreams, than of one who had met his death amid such fearful scenes as that field witnessed, the features being wholly without ghastliness or any impress of fear, horror or despair. He had died as he had lived—a hero, and excited the remark from those who had known him, and saw him there, 'You could almost imagine him standing before you.' Such was Custer at the time of his burial on the 28th of June, three days after the fight in which he had fallen, and I hope this assurance will dispose of the horrible tale of the mutilation and desecration of his remains.

"Of the 206 bodies buried on the field, there were very few I did not see, and beyond scalping, in possibly a majority of cases, there was little mutilation. Many of the bodies were not even scalped, and in the comparatively few cases of disfiguration it appeared to me as the result rather of a blow with a knife, hatchet or war-club to finish a wounded man, than deliberate mutilation. Many of Custer's men must have been disabled with wounds during the fight, and after the savages gained possession of the field, all such would probably be mainly killed in the manner indicated. The bodies were nearly all stripped, but it was an error to say that Kellogg, the correspondent, was the only one that escaped this treatment. I saw several entirely clothed—half a dozen at least—who, with Kellogg, appeared to owe their immunity to the fact that they had fallen some distance from the field of battle, so that the Indians had not cared to go to them, or had overlooked them when the plundering took place.

"The real mutilation occurred in the case of Reno's men who had fallen near the village. These had been visited by the squaws and children, and in some instances the bodies were frightfully butchered. Fortunately, not many were exposed to such a fate. Custer's field was some distance from the village, and appears not to have been visited by these hags, which probably explains the exemption from mutilation of those who had fallen there."

Lieut. James H. Bradley, at the time of writing the foregoing communication, was one of the best-known officers in the regular army—a writer of distinction, a keen observer and whose word is beyond dispute. He was killed the year following the Custer fight, while serving in the campaign against the Nez Perce Indians, at the battle of the Big Hole in Montana, while gallantly leading his men in a charge against the savages. Had he lived, history would have been greatly enriched by the manuscripts which he had under way. He kept a daily diary of the movements of his own command, the Seventh Infantry, from the time it left Fort Ellis, Montana, until the arrival of the command on the ill-fated Custer field, which disclosed the slaughtered troopers, and it teems with thrilling interest.

To Lieut. James H. Bradley, therefore, history is indebted for the actual discovery of the conditions existing on the Custer battlefield. All other stories are those recounted by men who saw the field after Lieut. Bradley had reported what he discovered.

CHAPTER 14

MEDAL OF HONOR HEROES IN CUSTER'S LAST FIGHT.

THAT GREATEST OF INDIAN FIGHTS ON the American continent, which occurred June 25-26, 1876, known variously as "Custer's last battle," and erroneously as "The Custer Massacre," developed many heroes, but none to whom the title is more apropos than the twenty-four troopers of the Seventh Cavalry who won Medals of Honor for extraordinarily-hazardous duty during the two days of this remarkable and thrilling engagement.

After Major Marcus A. Reno's command had recrossed the Little Big Horn River, from the stand of timber, where he had vainly, but heroically, attempted, with only 112 men (many of them raw recruits) to hold the Sioux hordes in check, and not receiving the promised support from Custer's command, he sought a more defensive position on the high hills on the east side of the stream. Reno's thrilling charge through about one thousand yelling savages who had surrounded his position in the timber, was a most desperate fight for life every inch of the way. But it was the only possible chance of saving his command, and he gamely and conscientiously took it, in preference to remaining in the timber, where certain annihilation would have been his portion had he retained the position many minutes longer.

As it was, Reno lost twenty-nine men killed and many wounded before he reached the hills, nearly one mile east. Here he was joined by Captains Benteen and McDougall, who, with the pack-train, carrying all the supplies and extra ammunition (some 24,000 rounds) had been sent by Custer off to the left at the time he divided his command. The pack-train was some miles behind Benteen's column in charge of Captain McDougall, and it was nearly an hour after Reno reached the hills before the pack-animals arrived. Lieutenant Hare, however, had succeeded in getting some of the ammunition mules hurried forward to Reno prior to this. The Reno command was, therefore, now well supplied with ammunition.

After Reno had crossed the river, the Indians suddenly left off attacking his command, instead of following it up to what undoubtedly would have been certain defeat for him had the Indians continued harassing him then, and swarmed down stream to concentrate their entire force against Custer, who, after Reno had started to attack the upper end of the great Indian camp, evidently decided that Reno could cope with the situation there, and started down stream, apparently looking for a ford where he could cross and attack the lower end of the village, containing approximately 15,000 souls—men, women and children. Although this village was known as "Sitting Bull's camp," that doughty warrior—or, to be strictly correct—great medicine man, had nothing to do with the fighting on the occasion of this great battle, but fled indiscriminately at the rattle of the first bullets of Reno's men through the tepees.

Why Custer failed to give Reno the promised support never will be known. If he had a battle plan he kept it to himself, or it may have materialized after Reno left him. At any rate, Reno was left to do the best he could alone.

Custer was quickly repulsed and his command wiped out to a man. The Indians, flushed with their easy victory, then once more turned their attention to Reno's command, which had occupied the time during the attack on Custer, to fortify themselves as well as circumstances would permit.

After the Indians had Reno once more completely surrounded, the fighting was terrific during the balance of the afternoon of June 25th—in fact, until 9 o'clock that night, as darkness came late in that section in June, while daylight appeared shortly after 2 in the morning. On the 26th the fighting again opened with redoubled fury, raging until nearly dark, when the savages, noting the approach of General Terry's troops up the Little Big Horn River, withdrew and scattered.

But during these two days of incessant and terrific warfare against a savage and relentless foe, twenty-four men of the Seventh Cavalry proved the mettle they were made of. Not that they were the only heroes of the battle of the Little Big Horn, but bcause they performed service of such a conspicuous character as to clearly distinguish them above any others—service that involved extreme jeopardy of life, and the performance of extraordinarily hazardous duty, thereby qualifying for and winning the Medal of Honor, awarded by the United States government only for bravery and gallantry above their comrades. It is right and fitting, therefore, that the names of these men should be written high on the scroll of fame.

After the ammunition mules had reached Major Reno's troops and his entire command had been served, a movement was made down stream in an attempt to either join Custer or to learn his fate. Reno's men, however, were set upon and driven back to their original position on the high hills.

During this retreat, one of the ammunition mules became frightened and stampeded straight toward the Indian lines. The animal carried two thousand rounds of cartridges, and it was highly important that this should not fall into the hands of the enemy.

Sergeant Richard P. Hanley, of C Troop, who had been detailed with the pack-train, therefore dashed forward after the frightened animal, urging his horse straight toward the Indian lines on the dead run, in an effort to head off and capture the mule before the Indians could gather in both mule and ammunition. "For fully twenty minutes, and under a most galling fire," reads the Medal of Honor government report, Hanley raced up and down between the two lines, with the bullets falling about him like hail, kicking up the dust around his horse's hoofs, while officers and troopers alike yelled and shouted at the intrepid and daring sergeant to 'let up and come on in.' But Hanley disregarded all commands and pleadings. He was determined to recapture that mule, and finally did so, escaping uninjured, and bringing the obstreperous animal back to the pack-train with the ammunition intact, to the accompaniment of the whoops and cheers of his comrades. For this nervy act, Sergeant Hanley was, on October 4th, 1878, awarded the Medal of Honor.

Sergeant Benjamin C. Criswell, of B Troop, also won the Medal of Honor "for rescuing the body of Lieutenant Benjamin Hodgson from within the enemy's lines, bringing up ammunition under a heavy fire and encouraging the men in the most exposed positions."

Sergeant Thomas Murray, of B Troop, brought rations to his hungry comrades on the firing line, passing to and fro several times through the fire of the enemy. This was on the 26th. On the previous day Murray had distinguished himself by bringing the pack-train within reach of the command and into a comparatively sheltered position—all this under a heavy fire from the Indians. For this gallantry Sergeant Murray also was rewarded with the Medal of Honor, October 5th, 1878.

Corporal Charles Cunningham, also of B Troop, was shot through the neck during the fighting on the 25th. Despite repeated orders to retire from the firing line, he pluckily refused to leave, and fought bravely throughout the entire engagement, saying that he "could do better on his belly with a gun in his hand on the firing-line, than on his back among the helpless in the rear." For his gallantry and pluck, he also was awarded the Medal of Honor, October 5th, 1878.

Private Henry Holden, of D Troop, repeatedly went for ammunition to supply the firing line, all the while exposed to

White Bull, sub-chief of the Northern Cheyennes, prominent in the Custer battle.

a merciless fire. Again and again he brought up cartridges that the carbines of his comrades might be continually kept belching lead into the ranks of the savages. His Medal of Honor was likewise awarded October 5th, 1878.

On the 26th, lack of water for the wounded finally became a desperate question. They were begging and pleading for it, and the situation was critical in the extreme. The day was scorching hot, and by noon the officers determined that heroic measures must be resorted to in order that the wounded might be supplied with the precious fluid for which they were so feverishly entreating.

Nineteen men volunteered to go for water. Four of them —Sergeant George H. Geiger of H Troop; Blacksmith Henry W. B. Mechling, Private Charles Windolph and Saddler Otto Voit, of H Troop—all expert marksmen, were detailed by their captain to take an exposed position outside the line and protect, as much as possible, the men who went to the stream for the precious water. They were instructed to keep up an incessant firing into the brush on the opposite side of the stream, where hordes of the savages were lying in wait with the expectation that the time would come when the troopers would be compelled to make a dash for water. These marksmen naturally drew the fire of the Indians, and bullets rained around them; but these four heroes pluckily held their exposed position nearly four hours, and it was due to their vigilance, reckless exposure of person and incessant and expert marksmanship, that none of the water-carriers were killed by the Indians, although one—Peter Thompson —was shot through the hand, but courageously went for water two or three times after receiving the wound.

The water carriers took with them several iron camp kettles, slipping singly from the right wing of Captain Benteen's line, and making a dash for the river. For some eighty yards before reaching the stream they had to traverse an exposed place, which brought them under the fire of the enemy. At this point they were enabled to obtain the shelter of a ravine which led down to within about fifty feet of the Little Big Horn River.

Then, while the four sharpshooters, from their exposed position above them, kept their carbines belching lead into the brush, the men would rush from the ravine, hastily dip their kettles into the stream and dash back to its shelter. The Indians were quick to divine the intent of the troopers, and the brush on the opposite bank of the Little Big Horn was ringed with the smoke of their guns, as they vainly attempted to shoot down the daring water carriers. But for the vigilance and skill of the four sharpshooters, doubtless many of the men would have been killed. There were many narrow escapes, however, and several of the camp kettles were perforated.

The names of these courageous water carriers who thus won the Medal of Honor (the sharpshooters were similarly honored) are: Neil Bancroft, Troop A, Seventh Cavalry; Abram J. Brant, Troop D, Seventh Cavalry; Thomas J. Callan, Troop B, Seventh Cavalry; Frederick Deetline, Troop D, Seventh Cavalry; Theodore W. Goldin, Troop G, Seventh Cavalry; David W. Harris, Troop A, Seventh Cavalry; William M. Harris, Troop D, Seventh Cavalry; Rufus D. Hutchinson, Troop B, Seventh Cavalry; James Pym, Troop B, Seventh Cavalry; Stanislaus Roy, Troop A, Seventh Cavalry; George Scott, Troop D, Seventh Cavalry; Thomas W. Stevens, Troop D, Seventh Cavalry; Frank Tolan, Troop D, Seventh Cavalry; Peter Thompson, Troop C, Seventh Cavalry; Charles H. Welch, Troop D, Seventh Cavalry.

CHAPTER 15

THE STORY OF "COMANCHE," SOLE SURVIVOR OF CUSTER FIGHT.

WHILE CUSTER'S LAST FIGHT on the Little Big Horn River, in southeastern Montana, is generally mentioned as the "battle of no survivors," this is not literally true.

One horse, "Comanche," the animal ridden by Capt. Myles W. Keogh was the "sole survivor" of the Custer column.

Comanche was a claybank gelding, and had been purchased by the Government in the spring of 1868, at St. Louis, along with other horses, for cavalry use. This particular animal was sent to the Seventh Cavalry, then stationed in camp near Ellis, Kansas. Comanche at that time was four or five years old. He was assigned to Troop I.

When General Sully's expedition against the southern Indians was organized at Fort Dodge, Kansas, in September, 1868, Capt. Myles Keogh was acting inspector-general on Sully's staff. He was attracted by Comanche's looks, and chose the animal for his field mount.

During one of the engagements of the Seventh Cavalry with Comanche Indians, on the Cimarron River—or the Beaver Fork—the horse was wounded while Keogh was riding him. It was from this particular engagement that he received the name of "Comanche."

Captain Keogh at once became greatly attached to the horse, which was thereafter known as "the captain's mount," and Keogh was riding him in the battle of the Little Big Horn.

It will be remembered that Major Reno was surrounded on the high bluffs on the east side of the Little Big Horn

269

River after his retreat from the river bottom, where his first engagement occurred. On these hills the Sioux maintained a constant siege from the afternoon of June 25th until late in the afternoon of the following day, when, noting the approaching troops of Generals Terry and Gibbon (who were to meet Custer about June 26th somewhere in the valley of the Little Big Horn) the Indians broke camp and scattered.

It was on the following day, June 27th, while General Terry's men were performing the last sad rites for their slaughtered comrades on the Custer battlefield, that Lieutenant H. I. Nowlan, field quartermaster on General Terry's staff, discovered Comanche wandering aimlessly about on the battlefield, wounded almost unto death, and so weak and emaciated that it was at first deemed the wise and humane thing to shoot the horse and put him out of his misery. Seven bullets had pierced the animal's body, yet the poor creature had clung tenaciously to life. Nowlan had been an intimate friend of Captain Keogh, and he immediately determined to save Comanche if such a thing were possible.

The badly wounded horse was tenderly conveyed to the steamer "Far West," lying at the junction of the Big and Little Horn Rivers, some fifteen miles from the battlefield. Here a comfortable stall was erected on the boat and everything possible done to make the animal's journey as easy as conditions would permit. Comanche's wounds were probed and he was most tenderly nursed on the down trip, being given as much attention as any of the wounded men.

Arriving at Bismarck, Comanche was conveyed across the river to Fort Abraham Lincoln, the post from which Custer and the Seventh Cavalry had so proudly and gallantly marched away just five weeks previously. Here the animal rapidly recovered.

There is a story told to the effect that after recovering from his wounds, Comanche was in great demand by the ladies at the post as a riding horse, and that great rivalry arose among them as to which should be awarded the honor of riding him. On several occasions, so goes the story, when riding parties went out from Fort Lincoln, considerable jealousy arose, which reached such a point that Colonel Sturgis, post commander, flatly refused to allow Comanche to again be ridden by anyone.

Comanche, horse ridden by Capt. Keogh, although wounded seven times in the Custer battle, became the only living survivor of Custer's command.

However, another story—doubtless the more correct one —is that Comanche never was ridden by anyone after the Custer fight, but that after he had recovered from his wounds sufficiently to be turned out to run as he willed, Colonel Sturgis issued the following order:

"Headquarters Seventh U.S. Cavalry,
Fort A. Lincoln, D. T.,
April 10, 1878.

"GENERAL ORDERS NO. 7:

(1)—The horse known as "Comanche," being the only living representative of the bloody tragedy of the Little Big Horn, June 25, 1876, his kind treatment and comfort shall be a matter of special pride and solicitude on the part of every member of the Seventh Cavalry, to the end that his life shall be preserved to the utmost limit. Wounded and scarred as he is, his very existence speaks in terms more eloquent than words, of the desperate struggle against overwhelming numbers of the hopeless conflict, and the heroic manner in which all went down on that fatal day.

(2)—The commanding officer of Company I will see that a special and comfortable stall is fitted up for him, and he will not again be ridden by any person whatsoever, under any circumstances, nor will he ever be put to any kind of work.

(3)—Hereafter, upon all occasions of ceremony of mounted regimental formation, Comanche, saddled, bridled and draped in mourning, and led by a mounted trooper of Company I, will be paraded by the regiment.

By command of Colonel Sturgis.

E. A. GARLINGTON,
First Lieutenant and adjt. Seventh Cavalry.

When the Seventh Cavalry was ordered to Fort Riley, Kansas, Comanche was taken along, and for many years the noble animal received the tenderest care it was possible to give him. In the winter of 1891 or '92, however, when Comanche was 28 years old, a fatal illness seized him, and he died, in spite of the best of expert treatment.

Comanche's death was sincerely mourned by the entire regiment, and the officers of the Seventh Cavalry determined to have the body of the beloved animal mounted and preserved.

Prof. Dyche, a naturalist connected with the University of Kansas, at Lawrence, made a proposition to the officers of the regiment to mount Comanche for $400, the officers to retain the mounted body, or he would mount the animal if presented to the State university, at no expense to the Seventh Cavalry.

Captain Nowlan called the officers together to decide the matter. As the regiment was changing stations more or less, and they had no way of transporting the mounted pet from place to place, it was decided to present the body to the Kansas University.

Prof. Dyche, therefore, took the body of Comanche to Lawrence and mounted it in a very creditable manner. It was on exhibition at the World's Fair at Chicago in 1893, where it was viewed by hundreds of thousands of persons.

In a letter some time ago to the author from the dean of the University of Kansas, he stated that the body of Comanche still stands in the museum, looking as lifelike as ever.

In the words of General E. S. Godfrey, "Comanche still lives."

CHAPTER 16

THE FAMOUS BRISBIN LETTER SHEDS NEW LIGHT ON THE CUSTER MYSTERY

The following letter—some portions deleted—was written by Major James S. Brisbin to General E. S. Godfrey, after the former had read the article Godfrey wrote for the CENTURY Magazine of January, 1892. Major Brisbin, in 1876, was an officer of the 2d Cavalry, operating with Genls. Gibbon and Terry in the Sioux campaign of 1876. This letter contains much valuable history and details the movements of the Gibbon-Terry forces in the Custer campaign. Many years ago, Gen. Godfrey sent a copy to the author. It is here reproduced for the first time, and forms a thrilling and interesting addition to the Gibbon-Terry-Custer movements in the 1876 campaign against the warring Sioux.—

The Author.

Red Wing, Minn., Jan. 1, 1892.

My dear Godfrey:

I have just finished reading your article in the January number of the CENTURY, on Custer's last battle. It is the most valuable contribution yet made to the history of that ill-fated battle, but I wish you had gone farther and given us all the facts.

Now, my dear Godfrey, *you, as well as I, and all of us know that Custer did disobey his orders, if not in letter then in spirit.* Terry intended, if he intended anything, that we should be in the battle with you. I was on the boat, (steamer Far West), Capt. Grant Marsh, the night of the 21st when the conference took place between Gibbon, Custer and Terry, to which you refer on page 363, second column, last paragraph, and I heard what passed. Terry had a map, and Custer's line of march up the Rosebud was blocked out on it by pins stuck in the table through the paper. Terry showed Custer his line of march, and being somewhat near-sighted, as you know, Terry asked me to mark the line, and I did so, with a blue pencil. Custer turned off that line of march from the Rosebud, just 20 miles short of the end of the pins and the blue line. Gibbon was there, and had gone out on the front deck of the steamer "Far West" for a few moments, to see some one, and gave some orders about getting scouts to go with Custer. Custer had remarked that his scouts did not know the country very well, and Gibbon had replied that he had scouts who knew it thoroughly, and Custer could have some. This is how Herendeen, Mitch Bouyer and the Crow Indian scouts came to be with Custer. They belonged to me with my battalion of the 2d Cavalry, and Gibbon claimed them, and gave them to Custer to guide him on his march. Herendeen was to come down the Tullock and communicate with Gibbon, Terry or myself when your column crossed that stream or channel. *Herendeen did report to Custer when you reached Tullock and said: "General, this is Tullock, and here is where I am to leave you and go down it to the other command."* Custer was riding on his horse at the time and Herendeen rode up beside him. Custer gave Herendeen no answer, but heard him and looked at him. Herendeen kept near the General for some time, expecting to be called and dispatched down the Tullock to us; but seeing that he was not wanted, he fell back and followed along; *nor did Custer ever speak to him again, though he knew Herendeen was there to go down the Tullock and communicate with us, by Terry's orders.* * * * He did not wish us to know where he was or what he was doing, for fear we would get some of the credit of the campaign. * * * He was then smarting under the rebuke of the President, and burning to do something to set himself up again. * * *

Col. James S. Brisbin, (Major 2nd Cavalry, 1876).

That Custer knew the strength of the Indians, I know, for at the mouth of the Rosebud, Gibbon and I had laid for days with our commands, and had picketed one side of the Yellowstone, while they had picketed the other. They had even crossed over and killed three of my men. Gibbon had sent Bradley over in the night, with scouts, to count them or get some idea of the strength of their camp, and Bradley had done so, being chased in and nearly captured by them. Bradley said their camp was seven (some) miles long, up Rosebud, and we all put them at 1000 to the mile, or 5000 souls, with 3000 fighting men, as they did not seem to have many squaws or children with them.

All this Custer knew, for I told him all about it and cautioned him to be careful. It was I who suggested to Terry the putting of all the cavalry together and going himself in command.

I said to Terry: "Why not put my cavalry with Custer's and go yourself in command?" He replied: "Custer is smarting under the rebuke of the President, and wants an independent command, and I wish to give him a chance to do something." Terry seemed troubled, and asked: "Don't you think Custer's regiment can handle them?" "No," I said, "there is enough for all of us—possibly Custer can whip them with the 7th Cavalry, but what is the use in taking any chances? Put all the cavalry together, and go yourself in command of it." He said, "I have had but little experience in Indian fighting, and Custer has had much, and is sure he can whip anything he meets." "General," I said, * * * "You underrate your own ability and overrate Custer's." He laughed and said, "I'll tell you what you may do; go to Custer and offer your cavalry, and if he says 'No', we will put the Montana Battalion of the 2d and 7th together."

"And you will go in command of the combined force?" I inquired. He hesitated and seemed to be thinking, turning the matter over and over in his mind. Seeing that he did not reply, and fearing he might send me with Custer, I made haste to say: "You will pardon me, General, if I speak plainly, but my affection and respect for you, as well as the care of the lives of my men and officers, always prompts me to do so in perilous times." He said, "I thank you, and you may always speak plainly to me, as it gives me no offense to have my officers frank with me." "Then," said I, "if I go with Custer, I want you to go in command, or not to send me and my battalion." * * * *

"Well, speak to him anyway about going with him, if you like, and see what he says." "And if he thinks well of it, and the columns are united, you will go in command of both?" I said. "Yes, I will," he replied.

This was how Custer came to be offered the battalion of the 2d Cavalry.

In the evening he came on the boat, and was on the front deck, talking to John Carland, 6th Infantry, when I went up to him and said: "General, do you feel quite strong enough with your 7th Cavalry to handle all the Indians you may meet? If not, myself and officers will be most happy to take service with you."

He replied quite briskly, "The 7th can handle anything it meets."

I was glad to hear him say so, and turned on my heel and went away at once. After I had gone, as Carland told me after Custer's death, the General said, "That was very clever in Brisbin to offer to go with me, but you know, Carland, this is to be a 7th Cavalry battle, and I want all the glory for the 7th Cavalry there is in it."

* * * *

You will remember how much young Low wanted to go with you and take his Gatling guns. I told Terry, and he thought well of it. I went again to Custer and at Low's request asked him if he might go. At first Custer said "yes", and it was understood that Low would go; but an hour later Custer changed his mind and came to me and said, "I don't want Low with me; I am afraid he will impede my march with his guns." I replied, "Low will keep up with you; he wants to go, and you had better take him along." Custer made no reply, but went into the boat and told Terry he did not want Low, repeating what he had said to me about Low impeding the march of his column.

And this is how Low came to be left behind.

I read the order you print as being the one given to Custer by Terry for his march. If that is the order Custer got, it is not the one copied in Terry's books at Department Head-quarters. You will remember that after Custer fell, Terry appointed me his chief of cavalry. I looked over all the papers affecting the march and battle of Little Big Horn, and took a copy of the order sending you up the Rosebud. That order now lies before me, and it says:

"You should proceed up Rosebud until you ascertain definitely the direction in which the trail above spoken of leads (Terry had already referred to the trail Reno followed). Should it be found, as it appears to be almost certain that it will be found, to turn toward the Little Big Horn, he thinks (that is, the Department Commander thinks) that you should still proceed southward, perhaps as far as the headwaters of the Tongue river, and *then* ("then" underscored in order) turn toward Little Big Horn, feeling constantly, however, to your left, so as to preclude the possibility of the escape of the Indians to the south or southeast, by passing around your left flank. *It is desired that you conform as nearly as possible to these instructions, and that you do not depart from them unless you see absolute necessity for doing so."* (The 'absolute necessity' mentioned here meant following the Indians.)

After you all marched from mouth of the Rosebud, Terry having turned his wild man loose, with the lives of 650 precious men in his hands, he became anxious. Gibbon was sick on the steamer with hepatic colic of the stomach and bowels, and the command of all the troops left behind devolved on me. I rushed the Montana column, which you will remember was on the north bank of the river, over to the south bank, and got ready to follow up Tullock as rapidly as possible. As is always the case, the embarkation of the troops and their transfer from the north to the south side of the Yellowstone, with their supplies and pack-train, was slower than anticipated, and I shall never forget Terry's anxiety and impatience to get on. It was the 23d before we got well up Tullock, and really ready to start. You had gone on the 22d. You will remember what hot days the 24th and 25th of June, 1876, were. I pushed and pushed, but the evening of the 25th found us on the Big Horn, twelve miles below the mouth of the Little Big Horn river. I had crossed over from Tullock, hoping to find smoother ground up Big Horn to Little Big Horn, but it was worse. Some of the infantrymen had neglected to fill their canteens in the morning before starting out, and as we took the divide between Tullock and Big Horn, the water became exhausted about noon, and the men suffered greatly from heat and thirst. I sent cavalrymen down to the Big Horn, their bodies and horses loaded with canteens, to fill for the infantrymen, and this relieved somewhat our condition, but at 2 o'clock I pulled down for the Big Horn, and reached it shortly before 4. I was in advance with my Montana Cavalry battalion and Doc Paulding and the other doctors sent me word that the infantrymen were played out, and could go no further that day.

The condition of the footmen was distressing, their feet being blistered, and every caisson and Gatling gun that came in was loaded down with exhausted men. I put my cavalrymen in the timber and went back to see what could be done. On the road I met Doc Paulding coming up to see me. He said the infantry was plumb played out, the men's feet blistered, and they—or many of them—could not walk further. He had ordered them to bathe their feet in the Big Horn.

I went back to my cavalry and told them to loosen the girths, unbridle and grass the animals, and cook meat and coffee, for we had had nothing to eat since 6 that morning.

While we were cooking, Terry came up. He had passed outside the infantry, and came off the ridge to me. He had heard of the condition of the infantry, and seemed worried and restless. A heavy cloud was coming up and overcasting the sky, and it had just begun to drop rain as he came into the timber. It looked as if a heavy storm was coming on, and the night would be a wet and disagreeable one.

I was sitting on a log with my poncho over me as Terry came up, dismounted and seated himself beside me. "How is your cavalry?" he asked.

"All right," I replied.

"Can it go further today?" he asked. I looked at him in surprise, and said, "Certainly it can go further, if you wish it."

"Then", he said, "we will go on. How far are we from the mouth of the Little Big Horn, do you think?

"About 11 or 12 miles," I said, "according to the best information I can get."

"Can we get there tonight with the cavalry?" he asked.

"We can try," I said.

"Well, then, we will go. When can we start?"

"General," I said, "a storm is coming up, and the night promises to be dark and wet and disagreeable. If anything is to be done we must do it at once. You go back to the infantry and stay there, and I will push on with the cavalry, and try to reach the Little Big Horn tonight."

"Very well," he said, "but I am going with you."

I saw he was sick, and remonstrated, but it did no good. Go he would. I then sounded "boots and saddles" and "to horse".

The men threw the meat out of the pans, and in four minutes the troops were in the saddle, and counting fours, ready to march.

Those who were on that dreadful night's march will never forget it. The rain soon began to fall, and darkness settled down over the earth, and the wind blew. We struggled on through the wet, mud and darkness, guided at times by the flashes of lightning.

At about 2 o'clock A.M. June 26th, we found ourselves on a hog-back overlooking the Big Horn. The precipice was 40 feet sheer above the water, the hog-back narrow and the sides very steep. We were wedged in on it, and it was too narrow even to counter-march the column. Terry and I made our way back to the rear. Nobody knew where we were, or how to get on. As we went back through the column, I heard a lot of Crow Indian scouts chattering, and asked Le Forge what they were saying. He replied that they were talking about the country, and one old fellow on a white pony claimed to know where we were. I at once called back. Terry had the old Indian brought up and questioned him. He said he had been on that hog-back before; he knew it, and also where the Little Big Horn was. He said just ahead, about a mile or so, there was a valley, and grass, water and timber on it.

We put the old Indian in our front and Terry and I followed him. We dragged the column up the ridge by the tail, putting the rear in front, and went ahead. We could just see the white pony in the darkness, and followed him closely. I lost Low's battery on the tail of my column, and also Tyler's troop. I halted, blew the bugles, but getting no response, we went on. The old Crow Indian went as straight as a bee-line to the little creek and valley, just across from Fort Custer (Brisbin here refers to the Fort Custer built in 1877— E.A.B.) and a mile and a half from the Little Big Horn. Here we halted, and the men, holding their bridle reins, lay down to get what rest they could. I crept under a big cottonwood with Ball, which had fallen down, and rested at one end off the ground. Here was a dry streak, and we crept up under the tree and slept as best we could.

It was soon daylight, and I rose with the first light. The rain had passed away, and the day promised to be fine, but hot. Low came in soon and said he had found the trail, and

Gen. A. H. Terry, Commander of the Custer Expedition
of 1876.

his guns were all right and were coming in. A body of men was seen in the valley about a mile below us and these turned out to be Tyler's troop, 2d Cavalry, who had come in and struck the valley soon after we did.

Terry was sleeping in an A-tent, his long legs and boots sticking out. All was going well, and I so reported to Hughes and Gibbs, who were up. Gibbs wanted to wake Terry, who had ordered that he should be waked at daylight, but I forbid it. "Why disturb him until we are ready to march? Let him sleep."

While I was talking, some of my scouts who had been pushing on at first streak of dawn, to find the Little Big Horn, came in and said the Little Big Horn was just over the hill, and only about a mile and a half from us. The first batch of scouts were almost immediately followed by a second lot, who dashed in and said there were Indians on the Little Big Horn bottom, just over the hill. The noise waked Terry; he berated me soundly for not waking him sooner. I mounted at once, and with Ball's troop rode up on the ridge. The others, with Terry, soon followed, and when we reached the top of the divide between the valley and the Little Big Horn, we saw the scouts coming in across the bottom with some Indians. They were "Curley" and two other Crows, who had been in the fight. They told us all of the 7th had been killed. We halted and waited for Freeman and the companies of the 7th Infantry. Freeman had been ordered to break camp at 3 A.M., and we could see him coming up the Big Horn about 3 miles to our rear. We sent word to him to hurry up, and halted. The steamer came up to the landing at Custer, and Gibbon, although still sick, mounted Jacobs' horse and came up on the hill to us. He relieved me from charge of the column and took command, and did not quit us again until after we reached you. * * * * He must have suffered greatly, but did not complain.

It was Taylor Muggins, my scout, who came to you on the hill. You say Harris, but it was Taylor, who was afterwards killed by a rough at Billings, Montana. Lieut. Jacobs of Gibbon's staff was the first man to see you on the hill. Ball had the advance, and Jacobs was riding ahead with the scouts. We all at first thought you were Indians. You ran about so, getting ready for us, who you also thought were the Sioux returning to attack you. The pack-train on the hill we took for a herd of Indian ponies.

Of the rest, you know, and describe it correctly.

I omitted to say that while Terry and I sat on the log in the woods on the morning of the 25th of June, 12 miles below the mouth of the Little Big Horn, after Terry had asked how my cavalry was, and if we could go on that night, he said, laying his hands on my shoulder, "You know I promised Custer we would be in the Little Big Horn valley on the 26th of June."

I replied, "And so we will, General."

"But," said he, "I would rather be there on the morning of the 26th than later. You know how Custer is. I feel uneasy about him and his command. Let us get on if possible tonight to the Little Big Horn, and be there tomorrow morning."

Terry had been uneasy all the time about you fellows, ever since you left, and he showed it in both his manner and conversation with me. Knowing Custer as I did, I fully appreciated and shared in Terry's anxiety for your welfare.

* * * *

Now, dear Godfrey, I have written this because I think it stresses some additional light on the battle in which you fellows came so near ending your days.

I would like to know what Moylan and Edgerly and those who were in that battle think of it. Edgerly once gave me the clearest idea of your part in the Little Big Horn I ever got, and I remember it to this day. * * * *

Write me, won't you?

Yours truly

Jas. S. Brisbin

U. S. Army

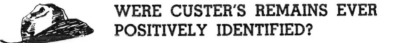

CHAPTER 17

WERE CUSTER'S REMAINS EVER POSITIVELY IDENTIFIED?

ARE THE REMAINS of what were popularly supposed to be those of Gen. George Armstrong Custer, which were taken from the battlefield of the Little Big Horn in June, 1877, a year after the fight with the Sioux, and which were buried at West Point, really those of the illustrious cavalry leader of the Seventh Regiment?

It is a question which probably never was satisfactorily determined. All published reports that ever have been given out state that, after Gen. Gibbon's troops, accompanied by detachments from Reno's command, went over to the Custer battlefield on Tuesday, June 27th, two days after the Custer fight, they "buried the dead." All told, there were two hundred and sixty officers and men killed in Custer's and Reno's commands. The survivors and the relief column had very few picks or shovels, for there had not been any such tools taken by Custer's troopers.

Sergt. M. C. Caddle of Troop I, under the command of Capt. Myles Keogh, was one of the men detailed from this troop to remain at Powder River when the expedition started, in charge of the Seventh Cavalry's property which had been left there. Every other trooper of Keogh's command was killed in the Custer fight.

In June, 1877, Caddle, due to his acquaintance with the officers and men of his regiment, and especially those of Keogh's troop, was detailed to accompany the burial party, under Col. Michael V. Sheridan, a brother of Gen. Phil. Sheridan. Sergt. Caddle states that when they arrived on the field they found all the skeletons *lying on top of the ground!* It would appear, therefore, that no serious attempt was made to inter the bodies of the dead on June 27, 1876—in fact, the accomplishment of the task would have been well-nigh impossible.

Properly to inter two hundred and sixty bodies in the hard prairie soil with the limited time and means at hand was almost out of the question. The graves—if any were dug— must have been very shallow; and doubtless the rains, together with the wolves or coyotes which undoubtedly were attracted to the spot, had uncovered and exposed to the elements the bodies of the troopers.

Be that as it may, Col. Sheridan and his party remained on the field for ten days, during which time the bones strewn about were placed in coffins. Each body when "buried" the year before had been marked with a stake at its head with a number to correspond with the name in the list which had been prepared immediately after the fight. Among these was one supposed to be that of Gen. Custer. It was placed in a coffin.

Immediately thereafter the remnants of a blouse was found under the remains, and in the pocket was a name, but it was not the name of Gen. Custer. It was a most disconcerting discovery to find that even the remains of Custer could not be satisfactorily identified, but Sergt. Caddle states that "they found another body and placed it in the coffin intended for the remains of Gen. Custer." He further adds—

"I think we got the right body the second time."

Gen. E. S. Godfrey, who was unquestionably one of the best living authorities of the Custer fight, was told by the officer in charge of the collection of the remains, that "in some cases the bones were somewhat removed from the places of burial, but that great care was taken in their collection."

It has been reported that when the officers killed with Custer were "buried," the grave was marked with a stake driven below the surface of the ground. The name of the officer was written on a slip of paper, and this paper was put into an empty cartridge-shell and driven on top of the stake. This probably is true, but it is also probably equally true that these bodies were dragged from their shallow graves in some manner, probably by wild animals, and scattered about promiscuously so that proper identification a year later was impossible.

It is also popularly supposed that the distribution of the headstones about the fenced monument on Custer Hill at the present time, represents the exact spot where certain of the officers fell in the fight, but there is nothing to substantiate this theory.

CHAPTER 18

PRIVATE GEORGE BERRY'S EXPERIENCE IN CUSTER CAMPAIGN OF 1876.

Recollections of Private George C. Berry, Company E, 7th Infantry, under command of Gen. John Gibbon. Mr. Berry wrote out these interesting facts of his experience, several years ago, for Attorney Oscar O. Mueller, of Lewistown, Montana, and through Mr. Mueller's permission they are here reproduced for the first time in print. Mr. Berry died April 13, 1939, while a resident of St. George, Utah. This data forms a most valuable addition to the Custer campaign, which ended so disastrously for Custer and his immediate command of five troops.—*The Author.*

"ALL OF THE 7TH INFANTRY was stationed in Montana in 1876—six companies at Fort Shaw, one company at Fort Benton, one company at Fort Ellis and two companies at Camp Baker. The latter post was renamed Fort Logan later after Captain W. A. Logan who was killed at the battle of the Big Hole in 1877 by Nez Perces under Chief Joseph. Col. John Gibbon was in command of the regiment at this time and early in 1876 six companies of his regiment started down the Yellowstone River.

"Co. 'E' left Camp Baker about the middle of March and I know that the first day out we shoveled fully two feet of snow off the ground to put up our tent which was of the common A type and supposed to hold four men, but we had lots of bedding as my bunkie was an old campaigner and knew what to expect. Our route at this time was across the Belt Mountains to the Missouri River which we crossed the next day at the Edmundson Ferry, and then up the river to

Fort Ellis which was near Bozeman. At Fort Ellis our company met a wagon train that was loaded for the Crow Agency and escorted it to its destination.

"The agency at that time was on a little creek on the south side of the Yellowstone River and quite a way back from that stream as it seems to me now. We made at least one camp after crossing the Yellowstone before we reached the Agency. (Agency then located southwest of Columbus at present site of Absarokee.) When we did get to the Agency we camped just outside of the stockade by the main gate and· as there was a large empty building that was also outside we used it for a cookhouse. Our company was to stay at the Agency until the rest of the Montana troops caught up.

"Someone brought us a load of cordwood, and shortly afterwards a couple of young Crow squaws going past asked for a couple of axes and soon had the wood ready for the cook stove a lot quicker than we would have done it ourselves. We offered to pay them for the work but they only asked for some soap which we supplied them with. While the squaws were chopping and splitting this wood one of the Agency employees went by and spoke to one of them in English and said: "Why Em, what are you doing here?' and she replied in the same language: 'We are just cutting this wood for these soldiers.'

"This was the same woman who lived with Major Reed at Reed's Fort near where Lewistown stands. She was a French halfbreed but the Indian predominated in her so much that anyone could be mistaken in her—that is, take her for an Indian. She afterwards sat beside me in the stockade that surrounds the buildings of the Agency and interpreted a speech that Chief Iron Bull was making to the Indians there assembled for one of their dances.

"This Chief Iron Bull was a big man and a sensible one too, and was recognized by the government as chief of the Crows. He had been to Washington. His talk as Emma Shane gave it to me was along the line of taking up ranches, that is he advised the Indians to do that, and said that he expected to locate one that summer and turn farmer, do as the white men were doing. Of course all of these doings were inside of the stockade and were mostly for the benefit of the white men and women of the Agency, as we were given to understand that the Indians engaged in this dance had been to other places and gone through the same performance.

"One of the things I remember quite well was the invitation by our company cooks to Iron Bull and squaw to have dinner at our cook house on a certain day. Well, about noon on the day set he and his squaw showed up, and from somewhere she produced a table cloth and spread it on the cook house floor and both seated themselves by it and as their dinner was all ready it was served to them, but they never touched a thing until one of the cooks handed them knives and forks. Now the soldiers engaged in serving this dinner would never think of the table cloth for Indians, but these two did.

"We were at the Agency about two weeks as I recollect now, when one morning some of our regiment appeared and told us that the rest of the command was down on the Yellowstone, so in a day or two we struck camp and moved down to them and found that Col. Gibbon had added the four companies of Cavalry that were stationed at Fort Ellis to his command. The wagon train that we escorted to the Agency had the supplies which the expedition was to use until we met the steamboats that were to meet us later, and a change in plans was the cause of our going to the Agency at all as the stuff we had stored there was moved to our new camp right away and taken down the river with us.

"Col. Gibbon also engaged a number of the Crow Indians to act as scouts, and among that number was Emma Shane, with several other squaws.

"The next time we made a camp to stay any length of time was at Fort Pease, which is nearly opposite the mouth of the Big Horn river, we of course, being on the north side of the Yellowstone. This Fort Pease it seems hadn't been built very long, and was used mostly as a wolfer's camp—that is the inhabitants had killed buffaloes and other game and inoculated the carcass with strychnine and left these bodies around on the prairie. After a time they skinned up the wolves and other varmints that had eaten of this bait. But the Indians got so bad the winter before at this place that the men sent one or two of their number up to Fort Ellis for help, and when the troops got down there the outfit packed up and went back to civilization with them. We found too, four, or five newly made graves at this post which no doubt were made for the bodies of men killed by the Indians.

"Before we got to Pease we had forded the Yellowstone on account of rough hills and country ahead of us. Now we had three pieces of artillery with us—two gatling guns and a twelve pounder. There was one of the boys, a young fellow of German extraction, who was just learning to talk English who sat next to me when we had just forded the river to the south side, and as most of our men were over, the teamsters were starting to bring our artillery and the wagons across. Now a gatling gun doesn't stand very high and as the first one went under the water my German friend exclaimed, 'Himmel, de're gose the doodlesock.'

"On another occasion this young fellow was found asleep on the picket line and when told that Sitting Bull might catch him that way sometime, wanted to know 'who that "sucking Bull" was, anyway.'

"In fording streams like the Yellowstone, Col. Gibbon usually sent part of the cavalry ahead, and had one of the cavalry men lead about three horses back, so that in that way we Infantrymen got over dry shod. Of course, the river was low at this time of the year, but we always crossed at a good ford and I think it was mostly on account of the supplies in the wagons. As soon as we passed the hills and rough country on the north side of the river we crossed again.

"Will say too that Col. Gibbon on his way down the Yel-

Lieut. A. E. Smith, commander Troop E, who was killed in the Custer battle.

lowstone took along with him four companies of the 2nd cavalry under Major Brisbin, that were stationed at Fort Ellis so that his command consisted of the cavalry, six companies of the 7th U.S. Infantry and the Crow Indians. I don't remember where we picked up the white men scouts we had along, of whom there were several, but Muggins Taylor, George Herendeen, and Mitch Boyer are the only ones whose names I can now recall. We also had some packers along, but I will tell you of them later, and we had Matt Carroll along with some of the teams that I think still belonged to the Diamond R outfit which at that time was the biggest freighting outfit in the then territory.

"This Matt Carroll is the same that the town of Carroll is named after, which town was situated on the Missouri River, the company to which he belonged at that time having built a road from Helena by way of White Sulphur Springs and the Judith Basin to the Missouri river. Lieut. Bradley was in charge of the scouts.

"We also found at Fort Pease some row-boats that the men who were there the fall and winter before had left there, and it fell to the lot of the company to which I belonged to take them on down the river.

"We were supposed to camp with the command every night and keep them in fresh meat, as game was more plentiful along the river than it was back a ways, so we took it slowly in the morning and I don't recall but one night that we camped away from the main outfit.

"Our next permanent camp was on the north side of the river, and as near as I can say now was above the Rosebud which comes in from the south. One thing that I do remember, though, was that on the last of May or the first of June it snowed all day, but it was a soft wet snow that melted as fast as it fell; but one of the boys had a letter from Camp Baker shortly after this and the writer stated that some of the boys went sleighing at that place in two feet of snow. This was the camp, too, that our scouts found the big camp of Indians on the Little Big Horn river that afterwards did up the Custer command.

"It was also the camp where a hunting party was killed by the Indians. It was made up of two soldiers of the 2nd Cavalry and one civilian, and if I remember rightly, the latter was one of the teamsters of the Diamond R. Anyhow, it was in the morning and I have an idea that the Indians were laying for our herd, but this hunting party walked into them. Our camp herd at that time contained most of the cavalry horses and all of the freight mules, besides quite a number of others, and would have made quite a haul for the hostiles if they could have gotten them across the river; but I have serious doubt of that as Col. Gibbon tried that when the scouts first found their camp, but the American horses of the cavalry drowned too easily.

"It was shortly after this that the steamboat 'Far West' put in an appearance, and so did General Terry and the 7th Cavalry, but the latter regiment was below us and on the south side of the Yellowstone, so we didn't get to see them until after the battle. Things moved pretty fast from this on. Gen. Terry, Col. Gibbon, and Col. Custer met and formed a plan of battle, but I do know that we gave at least five of our scouts to Custer and they were Geo. Herendeen, Mitch Boyer, Curley, Half Yellow face, and Fighting Lion. This last Indian is not mentioned in any of the histories I have read of this battle, at least not by that name, but I speak of him as I knew him, for the further reason that he was wounded in the charge down the river with Major Reno.

"Our command went back up the river to the mouth of the Big Horn and Gen. Terry accompanied us. He was a Brigadier General at this time, and in command of the department of Dakota which at that time included Minnesota, Dakota, Wyoming and Montana.

"We camped on the north side of the Yellowstone if I remember right, the first night, and it was the next morning that I saw our packers at work for the first time, as we were to change and use a pack outfit from here up the Big Horn river. The mules used were the same ones that had so far hauled our wagons, and as most of them had never had a pack on, most anyone can imagine what a time the packers had. It was fun for everyone but the packers and of course the mules, but Jack Bean, who was head packer, understood his business and made a better job of breaking these mules to pack than seemed possible.

"One of the Infantry companies was left in charge of our camp on the Yellowstone, as all of the wagons, harness, and a good deal of camp equipment was left behind, but I don't remember now which company it was.

"After we got ready and the mules had quit trying to buck their packs off, the steamer 'Far West' ferried us across the Yellowstone, as all the streams in this part of the country were very high by now.

"On the way up the Big Horn river we suddenly came across our Crow Indian scouts, and they told us that they had just been talking to Curley, who appeared to them on the west bank of the Big Horn and they, with our outfit, were on the east. Of course their talk was by the sign language and he advised them not to go in, as Custer and his men were all killed, and the hostiles were without number. This was the last we saw of our Indian scouts for a couple of weeks or more, excepting two that we found with Reno's men, and I will tell more of them later. This was in the forenoon of June 26, and about noon, or a little later, we forded the Little Horn, and I want to tell you the water was cold and nearly up to our necks although a good many of the soldiers thought it was close to one hundred in the shade that day.

"It was during this afternoon that the command reached some high ground and saw some smoke ahead on the Little Horn river, one of the officers as I remember, was Lieut. Woodruff, who shouted, 'I think Custer has got them, and the smoke we see is where he is trying to smoke some of them out.' We, of course, did not believe what Curley had told the other Crows from across the Big Horn that morning, but we did know that we were nearing the camp of the hostiles, as members of the cavalry were sent out to the flanks of the outfit, mostly on the higher hills, as the command kept right up the river bottom, it being easier walking for the Infantry. These cavalry men were instructed to ride in a circle whenever they saw anything suspicious, and too, I noticed they took to the highest ground that they could find in order, I suppose, to see over the country better.

"Some of the hostile Indians were pretty late in leaving their camp, as our flankers soon began to ride in circles, but it was getting late in the evening and we did not know what was ahead of us, so we camped just before dark. The Infantry camped in form of a hollow square, and nobody took any clothes off. Each man slept with his rifle beside him, and each one had a belt full of cartridges. This was on the 26th of June and I had served just four years, leaving me one year of a five year enlistment and of course, I remembered this date.

"Our officers knew by this time that something had gone wrong, as according to the talk among the soldiers this was the date we were to have met Custer and all hands were to tackle the Indian village together; but Custer, it seems, had ideas of his own on that matter, and I don't believe that he thought that enough Indians could be brought together to whip his regiment—that is with himself in command. We soldiers thought that Custer could not be beaten. I thought too that the officers of our regiment were disappointed in the turn affairs had taken, as they were a fighting bunch and most of them had risen from the ranks during the war of the Rebellion, especially the Captains. We were astir at daylight next morning and after breakfast started on our way up the river.

"Very soon after we started we came in sight of the Custer command on a sidehill to our left as we went up the river—every man laying where he fell, and as this is the only sight I had of this battle ground, I won't say much about it, only that it was three-fourths of a mile off our road and no one went to it as I remember now. Another thing that I remember was that stragglers from the hostile camp had disappeared altogether.

"We next went through the Indian camp ground, and it surely looked as though they left in a hurry, and lots of their camp equipage was left behind. I saw lodge poles, buffalo robes, pots and pans galore and in one place I saw a stack of new milk pans which no doubt had been taken from some settler, as gold had been found in the Black Hills and a rush in there had been started a year or so before '76.

"One of the last things we passed in the village was two complete tepées, covers on and all, which I was told afterward contained the bodies of seven Indians who had been killed in the battle, and their favorite ponies had been slain and were laying on the outside of these tepees. These Indians we were told were petty chiefs.

"After passing the Indian camp we soon came to the ground that Major Reno and his command fought over, and wherever we saw a batch of feathered arrows sticking up we knew that there the body of a trooper lay, especially those who had life in them after they had fallen. We were told that this was the work of squaws and young bucks that weren't old enough to go on the firing line.

"We did not see anyone that we knew at this time, as decomposition had already set in; the weather too, had been very warm. A Lieutenant named McIntosh was lying on his face directly in our line of march, and he had on a buckskin shirt with his name written or printed on it. A captain of our command who was on horseback was riding near me when we passed this body, and said that he knew McIntosh in life, and that the lieutenant was a part Delaware Indian himself. The captain who made these remarks was killed a year or so later at the battle of the Big Hole by the Nez Perce Indians.

"As soon as we got in sight of Reno's camp on the hills where he retreated and intrenched his command, we camped as usual about as near to them as we could get. It happened that on this particular day our company was in the lead, and on account of the bluffs and timber we were out of sight of his camp until we came just opposite to it, it being on the other side of the river. A man we called Reddy Stevenson whose time had expired the fall before this expedition, and who was not a good walker, had gone East and reenlisted for the cavalry and for this trip he was assigned to that regiment.

"We had hardly begun our camp preparations before five or six of the men on the hill came down to our camp, and among them was Reddy. They told us how glad they were to find that we were not Indians, as they at first thought, owing to the dust we kicked up on our line of march, and too, they asked if we knew what had become of Custer and his command. After we told them of the men we had seen lying to our left, and told them also about Curley's going down the Big Horn river and the talk he made to the other Crows across that river, they came to the conclusion that it was Custer's command, and that Curley, the Crow scout, was right and so far as learned he was the only one to escape. One of the men then turned loose on Custer and seemed to blame him for the outcome of the battle, but none of the men I heard speak of the matter had anything but praise for Capt. Benteen, who according to their story, managed things after they got together on the hills.

"General Terry had, so I was told, made an investigation of the battle shortly after we got there, but as we did not hear anything more of the matter, came to the conclusion that everyone had done their best, and that there were too many Indians for Custer's outfit.

"The first chore we did that morning was to bury the dead and haul off the horses that lay on the ground where we were camped, as we were camped on the ground that Reno fought over. Part of the cavalry went to bury the Custer men and part of them followed the Indian trail that leads away from the battle ground.

"The Indians, according to these men's story, went west, then south, then east and kept breaking up into small parties so that no one could follow; they said too, that a good many bloody rags were scattered over their trail.

"I next found the Crow scouts that Col. Gibbon had loaned to Custer, that is, those that fought with Reno. I found Half Yellow Face and Fighting Lion both together in a sort of tepee. Lion was trying to string some beads with one hand as he had been wounded in the other arm and was putting the beads on his sore arm, while Half Yellow Face was outside of the tepee rounding up some ponies that he had captured.

"Geo. Herendeen, whom I met later, had a plan of battle of his own which I thought visionary since his idea was to capture Indian ponies first and then go after the camp, but as there were more Indians than the troops could handle, anyway, it seemed to me that the plan followed was the best. I asked him how many ponies he thought there were and he said about 10,000. I also asked him what was the cause of the Indians pulling out in so much of a hurry when they found our command so close, and he said he thought they were out of ammunition.

"As I remember now all of the camp equipage left by the Indians was piled together and burned, at least we were told so, and none of it was in sight when we passed that way on our road out with Reno's wounded, of which he had about fifty.

"Our first attempt at this chore was by hand litter. These litters were made of green quaking-aspen poles, with the hide of the wounded horses that had to be killed, cut in strips and wound around these poles so as to carry a man. Now the weather was pretty warm and clear and it was planned to pack out the wounded only after sun down. Two men were supposed to carry one wounded man, and the infantry were assigned to this job. My partner said he weighed 125 pounds and I didn't weigh much more at that time.

"We were given to carry the first night, a man who said that when he was well he weighed 185 pounds. He was badly wounded, too, as he was shot in the small of the back, and didn't want to be put on the ground any oftener than could be avoided; but we had to set him down pretty often in order to rest, as there was no road, and after dark we kept tripping over weeds and sage brush. Pretty soon the cavalry were dismounted and told to help with the litter, four carrying and four resting; even then we made but three miles the first night.

"However, a change was made the next day, while we were lying in camp and mules or horses were used instead of men to carry the litters—that is, one horse or mule was put in front and one behind, and in that way the outfit moved more rapidly; in fact we made about 17 miles that night, and reached the steamboat which Capt. Marsh had run up the Big Horn river somewhere near where the Little Horn runs in that stream. It was between two and three o'clock in the morning when we arrived at the steamboat, and was daylight shortly after that, and if my memory serves me right the boat pulled out as soon as it got good daylight for Fort Lincoln, Dakota, which was at that time the headquarters of the 7th Cavalry.

"I nearly forgot to mention that one of the men who came down off the hill with Reddy Stevenson the morning we camped on Reno's battle ground, had two bullet marks on one side of his face and one on the other. That is, that the bullets had gone close to his head to plow marks as described, that I thought, there was one fellow that had luck.

"Many of the soldiers that came down from the hill were without shoes, some using gunnysacks to cover their feet. Their clothes were torn. They had been a long time on the march. They were a sorry looking lot."

CHAPTER 19

CHARLEY REYNOLDS, CUSTER'S CHIEF OF SCOUTS.

THE AMERICAN YOUTH of this day and age, who reads the stories of life in what was known as the "Far West" 75 years ago, has formed in his mind a conception of the appearance of the "scouts of the plains," and they are generally likened somewhat in this fashion:

A picturesque figure, dressed from head to foot in fringed buckskin, with wide sombrero, long hair, an eagle eye, a belt full of murderous bowies and revolvers and a thirst for Indian blood.

There were quite a few of that sort. Some of them drifted into the Wild West show business after the Indian had accepted the inevitable and become a reservation ward of Uncle Sam. Generally speaking, however, such specimens of the frontier were loud in proclaiming their own prowess; ever ready for newspaper notoriety, and were their own best press agents.

But the men who "did the business," who were the most reliable scouts, trailers, guides, hunters and plainsmen were chary of notoriety, avoided publicity, cared nothing for public praise and detested anything that smacked of braggadocio. And as a rule, they did not wear buckskin nor affect long hair.

Among this latter class was the subject of this sketch, Charles Alexander Reynolds, one of the bravest, most modest, unassuming and best-loved of all the plainsmen of the '70's, who met a tragic death with Reno's command in the battle of the Little Big Horn, June 25, 1876, in his early thirties.

Reynolds' fame as a hunter and scout was second to none among all the noted plainsmen of his time—indeed his prowess as a slayer of big game was marvelous, and the Indians looked upon him with awe and admiration, believing that he had supernatural aid on his hunts, as he would bring in game from sections of the country where their best hunters failed.

E. W. Howe, well known as the former editor of the Atchison (Kan.) Globe has this to say of Charley Reynolds:

"He was always a quiet man, and little could be learned of his exploits in the West. His disposition to say little caused the nickname of 'Lonesome Charley' to be given him, and it stuck. After he left home, in 1865, at rare intervals he sent his brother, William Reynolds, newspaper clippings. From one of these it was learned that he acted as guide for the Grand Duke Alexis during his memorable hunt in this country; also that he was employed at intervals as a Government scout.

"He never married. His brother says he used to talk of a girl he knew in New Mexico. He was possibly on his way to see her when attacked by the Indians, his partner killed and his outfit captured.

" 'Lonesome Charley' spent twelve years on the Plains and in the mountains, and yet little is known of him, except that he had the reputation of being a silent man, of great bravery, unusual sense and unimpeachable character. At intervals he would appear at army posts, remain awhile, and then drift away, no one knew where, except that it was known he had no partners; he hunted and trapped alone. When a campaign against the Indians was forming, his services were always in demand as a scout. When a notable person appeared on the frontier for a hunt, 'Lonesome Charley' was secured as a guide when he could be found. He was a noted character, but no one knew much about him; he had no intimates. For months he lived alone in the mountains; hunting and trapping. Romances have been written about him; about his dis-

Charley Reynolds, Custer's chief guide and scout. A noted frontiersman and hunter, he was killed in Reno's retreat from the river bottom.

appointment in love, which led to his melancholy disposition.
One story relates that he was engaged to be married to a
southern beauty—but this is all romance. His brother says
he never heard him mention any woman in connection with
love, except the girl in New Mexico, and this was probably
no more than a boyish fancy, a slight acquaintance. 'Lonesome Charley' was quiet as a boy.

"Dr. Reynolds, the father of 'Lonesome Charley,' died in 1868. In 1901 there were two sisters of Charley Reynolds living in Valley Falls, Kansas—Mrs. Lydia Hogan and Mrs. Malinda Allen.

"When 'Lonesome Charley' returned to Atchison County in 1861, he crossed the Plains alone. He early began the habit of being solitary—not because he was morose or disappointed, but because he was by nature a silent man."

Charley Reynolds and Capt. Grant Marsh, master of the steamboat "Far West," were firm friends. Joseph Mills Hanson, author of "The Conquest of the Missouri," has this to say of the great friendship between Capt. Marsh and Reynolds:

"Reynolds was chary of speech, seeming even surly on slight acquaintance, though such was not the case, for his disposition was cheerful and his generosity such that he would hesitate at no sacrifice for a friend. As a scout his services were of great value to the expedition, and the slaughter he wrought among the wild animals of the country caused continual astonishment to the soldiery, whom his rifle kept supplied with such a variety of choice game as would have tickled the palate of an epicure. The friendship existing between Capt. Marsh and 'Lonesome Charley' was close and warm, and it continued up to the day when the brave scout, after passing through countless dangers, laid down his life in the service of his country, and in the midst of the wild land which had so long been his home."

* * *

One of Reynolds' most intimate friends was Capt. Edward Allison, a noted scout and government interpreter, who had married into the Sioux tribe. In a letter to a friend in Potter, Kansas, written Dec. 30, 1913, he gives his recollections of 'Lonesome Charley':

"I met Charley Reynolds for the first time in 1873, when I joined Custer at Yankton, S. D., as interpreter, and accompanied him in that capacity on the long march up the Missouri Valley to Fort Rice. Charley was Custer's chief scout.

Every day we rode side by side, and at night our tents touched elbows. We prepared our meals over one campfire, and one set of cooking utensils answered for both.

"In 1875 I was employed as interpreter and chief of scouts at Fort Yates, thirty-five miles below Fort Rice, near the Standing Rock Indian agency. Fort Abraham Lincoln had been built, in the meantime, and there, opposite Bismarck, and twenty-two miles above Fort Rice, Custer was stationed, with Charley Reynolds still his chief of scouts. I had occasion frequently to visit Fort Lincoln, carrying dispatches between the posts, and I always stayed over night with Charley.

"Late that summer I was ordered by Gen. Carlin to proceed post haste to Bismarck and secure certain official papers which I would find on the person of one Eugene Waldorf, an employe of the agent at Standing Rock. My orders were that if he refused to surrender the papers, I should bring him, a prisoner, to Fort Yates, and if I needed help I would be assisted by Gen. Custer.

"I reached Lincoln in the dusk of the evening. I borrowed 'Lonesome Charley,' and immediately we crossed over to Bismarck. We found Waldorf with Tom Fortune, city marshal, and a few others of the gang of toughs that ruled Bismarck in those days, at the Red Chimney, a sporting house. I demanded the papers, and Waldorf handed them over without a word, but at this moment the city marshal, backed by the gang, threatened me with arrest for robbery. He had hardly opened his mouth when 'Lonesome' had him covered. Briefly, he made him get down on his hands and knees, disarmed him, and then drove the whole crowd upstairs and locked the stairway door. Then we quietly mounted our horses and rode back to the ferry and crossed again to Fort Lincoln. I was back in Fort Yates before daylight.

"I saw Charley two or three times that winter, and last when they were organizing in the spring of '76 for that awful march down the valley of death."

* * *

In Polson, Montana, lived Charles Edwin Reynolds, a nephew of the noted Charley Reynolds. In a letter to the author dated October 29th, 1925, Mr. Reynolds relates the following facts regarding his noted uncle.

"Part of the winter and spring of 1867 he spent at the home of my father, William Reynolds, three miles south of Pardee, Kansas. I was born in February of that year, and Uncle Charley left for the West in April. I had not been given a name at the time he was getting ready to leave. My mother has often told me that the day before he left, much of his attention was given to me. That day he asked my parents to allow him to give me a name. They consented, and he gave me the name of Charles Edwin Reynolds. He never liked his own middle name (Alexander). He was an admirer of Edwin M. Stanton, secretary of war throughout the Rebellion.

"When Uncle Charley left this time he never returned, and so far as we know, none of his relatives ever saw him again. He told them he expected to make money in the West, and should not return until he had enough to keep him comfortably. If he accumulated anything in the way of money or valuables, none of his relatives ever learned of it.

"I am sure there never was any mystery about him or of going West, nor was it on account of any disagreement with his family. It has been suggested by some who have written about him that he went West because of disappointment over a love affair, but his folks never actually knew that he was intrigued or in any way influenced by Cupid. He was very quiet, but not morose. On the contrary, he was quite genial, and a good conversationalist when interested, was well informed on current affairs, and better educated than most young men of his time. He was a real student of nature, had a keen eye and nothing escaped his notice. He was an expert horseman, and could almost instantly know a horse's disposition and ability by looking him over. I heard my father say that Charley could ride and conquer any horse, and father knew more about horses than any man I have known.

"His discharge papers, from service during the Civil War, were not recovered until several years after his death. A gentleman who gave his address as some place in Minnesota, advertised in the National Tribune that he had in his possession the discharge papers of one Charles A. Reynolds. Father wrote to him at once and soon received the discharge with a letter, in which the man stated that a friend of his had found it in an old satchel near some military post, the name of which I have forgotten.

"The first news we had of the Custer battle was from the Chicago papers, a copy of which was given my father by a friend and neighbor, Alexander Riley. I have never forgotten, although then a small boy, the look of agony on father's face as his eye ran down the casualty list and he reached the name of Charley Reynolds.

"After this, father received a letter from Major Reno, telling him Uncle Charley had been wounded, killed his horse and fought behind its body as long as he had ammunition, or until killed. He said there were many empty shells and dead Indians near his body, which was naked when found, having been stripped by the Indians. I am sure he was buried under the big monument erected on the battlefield, and his name appears on the monument.

"A bronze tablet upon which his name appears, has been placed at the spot where he was killed."

* * * * *

Some sixty-five years ago, James H. Taylor, then a well known newspaperman of the Dakotas, but prior to that time a hunter and trapper of considerable fame, wrote a most interesting western volume, entitled "Frontier and Indian Life." The book has been out of print and extremely rare for many years. From a copy owned by the author is gathered the following regarding Charley Reynolds and his early life on the frontier:

"One day in the early summer of 1870, there appeared at the lower Painted Woods of the then territory of Dakota, a young man about 24 years of age, swinging a Sharps rifle of 44 caliber over his shoulder, and leading a pony in pack. He unostentatiously gave his name as Charley Reynolds, and his occupation that of a professional huntsman.

"This young man was about five feet eight inches in height, heavy-set and somewhat round-shouldered. He had a pair of keen gray eyes, habituated to a restless, penetrating look, with rather unsociable, noncommunicative habit. His voice was soft in expression—almost feminine—and, what was more unusual among lovers of the border, he used no tobacco in any form, nor was he ever seen by his companions under the influence of intoxicating liquor.

"He had passed the previous winter around the old Grand River agency, and at Gayton's ranch, on the east bank of the Missouri River, nearly opposite the Standing Rock. In the early spring he moved up near Fort Rice, and while there, displayed first his remarkable gifts as a hunter that made him so much notoriety along the Upper Missouri country.

"He contracted with the post commissary to supply the garrison at Fort Rice with all the fresh meat needed at the post. His fame as a successful hunter spreading up the river, the officers of Fort Stevenson also requested him to furnish that post in like manner.

"It was while hunting in the Painted Woods that 'Reynolds luck' became a word of widespread familiarity among envious hunters, and varied studied expressions were indulged in by disappointed nimrods who could explain their own disappointment as being game stalkers decidedly out of luck.

"Reynolds' intuitive knowledge of the habits of wild animals, such as elk, antelope and deer, were marvelous, and could only have been gained by a very close study of the habits of those animals. He would very often say he would kill a deer or elk feeding at a certain place on a certain kind of herb or vine at a certain hour of the day; and he would almost invariably return from the hunt with a token of the accomplishment of his promise.

"The large amount of game killed by the solitary rifle of this extraordinary hunter became a subject of much discussion among the neighboring Indian tribes, who, to a certain extent, depended for food upon the very game which Reynolds was killing. The feeling particularly grew upon the Indians of the Fort Berthold agency, many of whom were themselves good hunters; but Reynolds so far eclipsed them all that they believed he was 'heap big medicine,' and possessed of unknown supernatural powers.

"The climax to the Indians' patience and forbearance was finally exhausted in the matter during the winter of 1874, when Reynolds started out from Fort Berthold on an elk hunt along the Little Missouri River, taking along as companion for the trip one Peter Buchamp, a half-breed Arickaree. At the mouth of Cherry Creek they came upon a herd of eight elk, and Reynolds killed them all without scarcely changing his position.

"After dressing them, they loaded as much of the meat on the wagon as it would hold, and then, 'caching' the balance against wolves, they returned to the agency. Buchamp was an intelligent half-breed, and disposed to play, at times, on the credulity of his red brothers. He half believed himself that Reynolds had some magic charm whereby he brought the game within reach.

"After his return from this hunt, Buchamp related to the Indians a wonderful story about the 'White-Hunter-Who-Never-Goes-Out-For-Nothing,' which name the Indians had bestowed upon Reynolds. Buchamp detailed to the Indians the story of finding the tracks of the elk. He then said that as soon as Reynolds had assured himself that the trail was fresh, he had taken from an inner pocket a black bottle, and poured out some of the contents along the trail. He then sat down on a log for the course of an hour or so, when every elk in the band returned in its own tracks, and Reynolds had nothing to do but shoot them down!

"As might have been expected, this story aroused the

jealous, famine-haunted savages to a pitch of superstitious fury. Reynolds, all unconscious of the gathering storm, was resting quietly at Trader Malnorie's house. Suddenly the place was surrounded by about two hundred Gros Ventres. The yelling Indians demanded that Reynolds give up the black bottle—that source of all the mischief, and the cause, so they supposed, of this decimation of the wild game thereabouts. The refusal of the bottle was death.

"Reynolds, of course, denied possession of any such magic charm, and some of the Indians drew their knives and made a rush for his team, hitched close by, with the evident intent of cutting the throats of his horses. Reynolds leveled his rifle at the mob, with the remark that the first Indian who touched a horse was a dead man. The aim of his well-known deadly gun had its effect, and the Indians slunk away."

*　*　*

At this point of his story, Taylor branches off into some of Reynolds' early life history:

"Charley Reynolds was born in Warren County, Ill., March 20, 1844.* His father was a physician with an extensive practice, and a man of fine mental attainments. During the last years of the residence of the Reynolds family in Illinois, Charley attended Abbington College. Just what started him out into the wild West is not certain, but at about the age of 16 he joined an emigrant train for California.

"Near the Platte River they were attacked by Indians. Some escaped, among them being Charley Reynolds. At Fort Kearney, Nebraska, the boy fell in with an old trapper named Green, who lived on an island in the Platte. But the habits of the old man bordered too much on the cannibal for the lad. One day the trapper found an Indian body in a tree, where the tribe had buried it in accordance with their

---

* There is some dispute as to the place and date of birth of Charley Reynolds, E. W. Howe, in the Atchison (Kan.) *Globe* names Stevensburg, Hardin Co., Ky., as the place, and 1842 the year. C. E. Reynolds of Polson, Mont., nephew of the scout, says his uncle was born in Elizabeth, Ky., in 1841.

usual custom. He shook the corpse down and used it for wolf bait. That capped the climax for Reynolds, and he departed in haste, Fort Laramie being his destination.

"Soon the great Civil War broke out, and Reynolds returned east and enlisted in a Kansas regiment. He served three years in the conflict, the greater part of the time being on scouting duty.

"After the war, he returned to Atchison County, Kansas, where he remained until the following summer, when he started out with a trader named Walmsley, with a load of goods, bound for southwestern Kansas. Near the Smoky Hill they were attacked by Indians, and the trader was killed. Reynolds took shelter in a wolfer's dugout, where he stood the savages off until nightfall. Then in the darkness he crept out and wriggled through the Indian line, making his way, by easy stages, down to Santa Fe, New Mexico.

"Here, it is stated, he fell in love with a pretty senorita and married her. It was a case, however, so the story goes, of 'too much mother-in-law,' and Reynolds finally quit the quarrelsome home and made his way back across the plains.

"During the summer of '66, Reynolds was hunting buffalo on the headwaters of the Republican. Hostile Indians kept him constantly on the lookout, and he had many narrow escapes. Not feeling justified in longer risking his scalp, Reynolds crossed over to Jack Morrow's ranch on the Platte —a well known spot in that day, where he remained through the winter, during which time he got into a difficulty with an army officer at Fort McPherson. Reynolds was a peaceable man, and never started a quarrel, but would not brook an insult. The officer made an unprovoked attack upon him, and when the smoke of battle had cleared away, was minus an arm.

"In the summer of '73, the Northern Pacific Railroad was surveyed up the Yellowstone Valley. General Stanley was sent with a force of men to protect them, and Reynolds accompanied the expedition as scout. In 1874, when Custer made his famous exploration of the Black Hills, Charley Reynolds was selected as the best man for chief scout and guide. This was the most important reconnaissance yet undertaken into the Sioux country. It was on this trip that Custer and Reynolds became so firmly attached to each other—a friendship which lasted during the remainder of their lives.

"The survey lasted all summer, and Reynolds had ample opportunity to prove his skill as a hunter, scout and guide. Always on the danger line, he proved his mettle in numerous skirmishes with the Indians.

"After Custer had entered the Black Hills, and gold was found, it became necessary to communicate the important news to the outside world. The greatest danger attended the carrying of it. The country everywhere was swarming with hostile Indians. Custer asked for a volunteer dispatch-bearer from his command to carry the news to Fort Laramie, over 150 miles distant. Nobody seemed in a hurry to undertake the task. Reynolds was sitting on a log near by, and as there were no volunteers, he quietly remarked:

" 'I'll go, General.'

"Custer objected. He needed Reynolds with the command, but the latter insisted upon going, and Custer reluctantly consented. When questioned as to how much of an escort he desired, Reynolds said he preferred going alone. He was given the best horse in the command, and after darkness had settled down, the intrepid scout started out. Two days later he rode up to the gates of Fort Laramie with his dispatches, and soon thereafter the civilized world was informed that gold had been found in the Black Hills, which started a stampede at once in that direction.

"Reynolds' fame as a guide spread rapidly. Hunting parties from the East, tourists from abroad, army officers and college professors in scientific research, all engaged Reynolds, because he was a man of intelligence, with a taste for scientific matters, and he was a general favorite with all. The fauna and flora and geological formations were familiar to him.

He became a devoted student and admirer of both the botanist and naturalist, and was in correspondence with some of the leading men in eastern universities on subjects that were dear to him.

"During Custer's expedition of 1873 there accompanied the command a Dr. Honzinger, the veterinary surgeon of the 7th Cavalry, and a Mr. Balleran, the sutler. They were men of scientific tastes, and often left the command to search for fossils. On one of these trips they were overtaken by Reynolds who warned them to return at once to the command, as he had just discovered fresh Indian signs. The men delayed, and were soon attacked and both killed and horribly mutilated.

"During the early part of the following winter, Custer sent Reynolds out on a scout. He attended a sun-dance of the Sioux, at which he overheard a young warrior known as Rain-in-the-Face boast of having personally killed both the veterinarian and the sutler. Obtaining further particulars, Reynolds at once sent word to Custer, who immediately ordered his brother, Captain Tom Custer, to arrest the Indian braggart and bring him to Fort Abraham Lincoln, headquarters of the 7th Cavalry.

"This was accomplished after Reynolds had pointed out the reputed murderer. The arrest was attended by considerable danger, but was successfully done. Rain-in-the-Face was taken to the guardhouse, from which he escaped in a few months, and made his way to the hostile camps along the Yellowstone, swearing eternal vengence against Tom Custer.

"When it became known, early in the spring of 1876, that an expedition was to be sent out against the hostiles, believed to be holding forth in the Big Horn country, Custer tendered Reynolds the position of chief guide of the expedition. The object of the undertaking was to compel all Indians to move onto reservations which the Government had set apart for them.

"Custer himself was not of the opinion that the warring

Sioux would offer much resistance when faced by military power; but Charley Reynolds gave it as his opinion that the Sioux would fight, and fight hard. He stated that he had observed the preparations which had been going on for some time; that they had been supplying themselves with plenty of ammunition and repeating rifles. He further stated that he believed the summer of 1876 would witness the greatest Indian battle ever fought upon this continent."

*   *   *

The world knows what a truthful prophecy was this declaration of Charley Reynolds. Little did Custer or Reynolds realize, however, that it would be their last Indian fight.

The battle of the Little Big Horn, or "Custer's last fight," as it is perhaps more generally called, is an item of American frontier history which has been attended by more speculation and surmising than any battle that ever occurred in all the Indian warfare of the West. When Custer divided his forces on that fatal June 25th, 1876, Charley Reynolds was detailed to accompany Major Reno's battalion, together with Billy Jackson, a half-breed scout, Fred F. Girard, an interpreter, Bloody Knife, Custer's favorite Arickaree Indian scout, and others of the 'Rees.

Let us now return to Taylor's narrative:

"It was in the earlier part of this fight with the Reno battalion that Charley Reynolds went down to his death. When the Indians were making a flanking assault, with the evident intention of cutting Reno's command in two parts, Charley Reynolds was standing nòt far from where Dr. H. R. Porter, one of the surgeons of the 7th Cavalry, was attending a dying soldier. The doctor was wearing a linen duster, and Reynolds, unmindful of his own danger, shouted to him:

" 'Look out, doctor, the Indians are shooting at you!'

"These were Reynolds' last words. A few minutes later, after fighting furiously against the swarming hordes of savages that poured out against them, the daring scout was shot

and instantly killed. That he died fighting is testified to from
the fact that over sixty empty cartridge shells were found
beside his body, the headless trunk of which was discovered
two or three days later, when Gen. Terry's troops took possession of the field to bury the dead."

*   *   *

At this point, the Taylor narrative states that Reynold's
body was afterward reinterred by a professor of Ann Arbor
University near the site of that Michigan institution. This is
an error, as the author tried in vain to verify it. Correspondence with the Ann Arbor authorities gave no light upon the
matter, the dean of the college stating that Reynolds was
not buried near Ann Arbor University, and that there must
be some mistake in such a statement. Further correspondence
with Supt. Asbury of Crow Agency, Montana, near the
battlefield, brought out the information that Reynolds' body
was buried on the side of the river on which the Reno forces
fought, and that the site had been appropriately marked.

*   *   *

Several years ago information was received from Supt. C. H.
Asbury at Crow Agency as follows: "DEAR MR. BRININ-
STOOL: I stated that Charley Reynolds' grave and burial site
was not exactly known, but in harking back, it occurred to me
that it had recently been marked with an iron tablet (about
1920), and I wrote to the custodian of the battlefield to find
out if I was correct in my surmise, and I find I was. Reynolds'
body was buried with the unrecognized dead under the battle
monument on the top of Custer Hill, so I am informed. The spot
where he was shot and killed is about one mile southeast of the
present railroad station of Garryowen, along the Burlington Railroad, which runs close to the battlefield, within a mile or so."

*   *   *

"In 1926, at the 50th anniversary of the Custer fight, the
author caused to be placed on the spot where Reynolds fell, a
large wooden cross, with his name thereon. This stood until
1938, when a fine cement marker was erected on the spot where
the cross had been placed. The man responsible for this splendid

achievement was George Osten, a prominent citizen of Billings, Montana, and friend of the author.

* * *

One of the finest testimonials to the character of Charley Reynolds is given by Mrs. Elizabeth Custer, widow of the general. In her interesting volume, "Boots and Saddles," she says:

"I wish I could recall more about the curious characters among us. Most of them had some strange history in the States that had been the cause of their seeking the wild life of the frontier. The one whose past we would have liked best to know was a man most valued by my husband. All the important scoutings and most difficult missions, where secrecy was required, were entrusted to him. We had no certain knowledge whether he had any family or friends anywhere, for he never spoke of them. He acknowledged once, in a brief moment of confidence, that he was a gentleman by birth. Startled, perhaps, by the look of curiosity that even a friend's face showed, he turned the conversation and said, 'Oh, what's the use to refer to it now?'

"We did not even know whether Charley Reynolds was his real name, or one he had assumed. Soon after we reached Dakota, the general began to employ him as a scout. He remained with him much of the time until he fell in the battle of the Little Big Horn. My husband had such genuine admiration for him that I soon learned to listen to everything pertaining to his life with marked interest. He was so shy that he hardly raised his eyes when I extended my hand at the general's introduction. He did not assume the picturesque dress—the long hair, the belt full of weapons, that are characteristic of the scout. His manner was perfectly simple and straightforward, and he could not be induced to talk about himself. He had large dark blue eyes and a frank face. I have known him to start out from Fort Lincoln when even our officers, accustomed as they are to hardships, were forbidden to go. Year after year he braved the awful winters of

Dakota alone. He had been the best shot and the most successful hunter in the territory for fifteen years.

"The year that the regiment explored the Black Hills, Charley Reynolds undertook to carry dispatches through to

Mrs. Elizabeth B. Custer, wife of General Custer.

Fort Laramie, over 150 miles distant. He had only his compass to guide him, for there were no trails. The country was infested with Indians, and he could only travel at night. During the day he hid his horse as well as he could in the underbrush, and lay down in the tall grass. In spite of these precautions he was sometimes so exposed that he could hear the voices of Indians passing near. The last nights of his march he was compelled to walk, as his horse was exhausted, and he found no water for hours. His lips became so parched and his throat so swollen that he could not close his mouth. In this condition he reached Fort Laramie and delivered his dispatches. It was from the people of the post that the general heard of his narrow escape. He came quietly back to his post at Fort Lincoln, and only confessed to his dangers when closely questioned by the general long afterward.

"When I think how gloriously he fell fighting for his country, with all the valor and fidelity of one of her own officers, my eyes fill with tears. He lies there on that battlefield unwept, unhonored and unsung. Had he worn all the insignia of the high rank and the decorations of an adoring country, he could not have led a braver life or died a more heroic death; yet he is chronicled as 'only a scout'."

Thus passed one of the West's great sons. Others may have won greater newspaper or magazine notoriety, but Charley Reynolds was not that sort. His quiet, unassuming manner endeard him to the hearts of all his associates, while his skill and fame as a mighty hunter, and his keen, intelligent insight as a scout and guide has been indelibly inscribed in Western history as a "top-notcher" in frontiersmanship.

CHAPTER 20

THE KIDDER MASSACRE OF 1867
IN CUSTER'S REGIME.

ONE OF THE STRANGE, unsolved mysteries
of the Great Plains of the West, in those days when Western
Kansas formed a part of the "Great American Desert," was
the massacre by Sioux Indians of Lieut. Lyman Kidder, an
Indian guide, and ten soldiers of the Second U. S. Cavalry,
on Beaver Creek, near Fort Wallace, on July 2, 1867. All the
evidence ever obtained as to the facts of their slaying was
purely circumstantial, although the trained eye of Billy
Comstock, Custer's guide in the searching party, was able
to decipher the probable events which led to the unfortunate
affair.

Lieut. Kidder was carrying important dispatches to Gen.
Geo. A. Custer, Seventh Cavalry, which had come to Fort
Sedgwick, Colorado Territory, from General Sherman.
Kidder was expected to meet Custer's command near the
forks of the Republican River, Kansas. His instructions were
that if he failed to find Custer in camp, to cut for and strike
his trail, and follow it at a rapid gait until he overtook the
command.

But little publicity has ever been given this unfortunate
affair. It occurred at a time when Custer was at the zenith
of his career as an Indian fighter, when on scouting duty
between the various frontier posts of Central and Western
Kansas.

Lyman Kidder was a first lieutenant during the struggle

323

between the North and the South. Following the Civil War he went to Dakota Territory, where his father was Associate Judge of the Supreme Court. It had been expected that young Kidder should follow the practice of law in his father's footsteps; but after the excitement of war days, the study of law was not to his liking, and he told his father he would prefer to return to army life.

Consequently, in February, 1867, President Andrew Johnson gave Kidder an appointment as second lieutenant in the United States Army, he being assigned to Fort Sedgwick, Colorado Territory, for which post he started on the 11th of June, following his appointment, with fond expectations of a great career as a soldier.

The following communication from the young officer was received by his parents shortly after his arrival at Fort Sedgwick:

"I arrived here safely this morning at 6 o'clock; intend to leave for Laramie at 9 a.m. There has been no Indian difficulty within the past week. I' wrote you from Omaha, asking for a remittance of $50 to be sent by express to Fort Laramie, D.T., via Omaha. I suppose my saber has arrived at Sioux City by this time by express from St. P. If so, I would like to have you see that it is forwarded to me."

Apparently, Lieut. Kidder was greatly pleased with his new station and the officers there with whom he was thrown in contact, as a few days later he again wrote his father:

"I am very much pleased with this post. I find the officers of the garrison very agreeable. Major Cain has treated me very handsomely since I have been here. I room and mess with him."

The young lieutenant had as yet seen no Indian warfare, nor had he any experience in dealing with the red man. It was a strange whim of fate that his first assignment "out on the trail" should also be his last, and that the real facts concerning the death of himself and his command should forever remain unsolved.

On the 29th of June, 1867, Lieut. Kidder was called into the Commanding Officer's quarters and detailed to carry some very important dispatches from General Sherman to General Custer. His written instructions from Post Commander C. H. Potter were as follows:

"You will proceed at once to the forks of the Republican, with an escort of ten (10) men of Co. M, Second U. S. Cavalry, where you will deliver to General Custer the dispatches with which you will be entrusted. Should General Custer have left that point, you will take his trail and overtake him. After delivering your dispatches you will return to this post. Until you reach General Custer you will travel as rapidly as possible."

Apparently Lieut. Kidder received these instructions at the time he was writing his letter of June 29th to his father, as he had hurriedly written a note which he pinned to the letter and which read:

"I start to the forks of the Republican tomorrow with ten men to carry dispatches to General Custer, to be absent seven days."

The soldiers who formed the escort were, with one exception, all young men and of small stature, half of them being under five feet in height. Four were 19 years of age, three were 23, one was 22, one was 21 and one 36. Five of them were native born, three were Irish and two Prussians. The distance to be covered by Kidder and his escort was approximately 100 miles, through an arid country, swarming with hostile Indians.

Lieut. Kidder himself was but 25 years of age. It will thus be noticed that with a single exception his detail was composed of mere boys. Why Commandant Potter should have selected such an inexperienced officer and such a youthful detachment for such hazardous duty—hazardous in the extreme, even for trained Indian fighters—when he must have realized it was plain suicide to send them through an Indian-infested country, is another of the mysteries of this affair.

Custer at this time was on scouting duty, and knew nothing of the sending of Lieut. Kidder to his supposed camp with the dispatches from General Sherman, until he reached a point about fifty miles west of Fort Sedgwick. At a place known as Riverside Station a telegraph wire was available. Custer was evidently expecting these dispatches to reach him in some manner, and from the Riverside Station camp he wired the commandant of Fort Sedgwick, and from him was greatly surprised to learn that Lieut. Kidder and a detail, guided by a famous Sioux friendly chief named Red Bead, had left that post to deliver the dispatches.

Custer immediately wired back that Lieut, Kidder had never reached his camp near the forks of the Republican, nor had he seen anything of him. He at once became greatly alarmed for the safety of the inexperienced young officer and his escort, realizing that doubtless Kidder was impressed with the importance of the dispatches in his possession, and that not finding Custer in camp at the forks of the Republican, he would immediately set out in an effort to overtake him. As the country through which he would necessarily have to travel was swarming with savages, watching every trail, and the entire command being composed of practically mere boys, unused to Indian fighting, the situation at once impressed Custer as being one of great peril.

On the 23d of the following August, General Custer wrote Judge Kidder a full explanation of his son's death, and the probable manner in which he and his escort had been overwhelmed. This letter forms a most interesting statement of the grave dangers of those early days, when Western Kansas was the scene of much bloody Indian warfare. It was written from Fort Riley:

"Yours of the 18th inst. is just received. In reply I will endeavor to state all the facts and circumstances connected with the finding of your son's remains.

"He, with ten men, one an Indian guide belonging to the Pawnees,* was sent as bearer of dispatches from Fort Sedgwick to the forks of the Republican River, where I was supposed to be encamped with my command. This point is distant from

---

* Custer was evidently in error here. Red Bead was of the Sioux tribe.

Sedgwick about 90 miles in a southeasterly direction. The dispatches of which your son was the bearer were important orders by telegraph from General Sherman.

"Unfortunately, upon the evening of the day of the departure of Lieut. Kidder from Fort Sedgwick, I broke camp and set out on a lengthened march westward, leaving the main southern trail which led to Fort Wallace, and over which a considerable force had passed twenty-four hours previous.

"I am thus minute in detail, as it was at this point that your son left my trail and followed the large trail toward Wallace. In returning from my scout, I marched for Wallace, striking the trail above referred to but a few miles south of the point at which I had left it.

"I at once discovered the trail of Lieut. Kidder and party, going toward Wallace, and knowing the dangerous country through which he must pass, and the probabilities of encountering an overwhelming force of savages, I became at once solicitous regarding his fate.

"The second day after striking the trail, we reached Beaver Creek at a point about forty miles northeast from Fort Wallace. Here we discovered evidences of a conflict. Two horses which had been slain recently excited my suspicions."

At this point, let us take a look at Custer's command at that time. Accompanying him as guide was the noted Billy Comstock, a frontiersman of great experience in Indian warfare, and who was thoroughly conversant with the country over which Custer's command was passing. He was frequently appealed to by Custer and his officers for an opinion, which, from his great experience on the plains, might give some encouragement regarding Kidder's safety.

But Comstock was chary of speech, and would give only a dubious shake of the head and avoid any direct answer. Finally, on the evening prior to the discovery of the slain Kidder party, Comstock unbosomed himself to General Custer and his officers as follows:

"Well, gentlemen, before a man can form any idea as to how this thing is likely to end, there are several things to take into consideration. For instance, no man need tell me any points about Indians. If I know anything, it's Indians. I know just how they'll do anything, and when they'll take to do it; but that don't settle the question, and I'll tell you why: If I knew this young lieutenant and what sort of a man he is, I could tell you mighty near to a certainty all you want to know, for you see, Indian hunting and Indian fighting is a trade all by itself, and like any other business, a man has to know what he's about. If he doesn't, he can't make a living at it. I have lots of confidence in the fighting sense of Red Bead, the Indian guide, and if that Indian can have his own way, there is a fair show of guiding him through all right; but as I said before, there lies the difficulty. Is this young lieutenant the kind of a man who is willing to take advice, even if it does come from an Indian? My experience with you army folks has always been that the youngsters from among you think they know the most, and this is particularly true if they have just come from West Point. If some of those youngsters know half as much as they think they know, you couldn't tell 'em anything. As to book-learning, I suppose they have got it all, but the fact of the matter is, they couldn't tell the difference between the trail of a war party and one made by a hunting party to save their necks. Half of 'em, when they first come into the Indian country, can't tell a squaw from a buck, just because both ride straddle-fashion—but they soon learn. But that's neither here nor there. I'm told that the lieutenant we're talking about is a newcomer, and that this is his first scout. If that is the case, it puts a mighty uncertain look on the whole thing, and 'twixt you and me, gentlemen, he'll be mighty lucky if he gets through all right. Tomorrow well strike the Wallace trail, and then I can soon mighty easily tell if he has gone that way.'

Let us now return to General Custer's letter to Judge Kidder:

"At the discovery of the two slain horses, I halted my command and grazed for a few hours, in the meantime sending out parties in different directions to discover further evidences of the engagement which had apparently taken place."

At this point the quick eyes of Comstock were not long in detecting pony tracks in the vicinity, and he easily conjectured that the Kidder detail had been sighted by a war-party of savages. It was in an open country, entirely devoid of ravines or gullies in which a detachment could stand off an Indian attack. Here the Indians could ride without any obstructions, and encircle their victims and draw their fire, while the command, from the character of the ground, would be unable to find anything from which to make a successful defense.

Comstock noted that shod horses and unshod ponies were here intermingled, all apparently moving at high speed, and proving that the Kidder party were doubtless endeavoring to escape by the speed of their mounts, or else were pushing them to the limit in hopes of reaching some point from which they could make a stand. Running away from Indians was, in the opinion of experienced Indian fighters, poor policy.

The Custer party followed along for several miles without any further evidences of a conflict. It must have been a race for life on the part of Kidder's command. As Custer's detail descended into a valley through which meandered a sickly stream called Beaver Creek, the banks of which were covered with a dense growth of tall wild grass, Comstock observed several buzzards lazily circling a short distance to the left of the trail, while a rank stench pervaded the atmosphere, as from decaying bodies.

Custer's letter to Judge Kidder continues:

"The horrible truth of the massacre of your son and his entire party, was soon rendered evident. Upon being informed that a number of bodies had been discovered hereby, I, in company with several of my officers, at once visited the spot.

"There were eleven bodies discovered, this being the number of your son's party.* I, as well as all the officers with me, endeavored to discover or distinguish the body of your son from those of his men. The Indians, however, had carried off everything which might indicate his rank, and our efforts were fruitless.

"I regretted this particularly, knowing what a satisfaction it would have been to his friends to have had it in their power to remove his remains at some future time. I caused a grave to be prepared on the spot where the lives of this little band had been given up, and consigned their remains to one common grave.

"From the large number of arrows picked up on the ground,

---

* Kidder's escort consisted of 10 troopers and the Indian guide—eleven in all.

and from other indications to be observed, it was evident that a desperate struggle had ensued before the Indians were successful in over-powering their victims.

"It is satisfactorily believed that the party which attacked your son was Roman Nose and his tribe of Cheyenne warriors† The ground near which the bodies of your son and his party lay, was thickly strewn with exploded metallic cartridges, showing conclusively that they had defended themselves a long time, and most gallantly, too, against their murderous enemies.

"Another proof of the determined gallantry exhibited by your lamented son and his little party, was the fact that the bodies, which were probably found as they fell, were lying near each other, thus proving that none had endeavored to flee or escape after being surrounded, but all had died nobly fighting to the last. No historian will ever chronicle the heroism which was probably here displayed. We can picture what determination, what bravery, what heroism must have inspired this devoted little band of martyrs when surrounded and assailed by a vastly overwhelming force of bloodthirsty, merciless and unrestrained barbarians, and that they manfully struggled to the last, equally devoid of hope or fear.

"Believe me, sir, although a stranger to you, and unknown to your son, I deeply sympathize with you and yours in this most sad and lamentable bereavement; and gladly would I tender to the wounds of your affliction such healing consolation as lies in the power of mortals to give; but I know how weak and futile must my efforts prove, and that in great bereavements like that to which you are now subjected, there is but one power, one source, to which we may hopefully look for that consolation you so much require.

"Very truly yours,
"G. A. Custer, Bvt. Maj.-Gen."

It was at first thought by Judge Kidder, upon receipt of this letter, that the chances of ever being able to locate and identify the remains of his son, were negligible. But he was determined to leave no stone unturned to bring about the recovery of his son's remains, rather than let them lie in an unmarked grave on the wild prairie lands of Western Kansas.

---

† It has also been related that the Kidder party were probably slain by Pawnee Killer's band of Sioux.

Accordingly, late in the fall of 1867, Judge Kidder journeyed to Fort Leavenworth, where Custer was then stationed, to have an interview with him.

Closeted with General Custer, Judge Kidder asked if there was not the faintest mark or fragment of his uniform available by which the body could be identified. Custer shook his head.

"No, there was not," was his reply. "Yet, since I now recall it, there was a mere trifle which attracted my attention—but I am sure your son could not have worn it. It was one of those ordinary checked overshirts so commonly worn on the plains. It had a peculiar collar-band."

Judge Kidder immediately became greatly excited, and asked more details about the shirt. It happened that General Custer had some cloth on hand very similar in appearance, which he showed the father. The Judge then stated that just before the young lieutenant left home for his station at Fort Sedgwick, his mother had made some shirts for him of material similar to that shown by General Custer.

Upon such a trifling bit of evidence, Judge Kidder journeyed 400 miles west of Fort Wallace, A friend of the writer of this article, Col. Homer W. Wheeler, for 40 years an officer in the Fifth U. S. Cavalry, but in 1867 a clerk in the post-trader's store at Fort Wallace, has often related to the writer the incident of Judge Kidder arriving at Wallace and asking for an escort to go out and endeavor to locate the grave of the Kidder party, and identify and rescue the remains of the martyred young lieutenant.

It was in bitter winter weather when Judge Kidder arrived at Fort Wallace, where, being furnished an escort, he started out to try and locate the grave. After a search of two days, their efforts were rewarded. The grave was located, and the remains of the young lieutenant identified by a simple checked collar-band in the faded shirt on the body.

Returning to Fort Wallace, Judge Kidder wrote home as follows:

"We went out to Beaver Creek, as I last wrote you we expected to, in two days. We found the grave—had traveled over it when covered with snow. In the morning we exhumed the bodies, and found our dear, dear Lyman's remains almost entire—the most so of any. I am positive I have his precious remains. It is enough for me to know that I am satisfied. His remains we put in a separate box. The others we brought in with us, and they will all be buried tomorrow morning in one honored grave, under martial orders, and with religious ceremonies.

"The team, a six-mule one, and an escort of twelve soldiers, will start tomorrow morning for the end of the railroad (Fort Hayes), which it will take about five days to reach. From the time I start on the railroad, it will take me five to six days to reach St. P. only, unless I am interrupted.

"There is not a house within 150 miles of here, except those that are merely holes in the ground, and except at military posts, nor a cord of wood growing. When we were out in the snow-storm, relying on buffalo chips for fuel, the snow covered and wet them so they were not fit for use. We had to cut up our wagon boxes for fuel to keep from perishing. Two soldiers went out from this point last night on special duty, and were expected to return within a short time, but have not been heard from. It is expected they have been frozen. The whole garrison is after them today. I am alone with the commandant."

Thus, by a simple bit of evidence, was Judge Kidder able to return to his Dakota home with the body of the son who died on the field of battle—the evidence of a mother's love making the means by which her son's body was recognized and reclaimed, when all others had failed.

CHAPTER 21

TREATMENT OF RED MEN—GEN. JOHN GIBBON'S OPINION.

ONE OF OUR GREATEST INDIAN FIGHT-ERS of the middle '70s, Gen. John Gibbon, 7th Infantry, has expressed his views in plain language of the government's treatment of the Indian in those days, in a manner which is far from commendatory to Uncle Sam and which, even today, is timely. Following the Custer fight and the Nez Perce campaign of 1877, Gen. Gibbon, that year, wrote a series of articles for the American Catholic Quarterly Review, dealing with the disastrous campaign of the Centennial Year, and in dealing with the subject of the unjust treatment of our red wards, he said:

"Wars are always costly, and, like commercial operations, the larger the transaction, the more cheaply, generally, they are conducted. And it may be safely asserted that, considering the circumstances, Indian wars are in proportion no more costly than any other kind of wars. It is very certain that in Indian wars the labor performed is far greater than in so-called civilized wars, while the troops engaged have not even the poor consolation of being credited with glory, a term which, upon the frontier, has long since been defined to signify 'being shot by an Indian from behind a rock, and having your name wrongly spelled in the newspapers.' Hence, if the American people do not wish to spend money, they should not go to war.

"Doubtless many well-meaning people will say, 'That is all

very well, but how are you going to avoid it?' This question
I will answer by asking another: How do you *ever* avoid
war? It can be avoided sometimes by the exercise of a spirit
of concession and justice, a spirit directly opposite to that
which has universally characterized the treatment of the red
man of this continent by the American people.

*"You cannot point to one single treaty made with the
Indians which has not, at some time or other, been violated by
the whites; and you can point to innumerable instances where
the Indian has been most outrageously swindled by the agents
of the government; and the great wonder is, not that we have
had so many wars, but that we have had so few.*

"The Indian, although a savage, is still a man, with probably quite as much instinctive sense of right and wrong as a
white man, and quite as sensible as the latter when wrongs
are perpetrated against him. He argues in this way: 'The
white man has come into *my* country and taken away everything which formerly belonged to *me*. He even drives off and
recklessly destroys the game which the Great Spirit has given
me to subsist on. He owes me something for this, but generally refuses to pay. Now and then we find the settlements
closing in around us, we succeed in getting him to promise
us a certain yearly amount of food and clothing, that our
wives and children may not starve or freeze to death; but
when his agents come to turn these over to us, we find the
quantity growing less and less every year, and the agents
growing rich upon what was intended to feed and clothe us.
We try to reach the ear of our Great Father to tell him of
our troubles, and how his agents defraud us, *but he is so far
away that our words do not reach him.* We cannot see our
wives and children starve, and year by year the danger be-
comes greater from the constant encroachment of the whites,
who insist upon settling upon the land guaranteed to us by
solemn treaty. Let us go to war, and force back the settlements of these intruders, or, if we must die, let us die like
men and warriors, not like dogs.'

Colonel John Gibbon, commanding 7th Infantry, whose column, with Custer's and Crook's, was expected to engage the Indians in a coordinated attack.

"Let the great people of America say whether or not the Indian is logical in his savage way, or whether or not the premises from which he argues are sound. None will dispute that his country has been overrun and taken from him for less than a 'mess of pottage'; and few will deny that the game on which he depends for subsistence is recklessly destroyed by the white man, so that in a few years more it will have entirely ceased to exist.

"None but Indian agents and their abettors will deny the fact that, with but few exceptions, *all such agents retire from their positions enriched by the spoils from the agencies,* and that, although exposures of these frauds have been made over and over again, none of these government agents are ever brought to punishment or made to disgorge their ill-gotten gains, *while the Indians are left to suffer for the actual necessaries of life.*

"When, then, the Indian, driven to desperation by neglect or want, and his sense of wrong, goes to war (and even a Christian will fight before he will starve) the army is called in to whip these 'wards of the nation' into subjection; and when the task is successfully accomplished—as it always is in the end—*the same old round of deceit and fraud commences again and continues until the next war is upon us;* but all the blame for these expensive wars is laid upon the military, supposed, by the 'Indian ring,' to be so bloodthirsty as never to be contented unless engaged in the delightful (?) task of chasing roving bands of Indians for thousands of miles through a wilderness, sometimes with the mercury frozen in the tube, for the purpose of bringing into subjection a people forced into war by the very agents of the government which makes war upon them!

"Let the American people remove this foul blot from their record by insisting that the red man shall be treated with something like justice, listening to the voice of reason and common humanity, and seeing to it that all the ample means provided by their liberality shall be expended on the Indians, instead of squandered and stolen under a system which is a disgrace to the age and the country.

"The small, miserable remnant of a race which once covered this whole continent can be retained in peaceful relations with the whites by simply expending for their benefit the funds appropriated every year by Congress. To feed and clothe them is cheaper in every way than to fight them, and if they are fed and clothed they will not fight.

"If, however, the people of the United States insist upon pretending to do *both,* let them cease to complain of the expense of one part of their bad system, and lay the responsibility for the results where it properly and justly belongs.

"Of the ultimate result of the struggle between civilization and barbarism, there can be no question. The complete extinction of the red man is in the end, certain. He may succeed in averting this for a time, and by such temporary triumphs as the Fetterman and Custer massacres postpone the fatal day, but ultimately the result will surely come; and as day by day and year by year the white settlements close in around his hunting-grounds, he is gradually becoming aware of his approaching doom.

"In the meantime he occupies a vast territory of comparatively unexplored country, into which the troops are obliged to seek him when active hostilities open. Of the geography of this region the troops are almost completely ignorant, and are not infrequently entirely at the mercy of incompetent guides, not only in their movements, but for the discovery of what is absolutely necessary to the success of such movements—water.

"Civilized warfare is conducted upon certain well-established principles, in which good maps of the country operated in, constitute a very important element. In addition to which there is always a stable 'objective point' to every campaign which the commander knows cannot be suddenly changed to some other place, and elude his combinations as an Indian village does.

"To the Indian, every foot of the country he is operating in is as familiar as are the paths of our flower gardens to us. He has traveled and hunted over it since childhood, knows every path, every pass in the mountains and every water-hole as thoroughly as the antelope or other wild animals which range through it. He knows exactly where he can go and where he cannot, where troops can come and will come, and where they cannot, and he knows the points from which he can safely watch the whole country, and give timely notice of the movements of troops, and direct those of his own camps so as to avoid an encounter, or concentrate to meet one.

"The best horseman in the world, he can, on his fleet little pony (the speed of which is a matter of wonder to the white man), pass over incredible distance in the shortest time, his mode of life accustoming him to any amount of fatigue and the greatest deprivations in the way of clothing and food. A piece of buffalo meat strung to his saddle, and the lightest possible amount of clothing, suffices him day or night for weeks, and even months together. With eyes, ears and even nose always on the alert, like any wild animal, he will discover signs of an approaching enemy more quickly and more certainly than can any white man, and will read the signs he meets with as a scholar will read the pages of an open book. He scents the smoke of a fire from a distance, and at early dawn will patiently watch from some prominent peak, as motionless as a bronze statue, the columns of smoke which, at that time of day, rise like pillars in the still, clear air, and tell him whether a large force is preparing its breakfast, or some small scouting party is out looking for his village.

"If his quick eye encounters horse-tracks, he can tell with unerring accuracy how many are in the party; whether the horses are ridden by white men or Indians; whether they are proceeding at a walk, a trot, a gallop or a run; whether they are acting cautiously or carelessly; how many of the horses are ridden and how many are without riders. He can tell whether the horses are tired or fresh, and whether they have traveled but a short distance or a very long one. The system of espionage of the Indians is probably the best in the world, and when time presses, and even the fleet-footed pony is not quick enough to convey information to their chiefs, they have a system of signals by using the smoke of fires or the reflected light of the sun with mirrors, by which the necessary intelligence is given at great distances.

"While troops entering the hostile country are watched by such a system, *they* move along almost without eyes, nothing beyond a very short distance from the moving column being seen or known, and the game of war is carried on very much on the principle of 'Blind Man's Buff.' The Indians can always, in summer, avoid a single column, or select their own time and place for meeting it. And they never do meet it unless they are prepared and have *all* the advantage on their side. The campaign of last year (1876) fully exemplified this. Hence, there are but two alternatives by which success can be attained: Operate against them in the winter time, when their movements are restricted, their watchfulness less efficient, and any 'signs' left by them in the snow are as plainly read by a white man as by an Indian; or else have in the field a number of columns, so that the moving Indian villages cannot avoid all of them, and have these columns cooperate under some common head, each of them being strong enough to take care of itself, and the Indians, if successful in eluding one, will in all probability be encountered by one of the others.

"One other important element enters into this system of warfare for which, as yet, no adequate provision has been made. This is the care of the wounded, who cannot, as in civilized warfare, be left in hospitals on the field of battle. An Indian is rarely defeated until he is dead, and he not only kills every one of his enemies he can find, but wreaks his vengeance on his dead body. Hence, a very small number of wounded men is sufficient to temporarily paralyze the offensive operations of a considerable body of troops. The Indians are better prepared in every way than our troops to carry off their wounded, and as they invariably do it, we might profit- ably take some lessons from them on the subject."

*   *   *

Apropos of this subject, the author believes that the reader will be interested in the statement of General George Crook, in his 1883 report at the time he was fighting the Apaches, and in General Phil Sheridan's views, as expressed in his report of July 7, 1886:

"From my experience of late years, I can state unhesitatingly that since the Indians have learned the strength and power of our people, in almost every Indian war which I have known anything about, the prime cause therefor has been either the failure of our Government to make good its pledges, or the wrongs perpetrated upon them by unscrupulous whites. . . . That the Indians are often robbed of their rations, and of the goods provided by the Government for their subsistence and support, by rascally Agents and other unscrupulous white men, is a fact within the knowledge of anyone having relations with them. . . . I have no knowledge of a case in record where a white man has been convicted and punished for defrauding an Indian."

—GEN. GEORGE CROOK

*　　*　　*

"The whole history of Indian wars in this country shows that they are generally directly traceable to the action of the Government in moving tribes from the locality where they had become established, and which they are always averse to leaving, for other ground, in the selection of which they had no part."

—GEN. PHIL SHERIDAN

*　　*　　*

ACKNOWLEDGMENTS

For valuable information, either through personal interviews, photographs or correspondence, the author gratefully expresses appreciation to the following persons, both living and dead:

GEN. E. S. GODFREY, 7th U. S. Cavalry.

COL. CHARLES A. VARNUM, 7th U. S. Cavalry.

GEN. H. L. SCOTT, U. S. Army. Noted Indian fighter.

CAPT. F. W. BENTEEN, 7th U. S. Cavalry, for valuable information in a long series of letters he wrote to Theodore W. Goldin, trooper of the 7th Cavalry, which letters were presented to the author by Trooper Goldin, many years ago.

COL. W. A. GRAHAM, then Judge Advocate, U. S. Army, author of "The Story of the Little Big Horn," for valuable data and the full report of the Reno Court of Inquiry.

LIEUT. E. A. GARLINGTON, Adjt., 7th U. S. Cavalry.

THEODORE W. GOLDIN, trooper, 7th U. S. Cavalry.

WILLIAM C. SLAPER, trooper, 7th U. S. Cavalry.

JOHN BURKMAN, trooper, 7th U. S. Cavalry.

JACOB HORNER, trooper, 7th U. S. Cavalry.

CHARLES WINDOLPH, trooper, 7th U. S. Cavalry.

WILLIAM C. BRISBIN, nephew of Major James S. Brisbin, 2d U. S. Cavalry.

CHARLEY REYNOLDS, nephew of Custer's Chief of Scouts, Charley Reynolds.

MRS. CORNELIA KNOWLES, sister of Major M. A. Reno, 7th U. S. Cavalry.

Miss Carrie M. Knowles, niece of Major M. A. Reno, 7th U. S. Cavalry.

D. F. Barry, noted photographer of leading Indian chiefs.

Mrs. Mary Little Nest, sister of "Mitch" Bouyer, Scout with Gen. Custer.

Andrew J. Fisk, Associated Press correspondent at Helena, Montana, who gave out first news of the Custer tragedy.

C. H. Asbury, former Agent at Crow Indian Reservation.

Miss Grace Harrington, daughter of Lieut. H. M. Harrington, 7th Cavalry, one of three officers of Custer's command whose bodies were never found.

Robert E. Strahorn, war correspondent with Gen. George Crook's command.

Capt. E. S. Luce, present Superintendent of Custer battlefield.

Fred Dustin, author of "The Custer Tragedy."

W. M. Camp, Chicago newspaperman, and historian of the Custer fight.

Dr. Chas. Kuhlman, author of "Legend into History—The Custer Mystery."

George G. Osten, who alone was responsible for the beautiful marker to Charley Reynolds, on the spot where he was killed.

Col. H. W. Wheeler, 5th Cavalry, U. S. A., author "The Frontier Trail."

Capt. Charles King, U. S. A. Author of "Campaigning With Crook."

D. L. Spotts, author of "Campaigning With Custer and the 19th Kansas Cavalry."

Capt. James H. Cook, author of "Fifty Years on the Old Frontier," personal friend of Chief Red Cloud and other noted Sioux leaders.

Gen. Jesse M. Lee, U. S. A., Military Agent in charge of the Brule Sioux at Spotted Tail Agency, close friend of Chief Crazy Horse.

Dr. V. T. McGillycuddy, noted Army Surgeon at Camp Robinson when Chief Crazy Horse was murdered.

Dr. Grace Raymond Hebard, noted Wyoming historian, co-author "The Bozeman Trail" and other volumes.

Mrs. Jesse M. Lee, for valuable information about Chiefs Crazy Horse and Spotted Tail.

MRS. MAUDE LEE RETHERS, daughter of Gen. and Mrs. Lee, for many stories of her child life at various frontier Army Posts and Indian Agencies and for gifts of beautiful bead work of the Indians and handsome Indian basketry, presented to the author.

GENERAL FRANK D. BALDWIN, U. S. A., noted Indian fighter.

MRS. ALCE BLACKWOOD BALDWIN, wife of Gen. Baldwin, author of "Memoirs of Major-General Frank D. Baldwin."

MRS. A. C. G. WILLIAMS-FOOTE, daughter of Gen. Baldwin.

GEN. W. C. BROWN, U. S. A.

DR. T. B. MARQUIS, author of "A Warrior Who Fought Custer."

GEN. ANSON MILLS, author of "My Story;" noted Indian fighter.

JAMES WILLARD SCHULTZ, author of "William Jackson, Indian Scout." Jackson scouted with Major Reno's battalion.

JOHN F. FINERTY, war correspondent with Gen. Crook's column, in the Rosebud fight and Slim Buttes engagement; author, "Warpath & Bivouac."

LUTHER STANDING BEAR, author of "My People, the Sioux."

MISS ANNIE OAKLEY, in defense of Crow Indian Scout "Curley," one of Custer's scouts.

Breinigsville, PA USA
16 December 2010
251565BV00002B/2/P